Dangerous Fun

The Social Lives
of Big Wave Surfers

UGO CORTE

The University of Chicago Press
Chicago and London

The University of Chicago Press, Chicago 60637
The University of Chicago Press, Ltd., London
© 2022 by The University of Chicago

31 30 29 28 27 26 25 24 23 22   1 2 3 4 5

ISBN-13: 978-0-226-81544-2 (cloth)
ISBN-13: 978-0-226-82045-3 (paper)
ISBN-13: 978-0-226-82044-6 (e-book)
DOI: https://doi.org/10.7208/chicago/9780226820446.001.0001

All photographs in this work are courtesy of the author.

Library of Congress Cataloging-in-Publication Data

Names: Corte, Ugo, author.
Title: Dangerous fun : the social lives of big wave surfers /
    Ugo Corte.
Description: Chicago ; London : The University of Chicago
    Press, 2022. | Includes bibliographical references and index.
Identifiers: LCCN 2021054316 | ISBN 9780226815442 (cloth) |
    ISBN 9780226820453 (paperback) | ISBN 9780226820446
    (ebook)
Subjects: LCSH: Surfers—Hawaii—Waimea Bay (Oahu) |
    Surfing—Social aspects.
Classification: LCC GV839.65.H3 C67 2022 |
    DDC 797.3/209969—dc23/eng/20211109
LC record available at https://lccn.loc.gov/2021054316

♾ This paper meets the requirements of ANSI/NISO Z39.48-1992
(Permanence of Paper).

DANGEROUS FUN

A Sergio

Contents

From Northern Europe to the North Shore of Oʻahu

As the third plane I have taken on this slightly more than twenty-two-hour journey is about to land, the pilot excuses the turbulence once more, announces the exotic air temperature on the ground, and then informs us that "we are approaching paradise, which is exactly where you're supposed to be." On this night in January the air is humid, it's hot, the wind is strong. Most passengers are in their T-shirts and shorts; some are also already wearing slippahs (Hawaiian slang for flip-flops), as if they can't wait to get into character. Most of us are smiling and feeling that our long journeys to the middle of the Pacific have been worthwhile.

The following morning, after spending a night at Lincoln Hall on the campus of the University of Hawaiʻi at Mānoa, I head out for the North Shore of the island. About forty-five minutes later I exit Kamehameha Highway, pass the pineapple fields, and then turn down the long road toward what surfers call the seven-mile miracle: seven miles of world-class surf spots. The road is nestled in a corridor of pine trees. Looking far out to sea in each direction—from Puaʻena Point and toward the east side of the island—the ocean looks like a series of avalanches marching toward the shore. Have I reached a ski resort? The surf looks gigantic, and each surf spot, except for one, is "blown out"—rendered disorderly by the wind. Only Waimea can handle that size and that wind. It's a sight I've never seen during what has already been an exceptional winter, with so many more than usual of these normally rare days. "A winter to remember," surfer/shaper and longtime resident Dennis Pang says, referring not only to the quantity of big waves, but also to the lack of wind. To reduce the chance of automobile accidents, the state had closed an 11.5-mile stretch of Kamehameha Highway from two to six p.m. anticipating high surf—an unprecedented[1] but justified precaution. The front page of the local paper displays a large image of a wave towering over several palm trees in the foreground, with the caption "Big Waves, Big Worries." But it might as well have added, "Big Excitement" (and heavy traffic)—and not only for the surfers, but for the larger community as well. And today the waves look even taller.

The Hawaiian Islands are known as the birthplace of surfing, and the North Shore of Oʻahu is renowned as holding the highest concentration of world-class surf spots on the globe—one after another, like pearls on a necklace, and most of them only a bike ride away. Pick up any surf map of the island and you will be amazed to learn that almost every single breaking wave and ripple along that entire storied shoreline has its own nomenclature. The names Waimea and Pipeline in particular have entered popular knowledge—the first as the birthplace of big wave surfing during the late fifties, and the second as the most photographed wave on the planet because its perfect tube, unfolding so close to the shore, allows easy access for transfixed audiences. On beaches like Pipeline the ground shakes when waves break and crash. Tune in to any radio station or TV channel in Hawaiʻi and you'll find a surf report with hourly updates.

Waimea Beach Park sits in front of the valley of the same name. Slowly approaching the Bay through traffic and looking down from the road above, I see a series of big rocks on each side, and a lifeguard tower in the middle of the beach. When I reach the other side of the Bay, I park my car next to a church. I try my pidgin with the gardener, greeting him with a "Howzit?" to which he responds with an upbeat, "Lifeguards plen[t]y busy today" (ending on a high intonation), before turning back to his work. I give a few dollars to his girlfriend who is sitting in front of a white plastic table in the shade collecting fees in a metal lunch box. I ask her if she goes to church. She says, "No." "Why not?" I probe. Seeming perfectly at ease answering my question, she smiles, letting me see before she speaks that she is missing a few teeth. "Because I'm a bad girl," she says—and both of us burst into a laugh. Then I cross the street, walk down the path, and join the crowd assembled at the guardrail. Cameras abound, filling the hands of professional photographers, aficionados, or retirees. I'm surprised by the look of the surfers walking down the trail to get to the water, and by those coming up the hill to reach their vehicles. As I would have expected, a few of them are strong-looking men in their twenties, but there are also many more who are much older; and while some of them are still looking fit, others are out of shape. There are a few women too, but not many. I only count four during the hours I'm there.

I'm also struck by the exceptional size of the waves crashing on the shore, and by how much water is moving into the Bay and then back out to the ocean. White, rather than blue or green, is the dominating color. Waves look so big that they seem to want to steamroll the people on the beach. Following their eyes, my gaze moves toward the horizon. More than two hundred yards offshore I spot a black patch that looks more like a series of tiny fishing boats than a group of surfers sitting on their surfboards. Lifting my powerful and heavy telephoto lens, I take a photograph and then I count them: thirty-five, plus four standing more toward the middle of the Bay, rather than nearer the church on the east side. I also see a handful of small houses and shacks close to the water, and a larger white house behind my back standing slightly higher above the road. There appears to be no action now except for the surfers trying to navigate getting into or out of the water. They provide crowd entertainment, as they often don't exit the water as smoothly as they have entered it. As the saying goes, "Once you enter the water, anything can happen," and the shore break at Waimea is notorious for its ruthlessness. So much so that some say that successfully "negotiating it is half the battle."

No waves are breaking far out, at least not now, but they certainly will if surfers are occupying a position nearby. Some twenty minutes later a series of four larger waves—the second set of the hour I was later told—slowly approaches from the horizon, moving menacingly toward the surf lineup—the spot where surfers wait for waves. The closer they get, the taller they grow. And from the dark blue ocean the color progressively lightens as they advance toward where surfers are waiting astride their boards. A few of them paddle to "the outside" to avoid having to deal with the set, following a surfer who initiates the escape, but the majority of surfers hold their ground. A young woman says to her mother, "Here comes a monster." The mother replies, "Oh my god!" And the daughter specifies, "That's the next one. Holy (holding her breath in suspense) . . . One, two, three, four, five . . . uhm . . . (short pause) dang: six guys!" As the wave steepens, five surfers paddle and catch it, riding alongside one another; another one joins them further down the line, dropping in on its "shoulder." As they ride it, they seem to be looking at one another to maintain distance by anticipating each other's trajectory as NASCAR drivers do. When some of them eventually reach its bottom after a long vertical drop from its curl, the wave looks at least four times as tall as they are. Then one of them begins losing his balance. He gets catapulted forward head first while his body stretches and twists halfway upside down, with his arms straightened as if hopelessly attempting to activate a superpower. Before shooting into the air his board hits another surfer, who then also falls. The impact looks painful. It looks like a mess. The surfer cartwheels without penetrating the water until the wave eventually hits him with its claw. The other three surfers ride until the wave flattens and eventually dies out into the deep water of the channel in the middle of the Bay. Overall, their ride lasts about ten seconds. And then, when it's over, they turn around and paddle back out to the lineup. Meanwhile, two lifeguards on a jet ski who were in the channel watching the action drive to the "impact zone," toward the two who collided, to check if they need any help. Those two surfers look rattled. The water is white and churning with foam, and it seems they are tangled up with one another. One who has broken the leash that tied him to his board accepts the invitation and gets driven back to the shore break on a sled on the back of the jet ski. Then the lifeguard takes the jet ski back into the channel to continue patrolling the action. Each wave in the set, except for one, also gets ridden by multiple surfers at once.

On the beach a group of five Brazilian surfers help one another put on their wetsuits and flotation vests. The oldest one points out toward the ocean, and two others listen attentively to his instructions while scanning the horizon. When dressed, they look like armored soldiers from ancient Rome. But they would look the same even if they weren't wearing padded vests. A female surfer wearing only a swimsuit walks past them alone, and they—along with four women sitting on towels nearby—turn their heads to follow her. An elderly man wearing a thick white mustache and a neoprene hood to protect his head from the sun comes ashore from surfing, and walks up the shore break toward the woman. As they maneuver their boards to avoid clashing them like two Hawaiian stilts would clash their beaks, the woman bends toward the man and places her left palm on his right shoulder. They laugh as they gesticulate at a long, steep "takeoff" on a wave, their mouths agape. They seem to be aware that they are being watched, and they may be playing to the crowd. Then they depart in opposite directions: one in, the other out. Conviviality. Switching players?

The South American surfers walk toward the shore, wait for a lull between waves, sprint toward the water, jump on their boards, and begin paddling out side by side. As they move further out, for a moment they look like a flock of birds, with the more experienced surfer spearheading their V formation. The Pacific Ocean looks relatively placid again, having returned to a state more in keeping with its misleading denomination after the set of waves have "unloaded" their might. A swimming surfer arrives at the shore break without a board, his broken leash dangling from his left ankle. He talks with a lifeguard on a quad bike who helps him locate his board among the dry rocks, then picks his way between them, sometimes crawling, to retrieve it. On his way back with a board that looks like it has been bitten by a shark, he stops by the guardrail next to three young women. "Aren't you scared?" they ask, to which he replies, "We train really hard, and then it gets to a point where it just gets really fun." He leans back smiling, placing his left hand on his hip, still tired from his swim back to shore. They chat for a while. Ricardo—who teaches a course called "Apnea & Surf Survival in Big Surf," notices my camera and turns toward me to ask: "Did you get my last ride?" I nod. "But you wiped out," I add. "That's OK," he says, "I almost prefer those pictures."

Introduction

This ethnography is about the social world of big wave surfing on the North Shore of Oʻahu in Hawaiʻi—particularly at Waimea, The Bay. It focuses on risk-taking, fun, failure, professionalization, and disengagement. To understand these themes and their connection I push for a sociology of small group episodes: stories of interactions I have seen unfold, experienced, or been told.

Modern recreational surfing differs from big wave surfing not just in form, but in the social interactions that typically occur in each social world. In his book *Surfing Life*, Mark Stranger argues that surfers are often fixed on their own individual pleasure: "participants are uninterested in any social interaction. . . . Instead, they are focused on the ocean for any sign that might give them an edge in what can be an aggressive competition for the waves."[1] Like other big wave surfers, Greg Long says that surfing is an individual sport, while what he does is a team sport requiring cooperation and interdependence. Discussing the camaraderie among members of this breed, Nathan Fletcher says: "I think you can truly connect because your guard is down, ʻcuz you're at nature's mercy so you can't really have your ego up. You got to lose all your culture, you got to lose all your history, everything that you bring to the table has to be set on the beach ʻcuz you're dealing with you and the ocean. It's not like you're a local (in an ironic tone). You're not gonna be like: ʻOh, this is my spot.ʼ"[2]

This book is based on the groups of men and women I met during my fieldwork in Hawaiʻi. These groups of friends and rivals who to a greater or lesser extent chase fun, respect, and excitement and ultimately create meaning, social cohesion, and boundaries. Individuals who aim at temporarily defeating the mundane by generating *collective effervescence*[3] and pushing their limits. In a few instances their intent is broader: expanding the borders of not only what they thought was possible, but what their community first considered insurmountable obstacles. Their quest consists of excitement, passion, meaning, respect, and for some, a dream of a livelihood around their addiction: surfing—being in the ocean. If you were to ask them "Why?" a common reply would be "For the love of the ocean." But there is certainly more to it, and I hope that this book introduces you to the captivating depths of this world.

My focus is not journalistic or historical, though it can be read in part as what anthropologists call a memory of a community. This book is also about a sociology of groups and how being part of small groups influences the risks we take, the amount and kind of fun we may or may not have, and the other situations we experience through a specific worldview. We are socialized through groups, and often we don't respond to an anonymous audience, as sociologist Erving Goffman famously argued, but rather, as Gary Alan Fine has contended, to other members of the small groups we know intimately.[4] We are impressed, we want to impress, we feel the most intense feelings—whether they be negative or positive—with the people closest to our hearts, near or under our skin, in our minds, and especially in our presence. Michael Farrell calls such groups *collaborative circles*[5]—primary groups of friends who try to make a dent in their field, particularly around projects that require much time, effort, and daring. Group projects that entail history: the making of history though memorable achievements that are based on intimate knowledge, trust, and idealization among group members. Put differently, to achieve long-term, highly uncertain goals, repeated interactions with close friends and collaborators generally matters more than passing interactions with an ephemeral audience. Each sequence of actions is built on previous actions and sequences. Novelty is needed to keep situations appealing, to keep boredom at bay, and to generate the approval we try to elicit from our collaborators. In his work on highly courageous and creative groups, Farrell argues that this idealization among unique small ensembles resembles other kinds of love,[6] such as the love within a squad of soldiers on a battlefield or among the members of a championship team. In these relationships individuals idealize one another and feel uplifted simply by being in the presence of the other person. As symbolic interactionists have put it, our behavior is learned partly by reading the response it generates in others. But the audience I address is not only of a generalized kind; it's composed of *significant others*,[7] whether they are family (in the colloquial sense of the term) or rivals.

Building on the writings of Émile Durkheim and Erving Goffman on the power and function of rituals, Randall Collins theorizes how the level of positive *emotional energy*[8] we dispose of—meaning: confidence, drive, initiative—is tied to the highly charged interactions we experience in co-presence whenever we are mutually focusing on a common object. Bodily rhythms, excitement, and knowledge are much stronger, and are amplified, when they are produced and transmitted face to face rather than through mediated communication. As Collins puts it: "full-body co-presence is multi-channel,"[9] making these kinds of interactions potentially the most intense. According to his theory of interaction ritual chains,[10] *emotional energy* is the primary motivating factor for action. These micro-communities of shared taste can be imagined as *coalitions in the mind*,[11] but they are also physically real and are contained within delineated spaces and activities: in the case of this study, at Waimea Bay and on the North Shore, and at other big wave surf locations. As *collaborative circles* they are likely to be found in what Farrell calls *magnet places*—geographical areas that attract novices and where divergent views within a field clash.[12] In these places the possibility of repeated interactions with distinctively ambitious and motivated individuals is maximized, as are the chances of finding the individuals with whom one may click, bond, and spark. Occasionally, voluntary interactions evolve into ritualized, periodic meetings in locales such as a café, a laboratory, or the home of a group of writers or social reformers.

While scholars in different fields have long explored risk and risk-taking, the novelty of my approach rests on detailing particularly consequential interactions which, in line with Goffman's work on *action*,[13] Anthony Giddens calls *fateful moments*:[14] "times when events come together in such a way that an individual stands, as it were, at a crossroads in his existence; or when a person learns of information with fateful consequences." I refer to the first of these qualifications of the concept's meaning. These moments both threaten one's security and well-being, and offer the potential to alter our life's trajectory. In my conceptualization, a fateful moment is one that leads to a transformative change in one's identity, a decision to step into a social role that is both desired and feared, and which, once chosen, changes one's self-concept irrevocably.

Further, I argue that when such moments are successful they are distinguished by intense interactions generating high levels of *emotional energy* that typically take place before and after the fateful moment. In this respect my work is primarily grounded on, but goes beyond, the theory of *interaction ritual chains* developed by Collins[15] coupled with research on inner speech to discuss internal rituals. Secondarily, it relies on Stephen Lyng's writings on *edgework*[16] while integrating it with new work on the sociology of fun by Fine and myself and research on interpersonal group dynamics by Farrell.

In his pioneering research on voluntary risk-taking, Lyng wrote that "[E]dgeworkers typically fall into a pattern of escalating risks that propel them toward a spiral of illicit action."[17] But how do individuals ratchet up their own performance and the level and kinds of risk that they take?[18] Lyng's answer is primarily rooted in the individual, in the sense that as they get closer to the edge and become habituated to specific risks, they modify their equipment or their approach or both to keep the activity exciting while they progress at it. As with theories of physiological addiction, the idea is that in order to keep the feeling of being on the edge, once tolerance to a stimulus has been reached, participants need to introduce more novelty and surprise, and one way to do so is by taking incrementally larger risks or qualitatively different kinds of risks.[19]

But how is risk-taking achieved interactionally and to what ends, besides *embodied pleasures* and individual satisfaction (Lyng) and a desire to impress an anonymous audience (Goffman)? And further, how does *edgework* change over the life course of an individual and the evolution of a field? In this book I advance the argument that risk-taking is intimately related to *emotional energy* and fun (*group pleasures*)—and by extension to excitement, as Jack Katz[20] has argued in relation to crime—but also to group cohesion. Building on the sociology of collaborative circles initiated by Farrell, and the theory of fun that I spearheaded with Fine, I detail how the concepts of *escalating reciprocity* and *individuation* are particularly productive in helping us to understand how individuals become involved in risk-taking, and how their approach changes over time[21] as a consequence of their level of expertise, their acquired status within the community, and innovations related to their field. And even though it's a common qualifier in studies of risk, I object to the adjective "voluntary" in Lyng's conceptualization. Instead, I show how group pressures contribute to explaining risk-taking, especially before an individual has aged and matured enough to consider which risks are worth taking and which may no longer be. But there is more: the addictive qualities of these high-sensation pursuits lead to feelings of personal and reciprocal obligation.

Describing big wave surfers while paraphrasing Herman Melville, sport writer Chris Dixon says that it's wrong to assume that what they do is chosen or optional. Such an interpretation would inevitably lead us to think that they are "crazy or utterly selfish and self-destructive." Instead, he suggests that they are "prisoners. They just don't seem to know it."[22]

In her journalistic book *The Wave*, Susan Casey describes a strong peer pressure that operates in distinctively cohesive small groups of big wave surfers. Talking about the "Strapped Crew" who pioneered tow-in surfing on Maui in the 1990s, she says that Brett Lickle's near-death experience provided him with a "ticket out" of the "gang." Probably exaggerating a little, Lickle told her: "There's so much peer pressure. . . . You can't just walk away . . . you just can't. But if you get shot up and almost die, they let you out."[23]

In this book I take a life course perspective. I begin by explaining how an individual generally gets involved in the activity, then progress through how he or she may take incrementally bigger risks in different pivotal episodes and moments, to when and how he or she eventually changes their line of action toward risk-taking (scaling up, scaling down, taking selective risks) and finally moves on. This approach reflects the range of individuals that I have observed, interacted with, and interviewed—the youngest being sixteen years old and the oldest, Peter Cole, being ninety at the time of writing. It has been estimated that there are about two hundred big wave surfers in the world. Some of them, like Aaron Gold, say that you can whittle that down to a top group of fifty guys that are the elite "pushing athletes" in this sport. But the number is increasing, as is the availability of safety devices that help surfers survive mishaps and come back home to their families. As one of the most dramatic examples, after a wipeout during a trip to Cloudbreak in Fiji, Aaron was not breathing for several minutes before his friends revived him on a supporting boat. The development and proliferation of safety devices and social media, as well as improvements in equipment, weather and wave forecasting, and knowledge of physiology, allow more people into the sport while also influencing how it's practiced.

How many women surf big waves? It depends on how you define "big," but the number is certainly growing. There are perhaps a dozen, as many as half of whom pursue this activity with the specific goal of becoming professional athletes. But because big wave surfers remain overwhelmingly male, I use the masculine pronoun unless I am specifically describing women.

This book is based upon one fall, four winters, and one spring that I spent on O'ahu. It relies on observations recorded through field notes, photographs, videos, and seventy-nine interviews with different big wave surfers who occupy various positions within this social world—including lifeguards. It's comparative on several levels.[24] For example, it contrasts risk-taking across participants' lifetimes, moving from novices to old hands. It also discusses how voluntary risk-taking relates to phases of professionalization of the sport, the various phases of participants' career development, gender, and technological developments.

To some extent it also employs embodied ethnography as described in Loïc Wacquant's *carnal approach*.[25] This perspective maintains that to gain a phenomenological, interactional, and experiential knowledge of a phenomenon, researchers must actively train to pursue it and eventually acquire some degree of proficiency. The body and its modification become a tool of inquiry. While I have surfed since my early teenage years and have competed in skateboarding, I never dreamed of or wanted to surf big waves. However, during my fieldwork I was pressured into paddling out on a surfboard on a big day at Waimea and seduced into surfing relatively "small" big waves for two winter seasons. And I also trained: physically by prone paddle boarding over two summers, and mentally by twice taking an intensive two-day course on apnea and survival in big surf on the North Shore of O'ahu. Like Wacquant and other ethnographers engaged in participant observation, I hold that this approach helped me better understand this social world and also provided me with opportunities to observe interactions I otherwise would not have been able to document. But unlike Wacquant, I can't claim to have reached expertise or even proficiency,[26] even though at times I wish I would have. It was only a memorable dip.

Toward the end of the data collection an informant admitted that the length of time I spent in the field justified opening up to me. Ethnographic quality largely depends on the depth and breadth of the relationships we form in the field, and the roles we manage to fulfill.[27] The words *quick* and *ethnography* are antonyms. My willingness to participate in the activities my informants were involved in also helped me to gain some of their trust. But most importantly, it helped me to taste, savor, and crave belonging, giving depth to my appreciation of their yearning. Sensorial approaches are also connected with an increased interest in using photo and video material to understand, describe, and communicate research to audiences beyond academia. I made use of each of these data gatherings, and you will find a number of photographs included here to enhance my story.

I begin each chapter by describing a character and a small group episode related to a specific theme that I subsequently elaborate and fit into a larger theoretical narrative. By focusing on rituals and processes that precede, contribute to, and follow on episodes of fateful moments in adolescence and adult life, I build a theory of the interpersonal dynamics that contribute to centeredness in a person who is weighing a difficult decision to step into a new "self" as a big wave surfer. And while I focus on surfing, I argue that the theory has the potential to be used in a wide range of studies of recreational careers outside one's everyday identity. Using numerous examples drawn from my experience as a participant observer and my interviews with men and women at various stages of their careers as surfers, I examine how mentors and peers contribute to the individual actor's psychological integration and will to take a transforming step. Specifically, in my theory of "becoming" I describe how a surfer forms the aspiration to be a surfer; the fateful moments experienced; the impact of a charismatic, supportive mentor on the fears and self-doubts of the novice; the impact of a set of peers and colleagues on the motivation to get through a fateful moment; the accumulation of achievements and injuries over a career; and the eventual decision to exit the role of active surfer.

But before we "get wet," I'll set the stage by introducing the social world of surfing generally, and big wave surfing in particular. While this historical section is based on an agglomeration of secondary, published sources, it also relies on a handful of the interviews I conducted. Its primary purpose is to briefly explain surfing and big wave surfing by placing them in a sociohistorical context while also describing the basic process of surfing. Put differently, this section is not a historical study, but an auxiliary part of my ethnography.

From the Cradle of Surfing to the World

Surfing is a traditional Hawaiian cultural activity, gifted to the world from that beautiful archipelago. Yet every indigenous culture that had an oceanic environment and fished in the sea did some form of wave riding—from Africa to South America. "That argument could go on forever," archeologist and surf professor Ian 'Akahi Masterson tells me. "Don't you ever get involved with that argument," anthropologist Ben Finney warned him decades ago when Finney was supervising Ian's master's thesis at the University of Hawai'i at Mānoa. Everywhere there was an ocean, people surfed in some rudimentary form or other. It is a basic adaptation to the marine environment. And we will never know who the first surfer was—whether it was a fisherman, or someone who saw a shark or dolphin ride a wave, or just someone trying to get to shore. Ian tells me: "Going out to sea in rough surf, catch food, and come back in? That certainly raised your status in the community hierarchy."

In the summer of 1907 George Freeth left Hawaiʻi to showcase surfing for large crowds along the California coast, in addition to working as a lifeguard. Promoters billed him as "the man who walked on water." And in 1912, his close friend, the Hawaiian Olympic swimmer Duke Kahanamoku, further popularized surfing with exhibitions both on the East and West Coasts of the United States, and eventually in Australia and New Zealand. According to writer David Davis, surfing initially "languished because outsiders did not 'get it.'"[28] Nonetheless, it provided a wondrous spectacle, just as seeing a tamer of tigers would. "Surfing was unstructured, ephemeral, and without written rules. There were no goals to score or points to make,"[29] and it appeared exclusively tied to Hawaiʻi, he added. As "The Duke" famously remarked: "The best surfer out there is the one having the most fun."

In ancient Hawaiʻi, surfing and its many different forms involved a number of rituals: from carving out boards in a specific way, to creating chants to try and raise the surf, to composing eulogies describing specific surf spots where a Hawaiian loved life. While the large majority of ancient rituals no longer exist, surfing for some is still a spiritual activity. As religion scholar Bron Taylor[30] notes, a segment of the global surfing community should be considered as a new religious movement. Taylor is referring to those surfers who since the late 1970s and early 1980s label themselves "soul surfers" in contrast to competitive surfers. "Do you surf to try to get rich and famous, or do you surf for yourself and your connection with nature?" Ian comments.

Surfing constituted an engrossing passion shared across different strata of the Hawaiian population: men, women, children, royalty, chiefs, and commoners, surfing even in their senior years. All of them not only devoting a large amount of time to riding waves, but also dropping any other activity when the surf rose up. Priests would pray for surf, and kites would be flown from the top of Diamond Head on the South Shore of Oʻahu to alert inlanders of pristine conditions. As surf historian John Clark writes, surfing "was one of the most beloved activities of the Hawaiian people,"[31] and by the 1800s several indigenous and non-Hawaiian writers described it as a "national pastime." Research by Ian Masterson and others further shows that women were not only highly respected in the lineup—where surfers wait for their opportunity to catch waves—but were also generally better surfers than men.[32] According to Masterson, women then had an edge compared to men because of the equipment: their lower center of gravity, in their hips, made it easier for them to ride the finless boards of that time, just as it made them, on average, better dancers than men. To maneuver a board with no fins requires gentle, subtle movements, just as steering a sailboat does. Women also benefitted from practicing hula, the original Hawaiian dance, and then transferring those skills and experiences to dancing on the waves.

In Hawaiian society surfing not only provided pleasure, fun, and social cohesion; it also afforded a way to influence the opposite sex, attain social and political status, and win prizes in competitions and money through gambling, which was a prominent kind of amusement for Hawaiians.[33]

Surfing in all its various forms became a foundational element of the social fabric of Hawaiian society for several reasons. First, the climate and the topography, and eventually, surfboard technology. The warm weather and the quantity and variety of surf breaks across the islands provided Hawaiians with an environment that allowed them not only to practice the activity often, but also to improve at it. Depending on different accounts, Hawaiians reached Hawai'i at least a thousand years ago. The island of O'ahu alone provided them with a truly vast array of different kinds of waves—south shore, north shore, west side, east side, literally hundreds and hundreds of breaks to choose from. Partially as a consequence of this profusion of opportunities, their skill level increased exponentially beyond any other population. As John Clark tells me, when they first arrived it's likely that they only bodysurfed waves (literally using their bodies to slide on waves) and bodyboarded (riding wooden planks to skim on their bellies), rather than gliding while standing up. Gradually increasing the size of surf boards arguably contributed to the beginning of riding waves standing on two feet.

The evolution of board manufacturing also influenced their increased skill level and led to surfers riding incrementally larger waves. Hawaiians experimented with different types of boards: big, small, with different shapes, all carved out of different types of wood. The *olo* boards, for example, were the largest; they looked like big telephone poles, and were reserved for royalty. In general, the larger the board, the easier it is to catch and surf both small and larger waves. Yet none of these solid wood, heavy boards had any fins on their bottom, and without even one fin it was difficult to angle the board on the wave without sliding out. As a consequence, most rides went straight into shore (which also allowed many surfers to ride alongside one another on a single wave), rather than across or along the wave one at a time as surfers do today. Yet we know that the most skilled ancient Hawaiians surfed on each side of the island and could execute turns on waves.

As historians Peter Westwick and Peter Neushul[34] note, the first Hawaiians who arrived on the islands (according to them, circa the fifth century AD from Polynesia, and around the twelfth century from Tahiti) were sailors from the most proficient seagoing populations the world has known. And because of the rough oceanic conditions they faced, they had to adapt further, ultimately becoming "some of the world's most accomplished watermen." In stark contrast to many populations who feared and avoided the sea (as is documented in many sources[35]), Hawaiians often felt more comfortable in the water than on land. Because of the warm weather, the plentiful supply of food, and a rich diet, Hawaiians were exceptionally healthy, which permitted them to pursue enthusiastically such physical activities as surfing.[36]

Pre-contact Hawaiians also devised an ingenious system of fish farming, which, along with agriculture, resulted in an abundant supply of food, affording them large amounts of leisure time to devote to surfing. As Westwick and Neushul further note, the annual festival Makahiki, which lasted for three months during the winter, meant they could spend fully a quarter of the year surfing, which ultimately contributed to their mastery.

This sociopolitical situation changed as Westerners made contact with Hawaiians. Prior to the Mahele (land division) of 1848, private property did not exist in Hawai'i. Hawaiian royalty controlled the lands, but the commoners could use most of them at the royalty's discretion. Hawaiian society was based on trading rather than a market economy. But in 1898 the forced annexation of Hawai'i by the United States and the launching of a cash economy through the sandalwood and whaling trades negatively impacted the time the indigenous population had for leisure activities like surfing. This modern colonization, still in place to this day, had repercussions that obviously extend beyond and deeper than the surf.

Émile Durkheim defines the religious ritual as primarily a means to establish and maintain solidarity among participants, but one that also provides a moral compass that guides their actions around the archetypical distinction between sacred and profane. Anthropologist Ben Finney and writer James Houston[37] describe how the death of King Kamehameha I in 1819 and the arrival of missionaries in Hawai'i in 1820 signaled the end of traditional life on the islands: "Religion had been the keystone of Hawai'i's cultural arch. With the removal of the gods and the power and stability of taboos, disorganization soon followed in the family, the class structure, farming and fishing, and in traditional crafts," including pastimes like surfing.

Contact with non-Hawaiian populations also resulted in epidemics of introduced diseases that decimated the indigenous Hawaiian population. The population of the most isolated group of islands in the world had no immunity against diseases like smallpox, measles, and cholera. According to Westwick and Neushul, prior to the arrival of Captain Cook on January 18, 1778, the Hawaiian population was estimated as at least 800,000; by the 1890s only about 40,000 indigenous Hawaiians remained. Though estimates vary from scholar to scholar, the tragic result is clear. Paraphrasing English writer David Lodge,[38] Hawai'i was a paradise stolen, raped, infected, developed, packaged, and sold. And Hawaiians survived, despite being unintentionally exterminated along with much of their culture. Hawaiians persisted, faring better in some parts of some of the islands more than in others, and maintaining a sovereignty movement fighting for Hawaiians' human right to be considered as something more than a purely decorative population for the tourism industry, as they have been since the 1893 overthrow of their monarchy by the government of the United States.

Disputing earlier accounts, scholars like political scientist Noenoe Silva[39] assert that Hawaiians actively resisted Western domination. And as historian Isaiah Helekunihi Walker[40] documents, the water and the surf represented and still represent one of the last spaces where Hawaiians, including those today that claim alliance or descent, whether opportunistically or not, can claim sovereignty. The water, the surf, is a liminal space where regular land laws are hard to implement—a fluid, contested space. As Helekunihi Walker puts it, a place of resistance, and "a window to Hawaiians' pre-colonial past."[41]

The bourgeoning tourism industry of the early 1900s, the development of Waikīkī as a tourist destination, and the popularization of swimming and surfboard development strongly contributed to surfing's revival and expansion. Referring to the beginning of the twentieth century, Finney and Houston write: "The history of the surfboard's evolution closely parallels the sport's revival. The two, in fact, depend on each other. As boards became more efficient and available, more people surfed; riding techniques improved."[42] In the mid-1950s surfing technology expanded further. Board manufacturing shifted from wood to polyurethane foam, cloth, and resin. This innovation made boards not only cheaper and faster to produce, but also easier to handle and to ride, thus contributing to surfing's popularity. Additionally, the modern expansion of the sport must be credited to photographic[43] and video material, and most recently, electronic media. And the invention of and subsequent improvements to wetsuits is still impacting the spread of the sport by providing access to surf even in frigid waters.

As surfing expanded across the world and lineups became more crowded, localism arose—that is, the demand for priority rights over waves by certain surfers who live near a surf spot and/or surf it religiously. According to Ian Masterson, localism arose because surfing culture had failed to integrate key aspects of Hawaiian culture, which entailed sharing norms both in and outside of the surf. Ultimately, even Hawai'i during the 1970s experienced heavy localism, partly as a result of visiting surfers from Australia and the mainland United States exploiting their power in the surf as if they could colonize it. As Masterson points out, in the 1960s and especially in the 1980s surf culture experienced the "culture of cool," which he says has "stuck with surfing into the 21st century," and which, he remarks, "wasn't very cool." The proliferation of contests, professional surfing, publications, and various other forms of media not only contributed to crowding in the surf; it also made surfing lineups in general more hostile toward newcomers, and spurred ever stiffer competition among surfers seeking to get more waves, the best waves, and to get their picture taken while riding them alone.

It's estimated that today there are about twenty million people surfing worldwide, and that number is increasing. Each location near an ocean or sea has developed its own surf culture, and such communities have also formed even in some places devoid of natural waves, making surfing a truly global phenomenon that permeates and influences popular culture at large. Surf parks have been and will continue to be built globally, and surfing made its debut as an Olympic sport at the 2021 Tokyo summer games.

Surfing 101: Waves and Process

But how does surfing work? These are the basics you need to better understand my tale.

Not counting rare phenomena like tsunamis and earthquakes, waves are generated by wind and gravity. Other factors held constant, the stronger, longer, and further from shore winds blow, the larger the waves will be. When waves meet a sufficient change in bathymetry (the topography of the ocean floor), they break, producing rideable surf. Sport historian Douglas Booth[44] writes that all big wave breaks are generated by a "radical variation in the marine contour, from deep to shallow," and that those changes of depth "can magnify wave energy and radically modify the form of a wave." It's exactly the interplay between changing bathymetry and different kinds of swells—for instance, the direction from which they originate and the point where they will encounter a reef—that determine the countless forms of waves. Wave speed, power, height, and thickness are also dependent on *period*—the number of seconds between two successive wave crests as they pass a stationary point. The longer the period, the more speed, height, and power a wave will carry. Each surf spot has a particular swell window—meaning a specific angle from which waves need to arrive to produce congenial (or, more rarely, epic) conditions. But top conditions for a particular spot also depend on period and wave height. And big waves, unicorns in this world, require an unusual combination of golden weatherly conditions; bathymetry; wind direction, duration, strength, and distance from shore; and swell angle. Surfers call these rarities "bombs"—referring to specific waves within a session, a "wave of the season" or "swell of the decade" or of the century, or the like. Each spot excels under different conditions, and each has a sweet spot where a myriad of factors intersect perfectly—sometimes only for a few hours. Different parts of the globe are more or less likely to be hit by swells during different seasons, and therefore most surfers travel, even if only by driving up and down a particular coast.

Surfers paddle to the *lineup* where they wait and chase waves to catch. To surf a wave, you have to be at the exact right place at the exact right time. More time in the water and more time watching and studying the ocean translate into the ability to predict the particular spot where waves will break during a session, and how they will likely behave. Not all surfers are similarly skilled, and not all pay as much attention to as many details as they should; yet like poker players counting cards and calculating the likelihood of certain hands, the top surfers count waves and how they play out during specific sessions and swells. The best surfers are those who can see rideable waves of quality coming in from the horizon before the others, and can then get themselves in position to take those waves. Further, they study and understand other surfers' strategies.

Different shore breaks at each spot entail different dangers, and negotiating them requires different approaches because of the currents, rocks, and other hazards. Waves generally arrive at fairly regular intervals ranging from a few minutes to thirty minutes or more, and in *sets* of three to seven waves. Between sets there may be smaller waves breaking closer to shore, or the ocean may be flat. This means that on big days surfers need to carefully time their entrance to and exit from the water to avoid being pushed back to shore or crushed by the waves breaking in the shore break. More than many other spots, Waimea shows you the power of the ocean right there on the shore. Depending on the direction the waves come from and their size, different waves break—and can be caught and ridden—at different spots. Surf spots vary as to how close to or far from shore they are located, but generally, the larger the waves, the further out they break and can be caught and ridden. Some big wave spots, like the Cortes Bank off the coast of Mexico, are located miles from shore and can only be accessed by boat. Others, like Waimea, are only a couple of hundred yards from shore—and past a certain size, waves there don't break further out as their size increases, but instead become more powerful and harder to ride. Spots are locations where the shallowness of the sea floor allows waves to curl enough to eventually begin breaking. Different waves of different sizes break in different places within the same spots.

Process

The *takeoff zone*, lineup, or peak is where surfers wait for waves to arrive. When a surfer sees a rideable-looking wave, he paddles toward it, trying to predict the perfect point of entry where if he paddles correctly toward the shore or aiming right or left in the direction of the breaking wave, he will be propelled by the wave energy and can merge with it. Think of it like a train that is at first self-propelled but, if it locks into the right rail, will be pulled along by a different kind of energy. As soon as his board catches enough speed to start to glide, the surfer pops up to his feet—the *take off*. The aim is not to ride straight toward the beach with the white water behind, but to ride at an angle, then come back toward the breaking wave, which is the larger source of energy, to acquire that energy from the wave and then zip away from the wave curl again. If the wave makes a big enough curl, a surfer may try to ride inside its tube, or at least get a quick head dip.

If the surfer *wipes out* or *gets caught inside* by an approaching wave that breaks before he can catch it, then he suffers a *hold down*. Hold downs can last from a few seconds to as much as twenty or thirty seconds. As Matt Warshaw writes: "Panic usually hits at thirty seconds, even for an expert. At fifty seconds, most surfers will be unconscious."[45] Especially in big surf, a surfer may be held down by more than one wave, greatly increasing the chance of drowning. At Waimea a ride can last from about ten seconds to forty-five seconds, but the length of ride varies from spot to spot, and from swell to swell.

Some surfers argue that most of surfing is paddling rather than riding, but really it's largely about waiting: waiting on shore scrutinizing weather forecasts and waiting for conditions to change, and waiting out on the water for waves to arrive. As writer Thomas Farber puts it, surfers stare "at the horizon as if able to will a wave to appear, as if to turn for even a moment might undermine the entire effort."[46]

From Gliding Together to One Person per Wave

As documented by John Clark,[47] ancient Hawaiians practiced at least six different forms of surfing: board surfing, outrigger canoe surfing, bodysurfing, bodyboarding, river surfing, and sand sliding—riding waves from shore back into the ocean initially with the body only. And we know that they often rode the same wave together, alongside one another. Even looking at old pictures of Waikīkī one can see many surfers on the same wave, sometimes even fifty or more at a time. In some activities on land, men and women were kept separate, so sharing a ride with the opposite sex afforded them the opportunity to flirt, which occasionally evolved into romantic encounters on shore. As Finney and Houston write: "equality and sexual freedom added zest to the sport and were important to its widespread popularity."[48] And historian Kevin Dawson[49] and others argue that surfing provided Polynesian women surfers an opportunity to exercise authority over choice of intimate partners and mates.

Up until the 1950s many surfers still used heavy, solid wood surfboards that didn't have fins, and for this reason weren't very maneuverable. It was difficult to angle either right or left and ride the face of the wave rather than in front of it going straight in toward the shore. That original style of riding involved swimming your board as far as possible to the lineup—not paddling on it because they weren't buoyant enough—which contributed to surfers' fitness, and then catching a wave and mostly just riding it in toward the shore as far as they could. In short, surfers were largely riding for distance, and when they held competitions that's mostly how they were judged.

This style of riding together on the same wave began to change in the 1950s with the introduction of foam and fiberglass boards with fins, which allowed more maneuvering. As surfboards became smaller and even more maneuverable (in what is known as the shortboard revolution), a new style consisting of riding closer to or actually in the curl of the wave—aptly named hot-dogging—rose to prominence, which contributed to the new norm of having only one person on a wave at a time. This new technology, coupled with surfers' wholesale adoption of the new style and the advent of modern surf contests, resulted in surfers switching to catching waves one surfer at a time, because they wanted the entire wave face to be their personal canvas.[50]

Surfing norms regarding wave priority are neither consistent from place to place nor formalized in any way, so they can be a source of contention, intimidation, and sometimes violence. The oceanic environment is constantly changing, the number of surfers is growing, but the number of waves stays the same—even though new surf spots continue to get discovered. And many of the norms conflict with one another.[51] But these informal norms help distribute waves, a prized resource, among surfers generally with remarkably little conflict.[52] They evolved from giving priority to the first person standing, to the person closest to the curl. One rule that is accepted by most people in the water is "Don't drop in. If I got the wave first, don't take off in front of me (or behind me); it's my wave." Unless you're surfing with friends or with people who are more receptive to sharing a wave with you, usually it's one person per wave. But there are certain places that accept more people on the wave. For example, at beginners' breaks like Waikīkī most people understand that there are beach concessions on the beach and that's where beginners go, and that's where surfing lessons happen. There you see lots of people on one wave just because that's all they can do: go straight. Surfers in these places temporarily go back to the old days even though they have the modern equipment.

Big wave surfing is also a *partial* exception to this norm, because large waves have more space, and thus they generally allow more riders to ride on the same wave at once. Also, until recently, big wave riders mostly used large boards without much turning. Waimea in particular is a big wave spot where surfers are usually more tolerant of sharing a ride. Partly this is because it's crowded. But another reason is that there are few big waves per hour and per day, and it is a fickle spot that doesn't "break" often enough during the few winter months when it actually can. And most riders go fairly straight, aiming toward the channel in the middle of the Bay, reminiscent of the ancient Hawaiian style of going for distance. As a wave Waimea mostly consists of one big drop, rather than a walling up long wave. Aside from occasionally offering a tubing wave, it doesn't allow much steering. Also, as in any big wave surf spot, once surfers begin paddling to catch such large waves, it's difficult to stop and pull back. Ian Masterson remembers as a fifteen-year-old asking veteran big wave rider Ken Bradshaw what it was like surfing Waimea with so many guys dropping in on the same wave at the same time. Ken allegedly replied:

> You see that coconut tree up there? Imagine there's guys dropping on a wave that big. You're not thinking about anything, you're thinking about making that wave! And as long as everybody makes the turn (at the bottom of the wave directing their boards toward the channel) you're OK. But the guy who goes straight is gonna ruin it for everybody behind. There's plenty of room for everybody on that wave.

Yet, a handful of surfers have told me that riding together hindered their performance. Ian, for example, says that "Eight out of my ten chances at getting barreled at Waimea were totally snuffed by people dropping straight down out of the sky." And talking about the joy of sharing rides, which I observed and also experienced, he says:

> You want to know what the best thing is at Waimea Bay? Even more than party waves? Having so few people out there. "Clark, it's your wave, go! Yeah!" Clark catches his wave. "Andrew! You go!" And then I catch a wave and then we sit off on the side after catching a couple of waves . . . to be able to rotate . . . now if you can get a wave by yourself at Waimea, what a cool thing. "Give a wave, take a wave," Pat Caldwell says. If I can sit on the side and watch one of my friends I have been surfing Waimea with, and maybe never even seen them on land, but they're some of my closest to heart friends because we do this together and it's real (his voice trembling)—(in a louder crescendo): the fear, the danger, the watching out for each other, the stoke, the passion, the morning jitters.

Big Wave Worlds

Contemporary big wave surfing originated in Hawai'i in the early 1940s and 1950s at Mākaha on the West side of O'ahu, and at Sunset and Waimea on the North Shore. We know that each of these spots had been surfed before, but we don't know what size the waves were. We also know that ancient Hawaiians surfed rather large waves, adapting their style to their rudimentary technology—for example, by taking off on the

A giant, perfect wave at Waimea with plenty of space lets four surfers ride it without obstructing each other.

shoulder of the wave and thus more on its slopy part, rather than close to its apex. And as John Clark tells me, the wave that the Olympic swimmer and surf ambassador Duke Kahanamoku rode in 1916 on the South Shore of O'ahu at a spot called Castles qualifies as big wave surfing. But how large do waves need to be to earn the label? Opinions vary and change as the sport progresses, just as the measuring of waves does. Some say that truly big waves start at 20/20—twenty feet measured from the trough to crest of an ocean swell with a twenty-second interval between waves. That would roughly equal falling from forty feet—or four stories, without counting the amount of water that would hit you next. But Clark Abbey, one of the most iconic Waimea surfers, thinks that there's a misconception about the Bay. "There is a mistaken identity that the Bay doesn't really break until it's twenty feet. The Bay is beautiful anywhere after fifteen feet. Once it gets over ten feet and it breaks outside the boil, the Bay becomes rideable. So, twelve to fifteen feet is great. When it's twenty to twenty-five, it starts closing out." And while some years it hardly breaks, there are other years when it breaks often.

Rather than size, others simply talk about big wave spots such as Waimea and the Outer Reefs on the North Shore of O'ahu, Jaws on Maui, Puerto Escondido in Mexico, Mavericks in Northern California, or Nazaré in Portugal. With exploration and improvements in the accuracy and availability of forecasting technologies, the list expands. There are surf spots that come to life only when the surf is unquestionably big—and sometimes wake up only because of a particularly rare swell direction. To be navigated successfully, conditions at such spots may require long, thick boards shaped narrowly in the nose and tail, called "guns." Still others, like the early 1940s surfing pioneer Buzzy Trent, talked about counting "increments of fear" rather than feet. Contemporary surfers like Sion Milosky, who drowned in 2011 surfing Mavericks in Half Moon Bay, California, are more direct: "I don't judge waves anymore. I don't put a size on it. It's small, big, really big, fucking big." Contest organizer Gary Linden is rumored to have said that regardless of surf size, big wave surfers are those gravitating toward the outside of the lineup waiting for the biggest waves of the day. Patience. Desire. Commitment. Passion. Craving. And for some, an obsession generating symptoms of chemical addiction that can negatively affect parts of your life besides getting you as high as some of the drugs you can buy.[53]

Surfers also distinguish between regular big waves and slabs—tall but also exceptionally thick waves breaking on very little water, like Shipstern's Bluff in Tasmania. They also differentiate between those who catch them by arm power alone (paddling, a pure form) and those who get towed into those waves by a jet ski (a profane form, unless conditions do not permit a surfer to successfully paddle into the waves—usually because of their exceptionally large size). Being towed by a jet ski allows surfers working in pairs (generally alternating between driving the ski and surfing) to catch larger waves than they could through paddling, as the speed required to catch the larger waves can sometimes only be attained with horsepower. Driver and surfer patrol outside of where waves are breaking (beyond the lineup), sometimes a mile or two out in the ocean, looking for a specific wave—for instance, a distinctly bigger wave within an already bigger set. Once they have identified it, the driver tows the surfer, feet strapped to his surfboard and standing up holding a tow rope, as if he were water skiing. The driver identifies the correct point of entry to the wave, places the surfer in the right position to ride down the slope before the wave starts breaking, and jets out to the side of the wave. The surfer lets go of the rope and rides the wave until completion or wipeout. Then the driver, who has monitored the ride, drives to where the surfer has ended up to take him back to safety offshore, away from the impact zone, or to the channel (where waves are not breaking because the seafloor is too deep). Once there, they rest and look for another wave, or switch roles. Alternatively, surfers can hire jet ski drivers to tow them into waves or to serve as lifeguards and rescue them if necessary when they are paddling into waves on their own.

Towing is *generally* regarded as safer and easier than paddling, and at particularly wild surf spots like Nazaré—where waves break all over the playing field and there's no safety channel—it's often the only option. As an informant put it: "I could tow my mother into a wave, while paddling requires much more mental and physical preparation . . . and it's also a lot more dangerous." While this statement is obviously an exaggeration that needs to be topographically and historically contextualized, there's truth in it.

As writer Jamie Brisick puts it in the photographic book *The Big Wave Riders of Hawaii: Aloha Spirit, Heritage & Respect*: "big wave surfing is a family within a family,"[54] the larger tribe being surfing, which Warshaw describes as having been "an uneasy conglomerate of many tribes"[55] (e.g., competitive vs. soulful; traveling vs. contest surfer; local vs. nonlocal). Yet even within this family there are many different subsets, such as big waves vs. slabs and paddling vs. tow-ins. There are also many small cliques of friends who not only help one another but also compete with other groups, especially when chasing big waves across the globe. To accomplish the missions big wave surfing entails, and to maximize the benefits of doing so—such as exclusivity of the accomplishment, which can bring monetary rewards—many resources need to be pulled together, and there are often last-minute necessities that add to the costs. It's also important to team up with friends you can count on and to have fine-tuned logistical procedures. While we are driving to catch a 5:00 a.m. flight from O'ahu to Maui to chase the first Jaws swell of the season, a surfer tells me that he waits to post on social media about his mission until it's already too late for others who might have been vacillating on the fence of indecision to get there: "Many are just waiting for a little encouragement to make the call. I've been there myself. It took me years to get to where I am today . . . lots of trial and error."

Group Pleasure

While one can argue that contemporary surfing is often a selfish activity leading to pleasure, which is personal and partially chemically induced (e.g., the adrenaline rush[56]), big wave surfing additionally tends to be more communal, leading to *group pleasure*—fun.[57] Professional surfer Garrett McNamara corrects me and says that big wave surfers are just as selfish as regular surfers, but they engage in "selfless acts" as when for example they try to save one another when things go wrong. But others disagree, and my focus is on situated behavior rather than on individual psychological traits. Because surfing big waves is a hazardous and difficult pursuit requiring much preparation, coordination, and collaboration—pro surfer Ross Clarke-Jones compares it to a military operation[58]—it's fair to argue that in general, surfing large waves "brings people together," as legendary Waimea surfer Chris Owens put it, while regular surfing usually doesn't. Many of the surfers I met told me that the experience is similar to going to war for a day. And I have also seen how on a big day, surfers operate like a platoon—the basic principle being that no one is left behind. For example, when a surfer takes off on a big wave, the whole lineup generally watches to see whether the surfer successfully makes the wave. If he doesn't, then they watch to see whether he comes up to the surface OK or not. If he doesn't, they're ready to jump in to try and save him. And as the day ends, surfers make sure to ride one wave in to the beach together to avoid leaving anyone in the lineup alone after sunset.

But big wave surfing is a group pleasure not only because surfers often depend on others to try and save them; surfers also motivate each other to paddle out and perform, and help one another read the ocean correctly to catch a wave. As many have told me, and as I have experienced, if one of your friends tells you to go—to take off—then you just have to go. And it's not only the danger and the risk associated with the activity, but also the fact that, as an outer reef surfer expressed, it's one of "the last pure" things left in surfing. This means that even though this specialized sport is growing fast, it's still subcultural and unpopular enough that those who seriously pursue it feel a shared sense of authenticity, exclusivity, and mutual respect.[59] Concomitantly, the sport of surfing is growing exponentially, and those working in the industry reasonably talk about a surf mania, of which big wave surfing is one of the last frontiers (along with others like cold water surfing).

As a surfer explained to me, at different swell sizes you will see different groups of surfers at the Outer Reefs, learning their limits and what kind of waves they are looking for. Surfers gradually learn where in the framework they feel comfortable, become more selective as they progress, and adjust their limits as they age by scaling down.

Catching a big wave is not only stressful, but also very difficult, and it requires (especially when paddling) perfect positioning—which in turn requires that surfers cooperate and help one another by cheering on those who may be better positioned to take off on a big wave. Besides luck, catching (or not catching) a big wave depends on many factors: commitment, the correct equipment, and physical strength, but also positioning and water knowledge, which tends to increase with experience and which also helps explain why some of the best at this specialization are not youngsters. Additionally, big waves are rare, which contributes to the sacrality of the experience but also to their preciousness and surfers' reluctance to let any of them get away unridden. "Was that the wave of my life?" some ask when they miss a singularly large wave by either being in the wrong position or deciding not to take the risk. For some this quest for "the wave of my life" becomes a lifelong pursuit that they know will be never-ending. An endless, perhaps unattainable quest, but one that might be good enough to provide you with a life trajectory and infuse you with enough meaning and drive to keep you going, sometimes for decades.

No matter how calculated many surfers at the top level have become, there's also still an element of gambling. Epitomizing this essential uncertainty, Chris Owens, who recently turned sixty and is an underground legend on the North Shore, says that "there are only so many times you can get away with it." Things will eventually go wrong. It's just a matter of time.

Finally, big waves are usually ridden by going fairly straight, either toward the bottom of the wave or at an angle—which, given the size of the waves, can allow many surfers to ride alongside each other. And if you know only one rule of surfing, it's probably this: taking off with someone else on the same wave is like sharing a toothbrush with a stranger—it can be done, but you probably shouldn't do it. Sometimes, though, surfing big waves means sharing a ride together or letting someone else have it because they are better positioned or because you want them to share in this adventure.

Waimea and Beyond

Waimea is the name of the wave, while The Bay is its topographical location. Three hundred feet above, ancient Hawaiians used to make animal and human sacrifices at a *heiau*—a place of worship to the Hawaiian gods. Below, a giant aquarium in the summer, and a place of rare giant surf in the winter. "A place of *mana*," says a Hawaiian who surfs and lifeguards there. A powerful spiritual place. Riding big waves was pioneered here in the late 1950s.

Since then Waimea has been considered the shrine of big wave surfing, and until modern innovations in big wave surfing technology and the introduction of safety apparatuses like jet skis and flotation devices worn by surfers it was also considered the ultimate proving ground in this specialty. More recently, with the discovery of different big waves around the world, it has come to be seen as a stepping-stone into a thriving surfing subdiscipline. Yet lately it has been referred to in niche media as the most underrated big wave spot.

What matters most for this introduction is that surfing big waves over the latter half of the twentieth century and through the first two decades of the twenty-first underwent a number of discernible changes which are ultimately pointing toward the professionalization of the activity—a process that screeched to a sudden halt in 2020 because of the COVID-19 pandemic.

First, as Matt Warshaw and others note, until the discovery in the early 1990s of a wave called Mavericks in northern California, big wave surfing was largely considered an underground, Hawaiian fringe aspect of the broader sport of surfing. Because Mavericks is located near the former editorial offices of *Surfer* and *Surfing Magazine*, its coverage in those publications helped popularize and commercialize the activity.

Second, tow-in surfing revolutionized the possibilities of big wave surfing by allowing surfers to ride waves they had for decades deemed too large to catch by "paddling in" under arm power alone. By 2011, with the invention and popularization of safety devices like flotation vests, tow-in surfing began to gradually be replaced by paddling in. Waimea is a spot where this transition never took place, as tow-in has never been allowed there.

Third, modern big wave surfing went through different phases of popularity and demographics. While the first Californian and Hawaiian surfers who committed to surfing Mākaha, Sunset, and Waimea in the late 1930s, 1940s, and 1950s[60] were a small group, big wave surfing went out of fashion because as the surf industry professionalized, it invested in "small" wave surfing. As surfing tournaments were being created, sporting equipment was being modified and improved; and as surfing was becoming a global phenomenon, a new surfing style was taking hold. As documented by scholars like Douglas Booth, the Hawaiian style of surfing involved dancing with the wave; but since the 1960s Californians and Australians advanced a new style that relied on shredding the wave to pieces with aggressive turns.[61] Because competitions and the surf industry are tightly coupled with surf media, Warshaw notes that "Waimea seemed a bygone surfbreak—it didn't make the cover of *Surfer* from 1967 to 1983—visited for the most part by surfers in their thirties and forties, and even fifties."[62] As Warshaw writes, during this period big wave surfers "weren't hip—and by association neither was their preferred form of riding."[63]

The distinctively big winter of 1982–83 brought big wave surfing back into the spotlight somewhat, yet the most dramatic increase in the publicity and popularity of the activity came with the advent of tow-in surfing in the 1990s. Since the early 2010s, the popularity of paddling into big waves rebounded, which led to the establishment of a big wave surfing competitive tour and technological advancements that made the activity safer and thus more approachable—but also more performance oriented.

The growing popularity of big wave surfing, whether in terms of active participants or spectators, is also an offshoot of the increasing popularity of surfing and other lifestyle sports like skateboarding, climbing, and snowboarding.

The Quiksilver Big Wave Invitational in Memory of Eddie Aikau[64] at Waimea Bay—the first competition specifically conceptualized for big wave surfing—represents the most meaningful event in the surfing world. Much of this book addresses a community of underground surfers who regularly ride the Bay, and the professionals who travel the world in the pursuit of big waves.

Plan of the Book

In chapter 1, "From Land to Water," I introduce the character of Phil Owen and recall my first experience with big waves at the Bay. This short chapter conveys my inner experience of becoming a surfer and participating in the interaction rituals of a small group of surfers led by Phil, a group that we will encounter again in chapter 2.

Chapter 2, "Beyond the Boil," dives into describing Phil, a sixty-year-old man who lives in a shack overlooking Waimea and has mentored several others besides me in riding big waves. I give an overview of Randall Collins's theory of interaction rituals, which serves as the larger theoretical frame I use in this book. Because it can be partially explained as a theory of situations, I take this unit of analysis as my starting point. For this reason, I also provide two detailed stories, cast in the form of dialogue between two groups of surfers who paddled out at Waimea on some of the largest waves of their lives during the El Niño year of 2016. One group is led by Phil, and the other by Chris Owens, who is another key figure at the Bay. I zoom in on the moments preceding the *action*:

from walking to the beach, to waiting for the right moment to paddle out, to eventually taking off on massive waves and making it safely back to shore. These stories show how fear is converted into excitement, commitment, and fun, and how mentors can help us achieve more than we dreamed we could. And they can lead us toward and through successful interactions constituted by *fateful moments*, or by a series of them.

Chapter 3, "Fun and Community," is written in a different style. It starts with Chris, a surfer whose reputation is similar to Phil's. But while Phil is content with his relative anonymity, Chris aims at being known beyond the underground scene. By introducing Chris's daily routine, I bring the reader closer to understanding the small community of the North Shore beyond what the tourists tend to see. There is poverty, alcoholism, violence, crime, and tragedy, but also communion and empathy. And there are still tensions and movements against colonization as a vestige of deep Hawaiian pride. Hawaiian culture and beliefs permeate the land and water and are expressed through such keywords as respect, aloha, and kōkua. Waves along with other commodities are exchanged. Big wave surfing provides a way to bring the original Polynesian ethos of sharing and fun back in.[65] The larger the waves grow, the more surfers tend to share them and collaborate to perform. Analytical in approach, this chapter describes a geographical area and its local culture, introduces a sociological theory of fun, and then uses field scenes and interview excerpts to illustrate the elements of that theory. Fun is one way to connect Collins's theory to ideas about group cultures, and thus with group history and future expectations. I show the communal, existential, and physiological aspects connected with the activity while introducing the idea of *interaction intensity variance*. Collins's theory is centered on situations and the ingredients that can lead to successful encounters producing high levels of emotional energy. But interaction ritual theory doesn't explore the impact of different kinds of physical environments on rituals, whereas I argue that the physical environment significantly affects the intensity of situations and, as a consequence, the emotional energy and solidarity among participants. I also discuss risk-taking in relation to embodied pleasures and fun. Surfing big waves is a way to find belonging, meaning, and a purpose, and for some a way out of drugs and alcohol. However, like other activities involving *flow*, it also has a dark side—a tendency toward a kind of physical addiction that undermines social relationships, and in certain cases leads male surfers to seek and enjoy various kinds of extreme pleasures.

Chapter 4, "Failing to Succeed, Failing to Become," introduces the idea of failing, and shows that regardless of the content and initial emotion, virtually any encounter can, under the right conditions, be shaped as a successful interaction. It describes the importance and meaning of a surfer's first "really bad pounding," by either falling and having a wave "squash you like a bug" or having the white water "mow you over" like a leaf swept up by a rake. It explains the significance of these moments in a big wave surfer's progression by focusing on internal rituals (inner dialogues and self-talk) and external rituals (interactions with significant others)—topics I will expand on in chapter 5.

Chapter 4 also introduces ideas about fear and safety, as well as mental and physical preparation, and how they have changed since the 1950s. In this line it addresses what sociologist Daniel Chambliss calls the "mundanity of excellence"—how qualitative differences in preparation distinguish top performers from those who possess similar talent but do not achieve noteworthy success.

The main character I present here is Jamie Sterling, a professional big wave surfer in his late thirties who suffered a dramatic wipeout early in his career, and years later (2011) won the world championship. I also describe the work of the lifeguards who patrol the heavy surf: Which main challenges do they face? How has their approach toward lifeguarding changed as technology has advanced?

Chapter 5, "Reciprocal Influence," examines how surfers stimulate one another into taking incrementally larger risks through two different types of group pressure: peer pressure and pushing against rivals. Surfers seek respect and approbation from their peers, and fear the shame that comes with the withholding of that approval.

It begins by narrating the relationship between Jamie Sterling and his childhood friend, Mark Healey, focusing on how they helped each other to become big wave surfers and eventually professional athletes. Here I detail the importance of idealization and what Michael Farrell calls *escalating reciprocity*—the dynamic that pushes members of a group to match and exceed each other's performance.

Unlike in pre-contact Hawai'i, in modern surfing women have been and to some extent are still considered outsiders in a male-dominated sport. In this chapter I include a discussion of women surfing big waves: first by centering on Keala Kennelly, who was the 2018 women's world champion, and then by focusing on Lynne Boyer, who had won the world championship in regular surfing twice in the 1970s, and was at that time also one of the best women in the world at surfing big waves. I discuss some of the challenges these women face, and the strategies they use to overcome them.

Chapter 6, "From Adventure to Entertainment and toward Sport," explores changes wrought on big wave surfing by the introduction and popularization of safety devices. It also analyzes different pathways through which athletes attempt to make a livelihood while pursuing this activity. The main character I describe here is the Brazilian Carlos Burle, who has won the Big Wave world title twice (1998, 2009), has recently retired from competitions, and has been pushing for the professionalization of the sport for three decades.

Conceptually this chapter discusses risk-taking, status, and reputation. Here I distinguish between *chargers* (surfers who are known to take high risks, sometimes with little or no chance of success) and *sharpshooters* (surfers who are much more selective in their approach toward risk and invest their efforts toward higher risk/higher reward opportunities). While contenders tend to be chargers, established professionals are more likely to be, or aspire to be, sharpshooters. In this part of the book I also discuss judging criteria, as well as how some professionals eventually realize that while they are just as likely to get hurt on a comparatively smaller wave as on an outstanding one, the latter could positively impact their careers, while the former wouldn't do very much. In this respect experienced surfers talk about "career waves"—waves that will be admired and remembered. Those *fateful moments* can thus become valuable episodes in a surfer's career while also marking breakthroughs within this social world.

Chapter 7, "One Last Ride," continues to look at when and how surfers change their approach toward risk, and when they eventually decide to quit or gracefully fade out. The last character I introduce is Eddie's brother, Clyde Aikau. I describe his last ride at the 2016 edition of The Eddie, delineating his game plan and how he decides to go back out for his second heat after having gotten seriously hurt in his first heat. During this event Clyde catalyzes *collective effervescence* and reverberates *emotional energy* from and toward the crowd and other participants. For a brief while he becomes a sacred object symbolizing Hawaiian cultural heritage, and the charismatic pastor of this ritual contributing to its success.

CHAPTER ONE
From Land to Water

I've put off buying a gun. Last season that thought didn't even cross my mind. But over the last two months I've borrowed one a few times—mostly against my will. Lately, and late in this season, perhaps because slightly more water experience and being in perceptibly better physical shape have infused me with confidence and joy, I've begun feeling the need to own my own, so that when conditions are right I can swiftly decide to use it, without hassles or (even worse) excuses.

It seems like a deal. Looking at pictures of it on Craigslist, Phil—who quickly found it when I voiced my interest in acquiring one—texts me that it is exactly what I need: "a ten-o," a ten-foot-long surfboard ideal for big waves, and from a shaper who is "experiencing his prime." His message ends with an encouraging "Pull the trigger!" But instead, I hang back.

A few days later I stumble upon the board stacked in the back of a surf shop at the Sugar Mill in Waialua, not far from the small locale where its shaper had built it. It feels bulky, heavy and cumbersome; clearly it's the largest tool in the store and looks more like a canoe than a regular surfboard. I can hardly hold it because of its weight, and it's so wide I can't quite wrap my arm around it. Still unconvinced, I decide again not to buy it. It feels like a foreign object, and I can hardly imagine getting used to handling it. So why get it? And do I *need* to get it?

A week later, frustrated by not being able to get hold of one during what look like playful big wave surfing conditions—which I end up nervously staring at for hours—I track down the board's owner through

Trevor Carlson, a professional big wave surfer I had interviewed whom I had also told about my quest, and for whom the board had originally been built. Already certain that the transaction will happen—I have finally made up my mind—I contact him, quickly negotiate the deal, and arrange to meet him. Giovanni, an Italian American engineer in his late twenties, tells me that he has taken this winter season off because of too many neck injuries. He needs to heal. I explain to him and one of his housemates—probably mostly for my own benefit—that I intend to use the board with caution and only in relatively safe conditions—on "small big waves." His friend complains about how crowded and danger- ous Waimea has become, but I remember that some of the elders have told me it's almost always been fairly busy. One of them who originally planned to start surfing there before he hurt his back calls it a zoo. And he's not alone. As I'm about to leave Giovanni pulls his phone out of his pocket and proudly (yet modestly and even somewhat nervously) shows me a photograph of himself riding the board on a truly steep, tall, and wide wall of thick water. It looks intimidating, and his performance is unmistakably impressive. Is he reminded of all the powerful experiences he has had using the board? "That was at one of the outer reefs," he says, without telling me exactly which one. His eyes are dreamy, fixed on that little screen displaying the image; I also stare, but wide-eyed. This young man is a true charger, I think to myself.

With some tweaking the board fits inside the Land Rover. Had it been one inch longer, it wouldn't have. Driving away realizing the most funda- mental implication of my action, my feet shake a little, timidly remind- ing me of the first time I actually *had to* use a gun, slightly over a year ago.

The 2016 winter season was the result of a weather pattern called El Niño that generally increases the likelihood of big surf. Incredibly, in this case the excellent conditions persisted for several months. Big wave surfers normally have to wait patiently, working to maintain their moti- vation, between the rare days of big swells. An elite few try to chase these swells across the globe by means of mentally and physically taxing last-minute travel arrangements. In 2016 they all had a different prob- lem: how to manage their time so as not to risk injury due to overuse. The season provided many opportunities to fine-tune equipment and to put years of preparation to use for the progression of the sport, but the longer it went on, the more injuries surfers sustained.

To surfers on the North Shore of Oʻahu, the winter of 2016 has been memorable. Big wave surfer, shaper, paddle boarder, former finalist, and one of the judges of the Eddie Aikau competition, Dennis Pang confidently says that it has been "unreal." He says that this, his thirty-fifth year living on the North Shore, has been the most amazing for surfing big waves: "The conditions have just been insane." Then he says that what is amazing is the quality and quantity: plenty of big surf, and with no wind. "When you got the wind, it's nuts. It's shitty." The time window in which it's even possible for Waimea to work by producing a rideable big wave is small, and the days each year when it actually works are very few. Some say that on average it only "breaks" well ten or fifteen times a year, and that the truly giant good days with light wind can be counted on the fingers of one hand, if there are any at all. It's fickle.

The surf report for Friday, January 15, 2016, is representative of this spectacular season: "Lots of activity, of course with this El Niño. Let's take a look . . . what an El Niño year!" the local forecaster exclaims, while referring to a "beast" of a swell being produced by hurricane-force winds close to Japan, which will reach Hawaiian shores as waves with light winds in the morning. And to make conditions even more special, that "thing" (as he calls it) is followed by another thing, and eventually many others. Every week from when I moved to the North Shore in January until April the surf ranges from "extra large" to "XXL," and from "very good" to "epic"—and this is by Hawaiian standards, which are well known for downplaying wave size. Even without such weather anomalies, this side of the planet is known for the powerful, perfect, and big waves that appear every year at this time. But some winters are better than others, and a few, like this one, are long remembered as outstanding.

Phil, a local gentleman in his early sixties, but closer in physical fitness and appearance to an athletic man in his early thirties (particularly in his upper body), has pushed others into big surf for decades. Seeing a picture of him, Lore (who used to be a boxer) calls him a genetic miracle. I've met several surfers who swear by his knowledge of the ocean and follow him religiously as he perfectly times *launching* from the shore break of the Bay out into the lineup. At least a handful mention him as the reason they started surfing big waves, in a few cases the largest waves of their life. By contrast, if you were to ask professional surfers, most would have no recollection of him. Many such talented surfers go undetected— and sometimes by choice. But Phil, like Chris, is a local standout to those who regularly surf the Bay or spots like Jocko's.

My first opportunity to become a "victim," as he says with a laugh, arrives on February 26, and with a generous warning of a few hours. Standing on the deck of his shack overlooking Waimea, Phil assertively and casually tells me, "We're paddling out this afternoon. Get back to the house by 14:00 o'clock." At that instant both of my feet shake as if I'm sensing a mild earthquake or as if I've suddenly received sad news. I feel as if I'm losing my balance, and I can't recall having experienced that feeling of panic before. (I did, however, feel a similar kind of dismay at 8:07 a.m. on January 13, 2018, when I woke up at Lincoln Hall on the University of Hawai'i Mānoa campus to the disturbing sound of this message: "BALLISTIC MISSILE THREAT INBOUND TO HAWAI'I. SEEK IMMEDIATE SHELTER. THIS IS NOT A DRILL.")

The previous day had seen the most significant and rare big wave surfing competition in the world unfold in spectacular and optimal conditions in front of roughly twenty-five thousand people congregated at Waimea Bay—the world's most iconic and picturesque big wave surfing spot. A perfect arena had temporarily welcomed twenty-five hand-picked surfers and spectators from all over the islands and as far away as Peru. I had heard that most flights from California had sold out quickly as soon as the 48-hour notice of The Eddie went out. By this morning the crowds had long gone home, but the waves remained—and so did the desire to ride them, mostly among the many who had not been invited to the competition, and who the day before could only surf before it started or after it ended at four in the afternoon.

John John Florence, who ended up winning the competition, said that when he received his invitation he felt both pride and fear, but didn't know which he felt more strongly. I try arguing with Phil about the implausibility of his idea, but each of my points (or at least the ones I felt comfortable voicing to someone who was at that point just an acquaintance) is met with patient but decisive reassurances, all implying the same thing: "Don't worry, it's going to be fine. Plus, there's nothing you can do about it." I even try to argue that there's a real possibility that I could get hurt, which could impact his reputation. That doesn't faze him in the slightest. Nothing seems to sway him—in fact, he's ignoring me. But I can see his upper lip twitching in mild amusement. If I really want to understand big wave surfing, he seems to be telling me, then I can't just listen to what other surfers tell me. I'll have to see it for myself, and to see it up close. And this means from the water, and on a surfboard—but from the safety of the channel next to where the waves break. Below the surface a flat ledge drops off into a valley in the middle of the Bay, impacting how the waves break and causing what surfers call a channel—a point where waves generally recede.

To run The Eddie, waves not only have to come from a certain direction congenial to the Bay's topography, but they also need to be at least twenty feet high in the open ocean—which translates to thirty- to forty-foot "faces" from the top to the bottom of the wave as surfers ride them—and for eight consecutive daylight hours. The Eddie "requires a perfect storm." Even on the North Shore of Hawai'i these criteria are not easily met, which helps imbue the event with a mystical connotation. Since its inception in 1984 this invitational contest—held to commemorate the first lifeguard at the Bay, Eddie Aikau, and by extension Hawaiian culture (i.e., courage, modesty, aloha, and also bravado) and the community of big wave surfers and surfers alike—has only run nine times, and a few argue that it has never before enjoyed such favorable conditions.

The day after The Eddie, the waves look big and perfect again, but smaller: eighteen- to twenty-foot faces, with occasional twenty-plus-footers rolling through. Or eight to twelve feet on the Hawaiian open ocean scale. While noticeably smaller than the day before, no expert would deny that these waves are still mountains of water and not small or "average" waves.

The shore break looks intimidating and challenging. Many surfers have snapped their thick boards trying to deal with it coming in or going out, or just been "rejected" back onto the beach and left to make the "walk of shame." A few weeks earlier even Kelly Slater, winner of an unprecedented eleven world titles in surfing and one edition of The Eddie, could not get past the shore break and had to give up.

No matter how important it might be for my project, merely seeing waves from the lineup seems not worth the risk. The potential reward is not equal to the hazard. And even though Phil reassures me that today the channel in the middle of the Bay will be a safe haven in which I can sit and observe, to my judgment there is still an undeniable element of real danger and a myriad of things that could go wrong, including the shore break. Why put myself at risk if I'm just going to observe? Just watching to try to understand this activity probably won't be enough for someone who can actually surf, albeit in serious fear of his safety. I find myself thinking that to make the effort worthwhile there has to be at least a fighting chance of me actually catching and riding one of those waves: to experience the thrill of the ride (and hopefully, at this point, not the agony of a wipeout). But that's not the plan—I'm only supposed to be *paddling out*.

I leave Phil's feeling seriously reluctant about his idea for the afternoon, but fairly confident in my two assets: first, my ingenuity in finding ways to convince him to spare me; and second, my donkey-like stubbornness. After all, I've succeeded at that before. A few years earlier, a tow-in surfer nicknamed "Crazy Robbie" had wanted to take me out to watch the giant surf on the back of a jet ski he claimed he had just fixed. This was just before sunset at a spot called Hammerheads, and after telling me days earlier that at this point in his career his "biggest kick" was not riding the wave, but saving his buddies. That evening I hid among the Hale'iwa harbor rocks. And it worked—luckily for me (or not), there was not enough daylight left for Robbie to find me and talk me into getting out there.

I close Phil's gate feeling that the whole idea is simply unrealistic. Then I walk across the street, hop over the guardrail, and make my way down the hill to the beach of the Bay. I stretch some, hoping that the feeling of sickness I still have from the early morning will subside. As I continue doing stretches, it starts to feel like I've partially hyperextended my groin, which adds to my uneasiness. "Great. I wasn't feeling one hundred percent and strong, and now I feel slightly injured too—and just because of some yoga!"

I walk back up the hill, grab my bike, and ride it to Foodland. I buy a yogurt, a coconut water, and a banana. Then, while standing in line to pay, I spot Shaun just a few customers ahead of me. He's limping—is he overdoing it?—which catches me by surprise. I met him yesterday and he didn't look so bad. He actually said he was better. I remember that a few days prior he'd suffered a minor injury on his job as a sky-diving instructor, and that he's taking sick leave. I don't think he's even wearing a T-shirt or slippers. How does he think nobody will know he's ditching work? The surf is perfect and he's sunburnt. Just as he's about to head out, he says: "Phil said you're coming out with us this afternoon." I fumblingly try to argue that this hasn't been agreed on yet, but he's clearly not interested in my reply. Giving no indication that he's heard anything I've said, he adds, walking away, "It'd be great if you could bring some ice to the house." Delighted to fulfill this simple request, I promptly bike back, balancing the largest bag of ice I could find on the handlebars.

Four men are gathered at the house, where a few of them store their guns. As I will find out, and unlike surfers in other conditions, big wave surfers tend to paddle out in groups. And usually there's a moment when those who are about to paddle out meet those who are on their way in, and they shake hands, hug, and exchange a few words about the session and the conditions. At Waimea, unlike most other surf spots I know of, it's typical to surf waves together. Big wave surfing is not like the more selfish and individualistic endeavor that regular surfing often is; it's usually more communal, not least because of the generally far greater danger and complexity of the endeavor, and the teamwork it takes for everyone to have the best chance of succeeding (or just surviving). Also, big wave surfing is still less popular, and the bigger the waves get, the fewer the surfers willing and able to surf them. Put differently: as the size of waves swells and the community shrinks, the social dynamics change—often deepening social bonds.

Most of the men are getting ready to go out. This means putting on safety equipment like vests—which for liability reasons are sold as impact-absorbing devices to protect surfers from being injured by either boards or the reef, rather than as flotation aids (which is mainly what surfers purchase them for)—as well as waxing their boards, discussing the surfing conditions, and talking about yesterday's exceptional waves and event.

Phil reaches under his house and pulls out an orange gun he thinks should work well for me—"it's a Cadillac," he says, meaning that it floats like a boat and paddles fast. It's ten-feet-ten, covered with dirt and spider webs. Phil says he saves it for truly giant days, adding with some regret that he should have used it yesterday. Then, looking through equipment other guys have left at the house, he finds a vest that will fit me. Since not everyone is using one, I assume he wants to minimize the chances of me getting hurt. Conversations are animated, punctuated by laughter, and perhaps charged with nervousness other than my own, even though the truly big day was yesterday, when Phil and his crew surfed the Bay after the competition ended. It had taken Phil more than twenty minutes to identify a long enough lull between sets of incoming waves that they could make it through the shore break rather than being rejected back onto the shore.

Neither Phil nor anyone else there has ever seen me surf: not big waves, not any waves. For that matter, they don't even know if I can swim, or if I can, how well. I've talked to some of them about surfing, but that's all I've done, and I certainly did not overstate my expertise—if anything, I downplayed it, as I tend to do. Timidly, I try to gauge their reactions, looking for any clues that will confirm that what I'm supposed to be doing is wrong—reckless, dangerous. By now some of my interviewees have talked to me about "steps": gradually learning how to surf larger waves at various spots, making steady progress over each winter season. Some old-timers in particular have complained that the increased production, distribution, and availability of safety equipment like flotation vests has led to unprepared surfers crowding previously elite grounds, increasing the level of danger for everyone. But to my surprise (and perhaps disappointment), I'm not seeing any sympathetic reaction. It all seems normal, or maybe everyone else is just gearing up.

I turn to Doug, whose kind midwestern manners tell me he might care. In the middle of the group that's chatting closely, I catch his attention, try to avoid everyone else's gaze, and mime to him what I want to say. I look at the vest I'm already wearing, then at him, and then back at the vest. By now I assume that everyone knows I've never surfed in these kinds of conditions and at this spot. Phil, I am sure, has told them. Instead of reacting as I'd hoped—with sympathy, surprise, and support— Doug slowly smiles with awe, and then, forgetting all about privately holding eye contact with me, turns to Phil and says, almost whispering, "Oh . . . he *will* see." I realize that all the hard work and just plain luck that brought me to this group and its leader, and allowed them to include me, have conspired with the propitious weather conditions to give me exactly what I wished for years ago. I am being introduced to a mysterious, powerful, binding, and exclusive practice. According to Doug, my life is about to change. I just don't know how yet. But he seems to know. Perhaps this is how he started as well.

My resolve to opt out fades as the time for paddling out draws near, and the momentum of being physically close to this tight-knit group of highly charged and confident friends sweeps me up. I surrender to my fate. To fight this would be futile, unless I were to resort to an extreme act like disappearing—which would feel to me (and probably to them) like an act of desertion. Decades earlier I successfully escaped boarding school, but that escape required an ingenious plan that hinged on a short period of time when I wasn't watched. I don't see any way out this time. The group pressure is too strong, and my own curiosity, excitement, and desire to be part of this mission and this cadre is too seductive. Between one hesitant moment and the next I instantaneously accept that I have to go out, that I am going out, and that this is what's going to happen regardless of how it will turn out. It may seem overly dramatic to say so, and in retrospect I think it is, but in this moment I think about the possibility of dying—and I don't care.

Phil tells me what I have to do, which basically entails following him and staying calm while being fully aware of my surroundings: my position, the current, other surfers. We watch waves breaking on the shore break for a few minutes until Phil—who, unlike me, has also been looking at the horizon—notices an "opportunity," and without warning springs toward the water. His sprint puts him a few important feet further ahead of me than I would have hoped. And I'm surprised by how soon he throws his board into the long carpet of foam that has just unfolded toward the beach as the last wave crashed to the shore. I do the same, but I'm still lagging behind. And because I've never used this board before, and am unfamiliar with its length and the buoyancy that makes it ride higher in the water than other boards, and because the padded vest affects my balance when I'm lying prone, I get thrown off by a small wave. I hastily get back on the board, as if I've spotted a shark nearby or I'm afraid a bigger wave is coming, and then begin paddling with all my might toward the channel, passing both Phil and Shaun. Perhaps astonished by my capabilities, Shaun comments that I really know how to paddle, but the fact is that I'm only this quick because the exceptional buoyancy of this large gun makes it glide with noticeable ease and speed. And because of my fear.

Phil is right: the waves today are not big enough to break into the channel, "closing it" and thus eliminating one of the few escape routes. As we paddle out, we stop to sit in different positions to gauge different viewpoints. As on land, and like every other time since I've known him that I've seen him observing the waves, Phil is in no rush here. Seeing surfers taking off on steep waves that look four or five times their own height, I scream my lungs out—from excitement, or probably to release some of the adrenaline that's already surging through my bloodstream. Unfazed, amused, or annoyed, Phil tells me to look at the Bay and "soak it all in." And I see that he's been right all along: this is a view that I could *never* have imagined.

From our current position in the ocean, Waimea Valley and the beach look stunning, but what I am most impressed by is how much water is moving into the basin of the Bay. Every time a wave detonates like an explosive at the "peak," where most surfers are, it moves on through the place where we're sitting and lifts us high up, but without breaking. Once the wave lifts us and passes us, I turn again toward the shore, and I can see how it creates a giant step of water between the lulls, and I can appreciate just how much water is actually moving toward the shore. And while I can't see the actual shore break from where I am, I can see the vast amount of water that washes up the beach before the wave's power is exhausted and the water recedes again. Each wave's power is partly released when it breaks out in the ocean, then gathered again in the form of white water that rushes toward the shore and eventually rises into a second wave, which then explodes again in the shore break. Energy that was originally generated miles from this specific point dissipates completely on the beach, and then is gone. Phil finds it intriguing that "the same energy that can kill you just vanishes forever a few moments after it meets you."

I feel relatively safe, and slightly embarrassed to be holding him back to look after me. I tell him to go to the peak to catch some waves, and assure him that I will be fine here—or so I hope. A few hours go by, during which from time to time I contemplate (with more than a little hope) going back to shore. Feelings of fear, cold from staying relatively still, and exhaustion almost overtake me a few times. And I've actually completed what I was assigned to do. So finally, mostly out of curiosity, possibly boredom, and a temporary sense of calm, I timidly try paddling to catch the slope of a wave as it approaches my location. It looks like a short hill. What surprises me is that while the wave is not breaking where I am—as is true of most of the waves here today (according to Phil's forecast)—my giant board nevertheless shows some signs of gliding even with only a few strokes. As I feel it skipping on the wave's surface (contrary to my expectations), I realize that with such a large gun there might actually be a chance that I could take off on a wave even from this sidelined position. More time goes by, only now I'm consciously trying to assess whether another wave of that kind might by chance meet me again in my corner. Another surfer paddles toward me and stops to sit near me. He strikes up a conversation, saying that the last time he surfed here was many months ago, maybe as a way of justifying why he isn't going to the peak. I reply that this is my first time, and perhaps wanting to display some competence, I add, "Maybe we'll get lucky"—implying that a rideable wave may come our way. In fact, though I don't say so out loud, I think I might have seen one a few moments earlier.

What feels like maybe forty-five seconds later, one of these opportunities materializes a few feet away from us. Without hesitation—and perhaps encouraged by having a partner now—I turn my board, shift from seated to prone position, and, as the wave approaches us, begin paddling to catch it. I notice then that the board is beginning to skip like it did before, but the skipping keeps going this time and the intervals get shorter, like a duck flapping its wings: flap . . . flap, flap, flap flap. As I give it a few more strokes I feel the wave lifting me, and I remember why this is called taking off. At this point I can tell that my safest bet is just to keep paddling harder and faster. Once you've turned on the engine, it's safer to keep going than to try to slam on the brakes, which could send you sailing over the handlebars and plunge you deep into the sea for who knows how long. Despite my fear, my body knows this from years of experience in smaller surf—so I keep paddling.

As I feel the wave carrying me, feel my board building speed, I instinctively know when it's fast enough and pop up to my feet. The board accelerates, and I'm surprised at how tall it sits on the water because of its exceptional buoyancy. And as I pass the halfway point down the face of the wave and feel the exhilaration of knowing that the hardest part is done—I caught it, I got up, I'm solid on my feet, and I won't nosedive now—I begin laughing uncontrollably and loudly, like I've never done before. I feel like no matter what—even if someone were to shoot me at this moment—there's simply no way at this point I can fall. That feeling of joy, excitement, and satisfaction lasts as I ride the wave successfully toward the beach and into the channel; then I find that it's filled me with enough energy to get back to prone position and paddle back out, and that I no longer have any desire to leave. Back in the lineup, I scream to Phil that I got one, but then I tell myself that riding just one might be considered luck, and I need *one more* as solid confirmation of what I think just happened.

I stay out in the lineup for what feels like at least another hour, and then I notice another wave that swings wide toward the edge of the channel where I am sitting. This one's different from the first one—it starts breaking on the main peak, technically making it a "shoulder" wave when it reaches me. I catch it, and toward the end of the ride I hear a voice calling my name. I see a surfer who is much deeper than me—meaning closer to the most critical part of the wave—screaming and waving at me with encouragement. I recognize Stevo, one of the surfers I'd interviewed a few days prior and with whom I feel a kind of connection. Being seen by him as I ride is an exhilarating experience that also makes me feel both proud of myself and safer in the surf. Stevo helps me time my passage through the shore break and out of the water. As we land on the beach we're talking about meeting at Phil's for a fire and barbecue; Stevo says he'll come later. I put on some dry clothes and drive to Foodland, and as I'm getting out of my car I see Stevo sitting at a table outside the Coffee Bean with one of his friends. As he sees me walking briskly in his direction, he gets up and opens his arms wide. I quicken my pace toward him, and we embrace. "That was awesome!" I shout. "You did great!" he says. We both start laughing. Bustling through the store picking up what I want, I feel a few inches taller—I can tell I'm holding my spine straight and my shoulders back. And I can't wait to get back to Phil's to meet him and the guys.

CHAPTER TWO

Beyond the Boil

Late spring 2016. Wrapping up the winter surf season on the North Shore of O'ahu. Phil and his friend Tracy organize an event for those who regularly surf the Bay but are not sponsored and don't take part in competitions. The Waimea Waterman's Ball is the working man's answer to the Big Wave Awards, which are equivalent to the Oscars for big wave surfing. Phil says: "Can you think of any other spot that has its own party to celebrate a season? And what a season this one has been!" And even though about a hundred and fifty people attend, most pro surfers I ask about it later didn't know about it.

The occasion celebrates those who've progressed the most during the season, those who've taken the worst wipeout or have ridden the largest waves. There's no prize money, and attendees pay only a small fee to help cover some of the catering costs. Many lifeguards object to paying, reckoning that having watched over and assisted surfers at the Bay is contribution enough for them. The only cost of admission for the others is having regularly surfed the Bay. Having sat next to the boil, swell after swell, clocking in when the ocean delivers, and "sending it"—committing oneself to the spot by being there, and by trying to make the waves. The boil[1] is that swirl of water above a series of submerged rocks out in the lineup, far out to sea where Waimea begins breaking, and the smaller wave Pinballs redirects the spotlight offshore. The boil may look like a small maelstrom, but the danger of it is not that you'll be sucked down to the bottom of the sea by its vortex. What makes it consequential is that it represents a shallow area of the reef that makes waves jack up, becoming difficult and sometimes close to impossible to ride, leading to many wipeouts as surfers attempt to ride over it.

On the left side, far from the boil, when waves are eighteen feet or less, there's a deep channel where one can sit on one's board and more or less safely watch the breaking waves at the peak—unless a larger set of waves comes in and closes out the whole Bay, which can happen unpredictably. "Closing out the Bay" happens when exceptionally large waves break from one side of the Bay to the other, leaving no channel through which surfers can escape.

And negotiating the shore break remains unavoidable: if you make it out, you still have to make it back to shore somehow. The best place to do so is called the "keyhole," next to the rocks on the right side of the Bay and just below Phil's house. Occasionally, waves break on the edge of the channel as well, but they are generally mellower—"chip shots," experienced surfers call them—and end in the relatively flat water, making the ride not only easier, but safer too. As surfers say about those waves, "they're more forgiving. It's an easier drop."

Like others, my friend Kevin says that surfing a spot repetitively lets you build an intimate relationship with the place, and with the regulars. Referring to the former element, William Finnegan[2] writes that "All surfers are oceanographers and in the area of breaking waves, all are engaged in advanced research. . . . The science of surfers is not pure obviously but heavily applied."

About the connection among regulars, Phil mentions what he calls "the *Cheers* theory," by which he means that surfers are habitual creatures and form communities around specific places—whether it's a bar, a street corner, or a surf spot. A place where, as the theme song to the TV show *Cheers* goes, "everybody knows your name, and they're always glad you came," and where "our troubles are all the same." Calvin Morrill and David Snow[3] write that these *anchored relationships* are characterized by "recurring interaction and interdependencies that develop between individuals over time but are tied to a particular public place and a narrow range of activities that do not, or rarely, spill over into private households and other domiciled settings." As Peggy Wireman[4] argues, these relationships are colored by qualities like "intense involvement, warmth, intimacy, sense of belonging, and rapport; mutual knowledge of character." Talking about Waimea, Phil says: "There's a tighter bond with people who surf there. Number one, because everybody goes on the same wave and nobody gets upset, or too upset. Some guys may get upset. It's not a free-for-all, but like a sharing. And at most spots, that isn't allowed." I comment: "Unless you go back hundreds of years." And Phil says: "Right. When I'm out there I go: 'Let's go together. Let's take this one together' . . . with someone that I trust (laughing). I stick to my game plan, you stick to yours, and as long as you make it, we're good. Sharing a wave, it's a bonding. It's exciting."

Silvia Nabuco feels that whenever she'd ditch surfing Sunset for Waimea it would seem like cheating. And when she would wipeout surfing a spot she had previously put in second place, she'd feel like she deserved it. Different surfers tend to populate different spots, and contribute at least as much as the quality of the waves to the spot's local culture.

As Daniel Nazer[5] argues, waves are a key resource in many surfers' lives, and they are administered by surfers with no state intervention, through informal norms that are fairly consistent across different parts of the world. These norms are directed toward efficiency, avoidance of congestion, and safety, and they essentially allow surfers to manage their commons.

Surf spots vary in terms of whether their lineup is aggressive or laid back. This quality is impacted by variation in surfing conditions from day to day and at specific times of the day, quality of waves, how close to or far from urban centers they are located, how difficult it is to paddle out, and how crowded or uncrowded they are. In addition, each spot has a specific pecking order that depends in part on factors such as personal ability, where a surfer lives, and how long he has surfed a specific break; seniority usually translates into a higher priority. Because waves are "resources without well-defined property rights," as Daniel Kaffine writes, high-quality waves provide an incentive for local surfers to claim authority over their use. According to Kaffine, the limited number of waves per hour means that surf breaks are a "congestible resource." "Locals recognize the benefits of high-quality waves and endogenously create strong property rights to capture them."[6]

Kevin also maintains that different personality types are attracted to different kinds of waves, just as the art scenes in Soho or Greenwich Village attract different people. Then he adds that sitting next to the boil at Waimea signals that you have become a member of the community—"all of a sudden you're on the main stage, on Broadway, rather than being in a high school play sitting in the channel." According to Kevin, Waimea is for the matador kind of surfers: those who enjoy not just surfing, but also getting into the arena and being watched. At other big wave surf spots you might be so far out that no one can identify you, or for that matter, even see you. Whatever you do at Waimea, everyone will see. There's a lot of chatter in the lineup, there's the fanfare after the surf session, there's the gossip. "There're so many phases before you're even out there," Phil adds.

> There's like knowing it's big and preparing. Your heart pumping. You're excited. You're walking down the road. And then entering the beach. And then waiting for a chance to paddle out. . . . Walking down the street, entering the beach and going through the crowd it's like you're a gladiator. Then, you got to paddle out—and talking about when it's big, hopefully you won't get cleaned out by a closeout. And once you're out there and you're ready to come in, that's a little tricky too. And walking up the beach when you're done, you're mentally and physically exhausted. There're so many little excitement factors. When I was younger I used to be nervous as hell, now that I'm older I get a kick out of it. People want to make eye contact. We surf a lot of spots that don't have this crowd participation.

And Kevin adds:

> Just the paddle out at Waimea will broaden your horizons in understanding what big wave surfing is about. And you know from where you're sitting at Waimea, on that pretty solid day . . . what the importance of thirty feet of distance is, and it will change your perspective of not only surfing, but life itself, you know. . . . How can thirty feet make a big difference? But it's literally like taking off in outer space. Once you go past the boil to the other side, not only physically are you confronting dangerous situations, but psychologically it's another factor that you have to deal with . . . but also on a community level. The surf lineup . . . community interaction. You're taking on a whole new identity once you've crossed that line. From the channel, across the boil to the other side, people look at you entirely different. You're a completely different person.

When waves at Waimea break at fifteen to eighteen feet, surfers who are committed enough sit right in front of the boil. When they get to twenty, twenty-five feet, then they sit beyond the boil, a little further out.

The prizes you win at an event like the Waterman's Ball are peer recognition, belonging, and the opportunity to celebrate those who have distinguished themselves. But such occasions also honor the wave itself, and by reflection its community: the few dozen regulars, some of

whom are lifeguards. Events like thes[...]
tradition and secure your role in the play[...]
more prominent role, or be sidelined in the[...]
Phil says:

> To me the wave is the star. You got to pick the right wav[...]
> wave is a canvas. You just happen to luck out, be there, and[...]
> right spot. The right moment, because this wave is created hou[...]
> from me. But of all the thousands of waves that come in, that part[...]
> wave is, can be, better than any other big wave.

Then he adds: "Surfers, in general, tend to be self-absorbed," partly implying that in large surf the case is different, but also communicating how much he enjoys sharing his passion with others. Talking about the day he took me out at Waimea, he says: "I'm glad you experienced it. When you write, you've lived it." But then, afraid that this was a one-time thing, I add: "I want to experience it more!" And he says: "Me and the boys will take care of you. They won't steer you wrong. You got to be aware of that rock sticking out. But you're a quick learner. I see you just pick things up . . . That's my job: to give you confidence like all these other guys . . . most surfers are so *focused on themselves*. They don't share the experience. They don't see the whole picture." Then I ask him if it's something that has come with age. And lightly laughing under his breath, he says:

> I've been doing this my whole life. I've been having little crews my whole
> life. A lot of guys who I've taken out in the last ten, fifteen, twenty years,
> when we communicate they always tell me they remember the experi-
> ences. It's normal for me. Surfers are selfish. All they're trying to get is
> their own game going.

This distinction reflects the difference between pleasure, which is personal, and fun, which is social. By sharing the experience through waves and adventures to be remembered, individuals like Phil add a layer of sociality to the activity, enhancing its enjoyment by helping it overflow from the water onto land and then reverberate through time.

Focusing on the wave also means that the best surfer is not the one forcing his or her will on the wave, but the one who best understands how it wants to be ridden. Each time we enter the ocean, each time we get in and get wet, we step away and literally turn our backs on civiliza-

lutionarily, as if to return
nd we usually leave every-
lmost reborn, cleansed, or
ls, stories, and excitement
ns calls this driving force
ce, enthusiasm, and drive
tuals just like the paddling
willingness to embrace the
ng from religious studies to
healing benefits of surfing,

al focus on the same object,
ads to intersubjectivity and
ike big wave surfing particu-

e provide opportunities to fasten
move up the ladder and get a
pecking order. Chuckling,

e and ride it. The
catch it at the
s away
icular

Interaction Rituals, Solidarity, and Emotional Energy

Randall Collins argues that what motivates us to act is a desire to maximize the *emotional energy* (EE) we gain from successful encounters, while at the same time learning how to avoid energy-draining situations and individuals. It's both physical and mental, and the two generally rise and fall together. In Collins's words, "The confidence of high-EE persons comes out as enthusiasm. You are up-beat, carrying around a positive mood that perks up yourself and others."[10]

Having a *trajectory*, a long-term goal in which you are deeply invested, also influences whether or not you have high energy. We can partly explain the ability of distinctively successful individuals to maintain a trajectory for long periods of time by the kind and series of interactions they are able to participate in. The capacity to choose and to control with whom you routinely spend your time impacts how you feel, what you think and cannot think, and whether you feel confident or low. Yet those situations are not evenly distributed across time, place, and space. On the other hand, those who are unsuccessful feel rightfully frustrated and stuck because they are cut off—whether they are aware of it or not—from these consequential interactions. Furthermore, individuals with a high level of EE are generally good observers and know which people and which kinds of situations to invest in, and who and what to smoothly overlook.[11] Put differently, they know how to avoid getting bogged down, and how to build and maintain momentum. They know how to dance through social interactions and when to politely refuse an invitation to the floor. According to Collins, Steve Jobs and Joan of Arc were masters at this game.[12] In his theory, the success of specific individuals and groups across history can thus be partly explained by the kinds of interactions they participate in and, as others like Ronald Burt[13] have already demonstrated in studying organizations, by the kinds of social networks they are part of, and their position within those networks, which also distribute knowledge, skills, and opportunities.

While *collective effervescence* is a group feeling based on an "intensification of shared experience"[14]—think of music concerts and religious or political meetings with strong audience participation—*emotional energy*, while collectively produced, is an individual outcome of a ritual broadly defined.[15] Each individual enters each social encounter with a certain amount of EE and walks away from it with more, less, or roughly the same amount. In this line the term "chains" implies that individuals enter new situations with a residue from previous encounters. A person's EE fluctuates upward or downward depending on "immediate and recent experiences in interactions" and "flows of EE are cumulative over long as well as short periods of time."[16]

According to Collins, a successful encounter—one potentially producing high amounts of EE—requires the following elements: a group of at least two individuals are in the same physical space, they are both focusing their attention on the same object or action, each becomes increasingly aware that the other is maintaining focus, and their shared mood intensifies so that they become attuned to one another. In his words, they become entrained—locked into a similar rhythm. Individuals start mirroring one another. John Parker and his collaborators describe vocal and bodily entrainment as "reciprocal synchronization and mirroring of voice and movement among co-located social actors."[17] Concomitantly, boundaries between insiders and outsiders need to be established so that participants feel included in an "elite" group. Boundaries help both the constitution of a group and its functioning—members learn and contribute to the rules of the related group culture,[18] and feel safe expressing themselves. In addition, they support the smoothness of action by minimizing potential ruptures, thus ensuring collegiality and reciprocity. As George Herbert Mead would say, there's a distinct satisfaction in being in situations where one can freely engage in "impulsive expression."[19]

For Collins, interaction ritual is above all a mechanism for converting an initial emotion—regardless of its kind, provided it's strong enough—via focus and rhythm entrainment, into another emotion, the confidence and vitality of EE. On the negative side is boredom: the feeling of being stuck, which drains EE. But we can theorize that an individual's inability, or unwillingness, to participate meaningfully in an interaction also drains EE. Three other factors that diminish energy are subordination, exclusion from a social interaction, and forced participation in a ritual with the requirement that you at least appear to be enjoying it.

The leader of the group typically sets the rhythm of the interaction and thus becomes its focus of attention—or, in other words, "the sacred object."[20] If this person dominates the situation by subordinating the others, he heightens his energy by draining theirs. Alternatively, he can amplify collective feelings and increase the energy of other group members by allowing them to be active participants. In such cases all members are recharged by the interaction, and ultimately the leader is the one experiencing the highest increase in *emotional energy*.

Situations vary in content, form, and intensity, and so do leaders' characteristics and styles; yet part of their success depends on being good at interaction rituals. Mentors are important in Collins's theory.[21] In his book *Interaction Ritual Chains* Collins argues that the status of mentors and the character and level of their feedback contribute to the emotional energy produced by the interaction. If the mentors validate their efforts, the protégés experience increases in emotional energy that motivate their desire to emulate the creativity of the mentors. Going beyond Collins, I argue that interaction rituals with peers, and not just those with mentors, are an important source of emotional energy. In addition, I introduce my theory of the effects of interaction rituals with mentors on novices in the midst of *fateful moments*. By unpacking Collins's concept of emotional energy I present a theory of how that interaction affects the protégé in fateful moments when the protégé is filled with self-doubt and fear in the face of an identity transition.

In what follows I describe two distinct intense episodes, focusing on *fateful moments* and identifying the interactional characteristics and leadership styles that contributed to their success. I start this discussion by focusing primarily on one leader: Phil. Next I investigate how a leader can sometimes be looked upon as a role model whose behavior needs more interpretation: Chris's example. In the last part of the chapter I highlight a number of analytical points related to these small group epi-

sodes and introduce the topic of the following chapter: fun. I conceptualize fun moments as successful encounters generating emotional energy
of similar measure across all participants.

* * *

Uncle Phil is a local legend. In his sixties, he's a senior who earns respect.
He doesn't just surf—he surfs very well regardless of his equipment and
wave size. Some say that if you see his truck parked somewhere, then
you'll know that's the best spot for the day. Phil is the youngest son of a
former 1950s–1960s North Shore policeman who eventually bought land
on Oʻahu and, working hard alongside his children, built homes to rent.
Phil's family owns a large property overlooking the famous break. The
house has a swimming pool, and a Jacuzzi, too. But while the big wave
celebration takes place there, Phil lives just below, in a small wooden
structure that lacks the view one could enjoy from a higher vantage
point. Phil says he's closer to the water, though, and he likes it there.
More than once we monitored waves at the Bay by lying cool on his
couch, watching a webcam streaming on his iPad. You could hardly find
a better location if you were looking to surf the Bay, and you can hardly
imagine growing up there without eventually being tempted to paddle
out. One of his three older brothers comments that "it was only a matter
of time." Phil has a recurring dream of being "cleaned out" by a humon-
gous rogue wave at the Bay. In the dream he looks at the wave approaching from the horizon and the only thing he can do is ditch his board and
dive. Then, talking to himself he says: "You just got to deal with it." And
after he gets rag-dolled for about fifteen seconds, and finally makes it to
the surface, he says to himself: "Oh, it wasn't that bad."

Phil and his family moved into the larger house above in 1972, and
along with his brothers he started surfing the Bay while he was in middle
school. He began with the smaller Pinballs, and then worked his way up
to Waimea. Stating the obvious, he says: "We were looking at it every
day." Then, he adds: "But then the thing about surfing Waimea when
it's big is you can't look at it . . . I mean you still have to time it (time
launching into the water between the sets, waiting for a break in their
arrivals on the shore), but you just got to go, you know? You just got
to walk down the beach and paddle out because otherwise you'll psych
yourself out." Continuing his description, he says that over the years he
has seen many surfers who, after having sat on the beach watching the
waves by the shore break all day, eventually just walk away. Scared. Hesi-

tant. Terrified. Defeated. Or, as a lifeguard tells me, courageous enough
to walk away.

When I ask about his house and surfing the Bay, Phil ironically says,
"I tell people I got a good parking spot." Rumor has it that decades ago
Eddie Aikau used to live in a smaller shack that is now part of Phil's yard,
a short walk from his lifeguard tower and from the break he loved to surf.
From the outside Phil's wooden house looks unkempt. It looks spartan on
the inside, yet it has everything he needs: a kitchen, a bathroom where
he can store several wetsuits and a few surfboards, a large flat screen TV,
a large patio, another Jacuzzi (which is now broken), a small bedroom,
a living area with a couch, and close to twenty surfboards stacked in a
corner. The other boards are either in the yard or under the house. Like
his house, the yard is a work in progress: piled-up wood, rusty metal
sheets, bikes. I wouldn't be surprised if someone stepped on a nail, or if
one of his animals died from eating something poisonous. Phil works
in construction, and there's always something better to do than fix his
own house or clean his junkyard, which also functions as a storage area
for his work projects. "Time just goes by, man," he says. When I ask him
about his living situation, he jokes that he's been camping all his life,
then specifies: "Gucci camping." But since 2016, when Amelia came into
his life, he has been renovating the house, for instance by installing a
stove and oven inside the house to replace the outdoor stovetop he had
used for years. Every time I showed up at the house, they always made
sure I was well fed.

Looking back at his youth and how pecking orders at different spots
change as older surfers phase out, he tells me that in those days he "just
wanted to take over" every spot he paddled out to—meaning, take the
best waves. That's what youth does until they get hurt enough times and
all the injuries start calling out, "Caution, Caution, Caution." Then you
start to hesitate, and someone younger comes up trying to replace you
because they haven't got hurt yet. "How did you maintain longevity?" I
ask. "You got to surf to keep it up," he says.

Phil is a featherweight, but a calm heavy hitter. Jock Sutherland says
he is a little too skinny. In regular size surf, he usually uses kid-size kinds
of boards. He has always been small. And when he was growing up and
was often getting some of the best waves, older guys would flip him over
as he was sitting on his board or paddling. They wouldn't hit him. Looking back on those years, he says: "I was like a little rat and they were so
upset." Contrastingly, Amelia tells me about growing up surfing on the
East Coast of the US during the 1970s. She recalls an episode when she

was thirteen years old, but looking more like nine, and she was surfing Cape Hatteras, on the Outer Banks in North Carolina. A group of guys paddles over and tells her: "You don't belong here. Girls shouldn't be surfing." To push further, one of them grabs her butt and tells her to get out of the water. Amelia explains: "I was a little bitty girl. This is the shit I had to put up with. Guys can be real assholes in the water. What I learned is that you got to be aggressive in the water: especially if you're a woman you got to prove yourself first. Prove that you can surf."

Phil and Amelia often surf together, and they are often the oldest in the lineup, at least on the North Shore. A couple of times I saw Amelia towing Phil out to the lineup at Chuns by having him hold on to her leash as he was kneeling on his board, like a pharaoh sitting in a horse-drawn carriage. An ironically designed scene that left some puzzled and others amused.

Thinking about the relatively low price of surfboards compared to other sporting equipment, he says: "The joy you'll get riding that board has no monetary value. You can't create that type of excitement. That's why we surf: because it's so damn fun, and that's why I remind people." When talking about pro surfers, who generally only surf for short periods perhaps to conserve energy or to emulate competition heats, he laughs: "I'd rather surf all day. I don't know what they do the rest of the day." But don't get me wrong, and let me set the record straight: Phil does work, and fairly hard too, but certainly much less than he did as an adolescent and young adult. Those who criticize him for having so much free time may understandably forget his age. Even Phil sometimes seems to think he's still in his thirties.

As a kid he enjoyed bringing home cats he'd found on the streets, until his mother told him he had to stop. "How many?" I ask. "Not that many," he says. "Not as many as I could have," he adds. "Maybe six." Under ten years old, he used to spend *hours* trying to get a cat to come to him. He tells me: "You got to win their trust, right?" "How did you do it?" I ask. "With food?" "No—be patient. Animals sense if you got to be nice to them or not. I just waited, and at that point take them home." "You kidnapped them!" I say. He chuckles: "Who knows where they lived, some probably had a home."

When I first met Phil, he owned two large pets and more than twenty cats, most of them inbred. Waimea is a white dog with dreadlocks on its belly, ice-blue eyes, and the temperament of a young hyperactive teenager that seems never to grow old. I've heard surfers referring to him as the happiest dog ever—and as a lover, when he tried humping my leg.

And just like a big foam of white water at the Bay, Waimea comes at you with relentless energy, over and over again. When Phil went to buy him, the dog picked him. "Just like with a woman," says Phil. "He's a little wild, but he's a good boy." A herder kind of dog, like Phil, who has brought together various crews over the years.

Cry Baby, or "Baby (for) short," is Waimea's best friend. A goat. It stays in the background, and you see it only sporadically. But if you turn your back, it sneaks up on you and will eat anything you leave unattended, a trait that also makes it particularly well-suited to its primary duty of keeping the grass short. Waimea's responsibility is to guard the property. But both animals, along with the cats, provide entertainment as well. Years ago Phil had another dog he named after Jockos—another favorite surfing spot of his, named after Jock Sutherland. He acted the part of Baby's older brother; at the time, Baby thought he was also a dog. While Phil was building his house, the two animals would head off to the beach together by themselves. Jockos would go for a swim, while Baby would just run around. Mark Dombroski, who was one of the senior lifeguards at the Bay at the time, remembers those incidents: "Finally we had to get his number and we would tie them to the lifeguard tower. I'd treat the goat like a chicken; it wouldn't bother anyone. A dog? OK. But a goat? They were partners. One of those bizarre things that happen here at the Bay."

At times Phil would load Baby into the back of his truck and go to Hale'iwa to take care of errands, leaving her in the truck. Phil recalls those times: "People would be taking pictures. It was awesome."

One day last year at around four a.m., Baby woke up Phil by screaming. A few days earlier the goat had been feeling unwell, and Phil speculates that he may have eaten something poisonous in the yard—maybe some paint. Phil got up to check on the goat, and within one minute the animal died. Thinking back on that moment, Phil says: "He was screaming to maybe see me one last time. It was super sad. He had this sadness in his eyes as if to say: 'I'm gonna go now.'"

If you ask, Phil will pull out a framed poster of the Waterman's Ball that's lying in a corner of his living room, beside the sofa. And you may notice, looking at the walls, that there are no pictures of him surfing. Phil says that he'll put up that poster eventually, but there's reason to doubt that will ever happen. In the four years I've known him the poster hasn't moved. On one of the walls, though, hangs a poster of The Eddie competition from decades ago, and on the front door is a sticker that reads: "EDDIE WOULD GO."

Phil's Crew

February 21, 2018. I'm talking to Kawika via social media, and he asks me about the book. "I'm working on the story of you paddling out on that huge day," I tell him. And he types back, "I don't think I'll ever forget that day." "What do you mean?" I prompt.

> I think it's like going to war for a day. Even though I never have. The anticipation, the uncertainty, the risk, the fear, the self-doubt, then the actual *run into the battle being the scariest part.* "The paddle out" esp for that spot at that size. I think after getting past all that, the actual fighting, "surfing" or "Trying to Surf," wasn't so bad. But then the triumph of coming home to "shore" alive and well and even with a couple waves successfully ridden, the accomplishment feeling is beyond most experiences. I think overcoming fear of death has to be a big key to the attraction. Like most of the fear is leading up to the actual catching of the waves. 80% before even walking from Phil's house. Esp after watching the best guys in the world getting pounded all day and closeouts.

The day we're talking about is the day The "Eddie Went" on February 25, 2016, the day before I was introduced to surfing the Bay. Phil, Kawika, Doug, and others waited all day for the competition to end at four in the afternoon so they could paddle out and have their own surf before dark.

Kawika is Hawaiian from his mum's side, but the light color of his eyes and skin is inherited from Scotland. He's a former professional bodyboarder, a believer, a preacher, a local entrepreneur. Unmistakably fit, but like many, claiming he is the most scared person out there. Look at the tail of any Hawaiian Airlines plane and you'll see the profile of his mother, Leinaala, when she was younger—Miss Hawai'i 1989. The tattoo on his chest reads: "Thy Kingdom Come." He has long curly hair bleached blond by the sun and saltwater, and he sometimes wears it in a man bun, drawing occasional derisive comments from people who don't know him. I once took part in a healing session he led for a small Christian group assembled at his house. Soft-spoken, island-time-relaxed, but also periodically stressed out by trying to keep the lemonade business he co-owns afloat.

"Where you from, Doug? Here?" I ask.

He laughs: "I grew up in Ohio. No ocean. It's like I didn't learn how to surf until I was twenty-one in Florida, between New Smyrna and Cocoa

Phil across the street from his house, walking down the trail toward the "keyhole" where he'll paddle out.

Beach. Nothing like this. A two-foot wave here (in Hawai'i) is a head-high wave there."

"Did you move to Hawai'i to surf big waves?" I ask.

"To pursue photography and to surf," he says. "To improve at surfing. Back home I was a mechanic."

Phil—judging by how fit he is, can you guess his age? If you were to take a picture with his head out of the frame, you couldn't tell. A Zen-like demeanor that suddenly transforms as he paddles to catch a wave into a fiercely focused glare. Not an ounce of fat on his body, like those who compete in racewalking. You'd have the same difficulty if you were judging by how excited he still is about surfing pretty much anything: from small windy waves to perfect giant surf, and anything in between. Years of experience growing up in this area translate into local knowledge as well as social recognition, especially at spots like Waimea, Laniākea, and Jockos, where he still sits comfortably in the front row of the pecking order.

Informal Mentoring

It may seem a stretch to talk about mentoring in surfing—so much so that when I mentioned it during a scholarly presentation, a professor who seemed to always be on her phone doing something else rather than participating started to laugh. But mentoring is how most get here, even though they have many different motivations. And by here I mean big surf.

Kawika says he has been away from the islands for eleven years. While he is scared of large waves, he's certainly capable and physically ready even without training, and he could easily climb in the pecking order of the surfing lineup because of his partly indigenous origin. There is a precarious *social order* at any surf spot on the planet, and more so at some spots than others.

As Phil explains to me, many of the surf breaks in Honolulu—where waves are usually smaller and less powerful than on the North Shore—are dominated by packs of surfers acting like wolves. He says: "They'll guard it with their lives and they won't allow you in. They'll outmaneuver you or something if they've never seen you before. They'll try to scare you away."

When talking about Waimea—a spot professional surfers surf only in exceptional conditions when everywhere else on the North Shore is a mess, or during The Eddie—Kawika's voice rises in pitch. Emotional. He explains to me some of what his family and his people lost with Hawai'i's overthrow by the United States. Then he says: "I may sound egotistical, but I'm more doubting myself, the crowds, and the danger of collisions. Once I get over that I'll be able to get a lot higher in the pecking order because of my ancestors." The water: one of the last arenas in which Hawaiians can maintain and even reclaim their original sovereignty. But Waimea is populated mostly by non-professional surfers from the mainland who have made it their own, rather than by locally born surfers. As a community Waimea is pretty open. Under eighteen feet it's pretty safe. At other spots, though, you might get cleaned up by unexpected larger waves. "With the buoys you would know it pretty much," Kawika says.

The Day The Eddie Went

"Those were the biggest waves I've ever surfed," Kawika says firmly a week later, echoing others who paddled out that day. I ask him: "Did Phil play any part in it?" "That's huge," he replies. "He made sure I had no excuses, calling me days before making sure my board was waxed, and that I was available. He knows I want it." I ask him: "Why did you trust him?" He says: "All a mentor does is he helps you to trust yourself. It helps being trustworthy, the kind of person he is, and his experience. A good mentor really brings out the ability to trust yourself. I know the feeling you get when you get over it. I can't remember one time I regretted it, even when I got hurt. Having him there is almost like a pacifier. Especially in bigger days he's creating a place of safety."

Kawika recalls being scared from the moment he woke up that morning, and his fear continued as the day progressed and he watched the online livestreaming of The Eddie competition. Then, as the swell grew, his fear almost subsided because he thought that when the time came it would be too big for them to paddle out. In fact, during the afternoon the Bay saw a series of waves "annihilating the channel." Jet skis employed for safety at one point gassed out to the horizon, leaving surfers "scratching"—meaning trying to paddle over the large waves to avoid being caught inside. In another instance, with no possibility of making it out to sea fast enough, drivers decided to jet toward the beach to outrun the power of the white water—which they did, providing excitement for the large crowd gathered on the shore. The scariest part, Kawika reflects, was not necessarily surfing the waves, but trying to avoid getting a close-out set on the head while paddling out from shore.

Around three o'clock Phil phoned him, saying: "It seems doable." Kawika's fear skyrocketed, and the battle to remain calm that began early in the morning resumed. That battle lasted through the eventual paddling out, and indeed throughout the entire surf session, and it ended only when he finally found himself safely back on shore.

All of us face situations in which we doubt ourselves. We find ourselves facing *fateful moments* and looking for cues from people near us, and also looking inside ourselves asking whether we should retreat—perhaps often the case—or proceed. And if we should proceed, in which manner. When we look for cues we may express our doubts directly, for example by asking a question: "Do you think that this is a good idea?" Or we may give off subtle signals that we are in doubt, as I did at Phil's before paddling out at Waimea for the first time. Gestures and general demeanor are two pathways of such communication. In using them we're asking the other person to either confirm or disconfirm our hesitation, and to give us valuable information we might then use to better assess our situation and make the best decision.

Below I provide three illustrations, the first two of which pertain to Phil's crew. Then I present another small group story, in which the mentorship role is filled by Chris Owens. The stories are of two kinds: disconfirming and confirming doubt about whether to engage in risk-taking. The first focuses on Doug, and it reveals that he is not content with the numerous interactions through which he seeks confirmation that he can surf in these conditions despite having collided with another surfer during the paddle out, severely damaging his surfboard. In the other, Kawika is looking for hints to confirm his feeling that the mission should be called off. The final episode describes the uncertainty two young, really good surfers feel trying to decide whether they should paddle out at the Bay on the biggest day of their lives, and shows how Chris helped them gain the confidence they needed. As in Doug's example, the two young surfers are looking for signals confirming that what they want to do is possible.

On the Beach

After picking up the boards at Phil's, the group walks toward the beach below his house to paddle out. We cross the road and walk down the trail in single file. Phil is leading the way and setting the pace; I am last in line. A few leftovers of the contest crowd are still on the beach, while the rest are stuck in traffic or leaving. Those walking in the opposite direction step aside to let us pass by. Deference.

Most of the inhabitants of O'ahu do not live on the North Shore, where the scarcity of jobs counterbalances the attraction of the quantity and quality of surf during the winter—a constant distraction for the majority whose occupation is not surfing. According to some, this availability doesn't make it easier for the individuals who live there to successfully split their time between surfing and work; in fact, it seriously hinders their ability to keep a balanced life and to maintain family responsibilities. Kevin tells me about the many colorful characters on the North Shore—a fact he enjoys. Then he fills me in on the other side of the coin: "Many people move here trying to escape their problems. This is paradise, right? But eventually those problems catch up on them. You'd be surprised about the number of alcoholics and drug addicts we have here."

It's late afternoon, but the sun is still blazing. To make shade, some of The Eddie's remaining spectators are using small umbrellas, while others have wrapped their T-shirts around their heads. They look tired, but also relaxed, as they wait out the heavy traffic. Phil and his group are standing close to the shore, monitoring the horizon. Phil uses his surfboard as a shield to block the sun, and stands with his left foot bent slightly forward. Doug and Kawika mimic his pose. Kawika's lips tighten as he moves his feet parallel, signaling steadiness. Two other surfers join them. An exceptionally large set of waves breaks far out and rolls in; when it eventually reaches the shore, it catches the people on the beach by surprise. Suddenly a beach day turns into what looks like a rave party—

foam gets everywhere, and people find themselves standing in knee-high water that resembles snow. At first they look worried, but as the receding waves wash the danger back to the ocean, their frowns turn into smiles while they try to rescue gear that has been drenched or that seems likely to be dragged out to sea. This is a comparatively small shock, and hopefully a reminder of the unpredictability of the water. For Phil's group the excitement is in the exceptional size of that set, although it heightens the fear for some of them. The group's focus intensifies. Every year on the North Shore tourists have to be rescued (or drown) because they see flat water, turn their back to the ocean, and don't anticipate large sets suddenly hitting the shore. The group is more apprehensive. It's their duty to respond—lifeguards are on the opposite side of the Bay. The group quickly moves toward the rocks on the right, making sure that everyone is OK and trying to help them gather some of the items that are floating out. Like other tourists, traveling surfers sometimes get caught inside by surprise and almost drown, especially during rising swells. I don't know of any other place where waves can rise up as quickly and as much as they do on the North Shore.

Looking back, Kawika says:

> That's what threw me off. All those bombs that came in, and they started washing off on the beach and took everyone's stuff. So, I got my big board on one hand and I'm picking up people's backpacks, hydro flasks, and stuff, and by the time that thing ended I was a little bit of breathing hard, you know. And it wasn't long after that I see these guys running out and I'm like: "Ah, ah . . . OK, we're going."

Doug recalls that moment:

> Kawika is picking up all sorts of people's crap. I'm picking up a case of Red Bull off the ground like it has exploded. A backpack is floating in the water. Slippers: I saw them going toward the ocean with a pair of flippers. I saw some going toward the ocean next to a backpack. I'm going to try to get to the backpack first, but Kawika got it first. We're all sitting there like trying to zone out, trying not to think about the crowd. Not to think too much.

Kawika then says to Doug, who is standing next to him: "Ah, man it is huge" (in a tone that is equal parts surprise and fear). Trying to talk him out of giving up, Doug replies: "Don't worry. We're just gonna go.

We're gonna get out there." As he utters these words, he sees the biggest closeout sets he has ever seen at the Bay.

Then the group goes back to waiting in the same spot where they'd been before the large set came. Kawika is mumbling to himself, "this is not a good idea," and then, as if implying an additional question, says, "Phil, I don't know about this." Phil ignores him, not letting Kawika change his rhythm or distract his focus. His gaze is fixed on the horizon. His mouth is slightly open. Over all, twenty minutes of waiting have passed since they stepped onto the beach. At this point another surfer joins Kawika, Phil, Doug, and the two other surfers. One of them bends on his knees, another squats, laying his board across his knees and tilting his head down. Kawika sits, puts his surfboard on the sand, and lays his left arm across it for support. They're all exhausted from the waiting, the fear, and the sun, and from having helped people keep their stuff from washing away. Phil is still the only one standing tall, and he has moved closer to the shore break. Doug has followed him and is also standing up, but he crouches a little in anticipation of the sprint toward the water should a momentary opportunity between the sets materialize. He is anticipating Phil's call. Then, in the corner of his eye, Doug sees movement and hears Phil, who is standing next to him, saying "Let's go!" Everyone in the group, plus the surfer who had joined them, follow, but

When it's huge and it's pulsing, lulls may be short-lived, hard to detect, or nonexistent, making it much harder for surfers to reach the lineup.

they're a few steps behind Phil. Kawika is clearly way behind them, and he almost falls as he's getting up.

Doug says he barely remembers that moment, because by then he was close to blacking out. The group runs down the beach for about thirty or forty feet. No one hesitates except for Kawika. Everyone starts bolting. And then they all launch into a carpet of white, foamy water toward the lineup. Doug recalls not even knowing what was happening out in front: "I didn't even take the time to see if I wanted to paddle out or not. I just went. All instinct. I didn't even look if there was a wave that I should dodge." Doug and the other group members blindly trust Phil's decision. Then, when the first waves of the set reach them, not being able to duck-dive such huge boards or to make it over the top because the waves have already broken, Doug and the others bail off their boards and dive, hoping to make it through. During the time underwater Doug is thinking: "I hope nobody's boards hit mine, or mine hits theirs, or it hits me." And then the board of the guy in front of him and to the right smacks his. Doug pops up after the wave rumbles over him and notices that one of his three fins is pushed in—basically about to snap off his board. He says: "Fuck! Oh my gosh, not today!" Later that day, when we gather by the fire at Phil's, Doug talks about that moment: "This is the only day that I really . . . (short pause) . . . the day I've been . . . everything has been building up to. And I'm bumming . . . I get my board and I'm looking at it, taking way too much time. And it was probably only ten or fifteen seconds, probably not even five or ten seconds." Phil calmly interrupts him: "Which is a lot."

Then everybody else, all of them having ditched their boards to the side to keep from being pushed back too much toward the shore break, begins grabbing their boards, getting on top of them, and paddling out again offshore. By this time Doug has lost considerable ground, and he ends up about thirty feet behind them.

Paddling out, they pass the first obstacle, the first sandbar wave, and as they're getting a little further out, the waves keep coming—and they're a little bigger. And they keep getting bigger. That evening Phil recalls that moment, and laughingly says, "And I'm thinking to myself: this shouldn't be happening. We should have passed it. And it got worse and worse until we got to the middle of the Bay. This wasn't part of the plan." Even though Phil is surprised, he doesn't show his feelings in the moment, in the surf; instead he remains poised.

Doug tries unsuccessfully to reach the group, but he succeeds in making it out beyond the shore break, away from the impact zone and to the lineup. As the group hits the middle area of the Bay, Doug recalls, "it's just churning. There's a huge rip current and my board is being pushed sideways and going underwater in the foam." The water isn't as dense when there are bubbles in it, so boards are sinking rather than gliding, and Doug's board in particular can't seem to go straight, perhaps because its fins are busted. Savoring the tale, Phil agrees: "True, true."

Doug and the others get sucked all the way over to the left side of the Bay. This is a very dangerous spot to be in, because of the rocks and because there's no beach. Lifeguards on a jet ski come up to the group and say: "You guys just got to go!" letting them know they all need to paddle faster to get to a safer zone. Everyone is exhausted, out of breath, hurting. Doug says: "By then each wave that comes I feel like it's gonna break on me. Everybody else got past me and I had to jump off my board again. If I would have been five or ten yards further, I don't know if I would have made it out."

When they're telling the story that evening, the whole group erupts in nervous laughter at this point. The group eventually reaches the lineup, passes the crowd waiting in the lineup, and goes further out. Then they sit next to one another to regroup, rest, and catch their breath. In other words, they don't want to have to "scratch again" to go over another set. Doug punctuates this part of the story by saying: "And that was (just) the paddle out."

"What happened afterwards?" I ask. Doug says: "I flip my board again, and I'm pissed, bummed, upset, all these emotions going through my mind. Crap, can I still surf? What do I do?" And Phil tells him: "Just hang, and at least see a set. You're out here." This is a subtle command.

Doug then starts to approach other people in the lineup to try and figure out what he should do, starting conversations with "Hey man, how are you?" The typical response he gets is "Good, and how are you?" He says, "Oh man, I'm bummed. My fin just broke." But a lot of the other people are on edge too, wide-eyed because of the conditions, and they don't have the time to truly engage in the conversation Doug seems to need to have. Instead they try to focus and stay calm. Next, Doug asks Phil again, and Phil says: "The board doesn't look good. Hang, and if anything catch a ride in with a jet ski." More people echo what Phil says: "You should just wait on a ski and take a ride in if you don't want to catch a wave on that thing." As he recalls those instances, Doug says, exasperated, "And I'm like: I can't have that as an answer. *I can't take that!*"

About an hour goes by. The last guy he paddles up to to ask about what to do is a young surfer, Luke Shepardson, who according to many has been surfing the best this season, which secures him a spot as an alternate on the list of invitees for the next Eddie. "I flip the board. I grab the fin and I pull it up and it's like an inch up, and then it's in my hands. It just snaps off." And Doug says to Luke: "What do you think I should do?" And Luke is like: "Dude, you should call a ski over, and catch a ride in, or you could go straight on a smaller one." Heartened by the response, Doug triumphantly says: "I want to go straight!" And then he takes off on a shoulder of a smaller wave with Luke. And they ride it together. "And that was the beginning," Doug says, adding that he ended up riding two other waves that day. Phil says: "I saw you paddling out smiling from fifty yards away. You look back at me and I am going: 'Look, Kawika, he's smiling.'" Doug concludes his part of the story, saying: "It went from miserable to stoked. Yeah . . . absolutely stoked."

I ask him if Phil played any part in it, and he says: "I talked to him a little bit, but I was trying not to. I didn't want to bum anybody out. I felt like my energy was so negative. I was trying not to go on with it, but I couldn't help it. I said to Phil: 'I want to stay out.' And he said: 'Yeah, you should stay out a little bit. Watch and enjoy the experience. Be part of it. You made the paddle out'"—meaning Doug had completed one of the hardest parts of the mission. This is a case where Phil commends Doug for what he has already accomplished.

Then, as we continue trying to recollect different angles of the story, I ask Phil: "Did it get as big as you thought it was gonna get?" And he says: "I thought it was gonna get much bigger. I thought it was gonna be beyond surfable at one point. That's what I was waiting to see." (I, of course, was waiting on the beach at that moment, not sharing his concern.) "If it was gonna get too big where we couldn't surf, but it was just on the edge. I was watching it for a while, and then it looked doable."

Kawika's Take

As Phil starts rallying up the troops at his house, Kawika tells him: "I don't really want to go out." Phil replies: "Put your stuff on (your wetsuit and life vest). Let's walk down. You can always make a decision on the beach. We're just going to assess it." As the group walks down from the road to the beach, there's no more talk about making a decision, and Phil simply says: "When I say go, you just go and paddle as fast as you can." A week later I tell Kawika that that's a lot like what happened when Phil took me out at the Bay. I said that when I recalled my experience, another surfer told me that when Phil says "assess it," it means "we're going." Kawika then says: "He shouldn't have told you that. He shouldn't have told you Phil's tactics."

Kawika picks up the story at the point where he's reached the lineup, and says: "I was sitting so far over on the side. My biggest concern was that I didn't want to get a closeout set. As soon as the bigger bombs came, I'd just be paddling for the horizon. And Phil kept saying: 'It's coming,' meaning 'stay focused.'" Kawika continues: "And it's probably gonna come, so you have to have that kind of mindset." No matter how forecasting has improved there's always going to be that rogue wave that breaks fifty yards out. And neither Phil nor any other surfer, no matter how experienced, can predict exactly what will happen, and when. The only way to know with more precision what's coming would be to have someone on a higher vantage point informing surfers of waves approaching from the horizon—an idea Nicole McNamara put into practice while assisting her husband surfing Nazaré in Portugal. They had walkie-talkies, and she would even suggest which of the waves in a set was likely to be bigger.

Comparing his mental and physical condition to that of professionals, Kawika says:

> I probably surfed Waimea five or six times at least 12 feet or bigger, but this was much bigger than anything I have ever surfed in my life. Guys like Mark Healey, they already had a thousand twenty-footers on their heads. They know they can do it. I don't train. I can hold my breath for like two minutes sitting here relaxing. Waimea at 20 feet is big, but it's still very controlled and mellow. When it gets to 25 plus, as it was today, it turns into another location. It's like you're on a different planet. It's a whole different animal.

In the evening, around the fire, Phil turns with a smirk on his face that looks ready to turn to laughter and asks: "Kawika, what were you thinking on the beach? I was reading your mind." And the following exchange ensues:

> KAWIKA: I thought I was trying to read *your* mind. It's funny you even
>   say that. When that set started bombing nonstop for fifteen minutes
>   I was trying to think: "Is Phil actually having second thoughts?" I was
>   almost hoping he was, but he wasn't, unfortunately . . . but I was think-
>   ing . . . I was like, he was shaking his head probably more frustrated we
>   were sitting there. Or standing there for 20 minutes . . . but when I was

doing the self-talk, you know what I was saying? And I know it's going to sound weird. I was telling myself: "This is your destiny. This is your identity. This is where you're supposed to be. This is meant to be." I had to tell myself that. I went through a big transition out there. Huge. I went from light-headed, almost ready to throw up, wanting the jet skis to take me in immediately, to actually being able to breathe, looking around, thinking maybe I'll catch a wave (laughing nervously).

PHIL: I told you you got to get a chip shot, and then you'll feel better.

KAWIKA: (addressing the rest of the group to include them in the conversation, and implying that a chip shot on such a huge day still meant a gigantic wave) Yeah, he started saying chip shot . . . yeah, I can handle a chip shot (laughing ironically).

PHIL: Yeah. (Pause) Get one under your belt (affirmatively).

KAWIKA: I was scaaared (emphasizing the weight of the situation). I would be the first guy to tell you how scared I was.

PHIL: No, I knew you were scared, and I wanted to give you confidence (in a tone emphasizing its self-evidence).

KAWIKA: (assertively) That's good you know me.

DOUG: (interrupting, as he feels sorry and slightly resentful that he couldn't do more) Dude, I did not know what to say. I tried everything. I saw you talking to a lifeguard. I heard you talking to yourself.

KAWIKA: Yeah, I told them: "Don't leave me here!" The first day I saw my friend Kai working. And as soon as I got to the outside I told him: "I'm almost sure I'm out of my league. I'm gonna let you guys know that I'm sorry. I'm sorry." I was apologizing ahead of time. "You guys are gonna have to take me in."

UGO: What did he say?

KAWIKA: He looked at me kinda weird, he didn't know if I was joking. Then they came around twenty or thirty minutes later and I told them again: "Don't leave me out here! You have to take me in." And they said: "OK, OK . . . just let us know when you wanna go in," and I was like—

DOUG: (interrupting again) And how long have you been surfing? (highlighting the fact that Kawika is a great surfer, and also much better than he is himself).

PHIL: And that's when I told him you got to get a chip shot. But I was reading your mind on the beach. That's why I knew we had to get out there soon. I'm thinking to myself: Kawika is about to walk back to the house, and I'm gonna lose my crew (laughing).

KAWIKA: That is so funny. So true. I was telling Doug: "Hey, two minutes into these sets I think it's changing, pulsing again." And I can see Phil.

I was happy to walk up (the beach to the house), take off my wetsuit, jump into Phil's cold shower, relax. It was a battle. Seriously, from then on, and it didn't stop. You know what it was? And this is stating the very obvious: it was a mental battle from the moment Phil told me: "Hey, just come over, we're gonna look at it . . . do the last assessment with Doug." And then I said to Natalie (his former wife): "I think I have to go over there." I forgot about my water. I forgot my chia seeds. I should have been drinking and stuff. And I'm like: "I'm just gonna go over and just look at it. I don't think they're gonna go out because it's too crazy out there."

Back in the lineup, Phil paddled over to him and said: "You have the best seat in the house. You might as well enjoy it for a bit," trying to get him thinking about something other than the fear, maybe focus on the positives. (This is the same strategy he used with me and with Doug.) Kawika describes how he eventually caught his first wave thinking that if he could get it, he would try to get out of the water. After his conversation with Phil about taking a chip shot, all of a sudden a wave shifts over to the channel, and Kawika instinctively turns around, catches it, and rides it. But the wave isn't big enough for him to ride it all the way in to get out of the water. It is, however, enough to help him realize that he can—and wants to—continue surfing. He says:

It's so funny how you can ride a wave and it can change . . . you can be on the outside thinking, I'm going to get one wave and ride it back to shore, but the feeling you get from riding that wave, by the time I kicked out I was like, "I want to ride another one" (uncontrollable laughter by the whole group). It's amazing how your mindset can shift.

Sipping a screwdriver from his glass, Phil says: "The chip shots warm you up" (in a proud tone that conveys his satisfaction with how his strategy worked on Kawika).

Kawika's former wife then says, "You've finally found your match." What she means is that Kawika has always tried to get people to push their limits, and now he has found someone who has put him in that position. Kawika then adds:

To help people overcome their fears, you also have to be a salesman. Phil has more authority and years behind him, so he's like a Yoda; he doesn't have to say a lot. I have to convince people. I have to be more manipulative, for lack of a better word. I think you should always have a mentor and people you're mentoring.

He concludes: "So much is fear of the unknown. Don't get me wrong, I'm stoked, but I would have been even happier if I would have got a wipeout too, to know I can survive it, and that I need to train harder."

Noa, Mo, and Chris on the Day The Eddie Didn't Go

One evening, after finishing some homemade pizza and drinking some Italian red wine, Noa tells me, his brother Johnny, and his mum and dad, "I wouldn't have gone out if it wasn't for Chris Owens." Noa and Mo are two professional stand up paddle board surfers in their early twenties who grew up on the North Shore. They cemented their friendship while traveling the world for competitions. The day Noa is talking about, a few weeks before the episode described above, The Eddie could have run, but didn't. The main organizers predicted that the swell wouldn't reach the coast until midday, which wouldn't allow enough time for the eight-hour contest to be held. According to some, like the oldest competitor, Clyde Aikau, surfing conditions turned out to be even bigger than the day of The Eddie.

On the morning in question, not in a rush, Noa wakes up early and then drives up to the mountains to watch the swell rise and to wait for the right time to paddle out to surf. Looking at the horizon on his right, he sees some twenty-foot sets coming through at an outer reef called Phantoms. He sees some guys "get smoked" by the waves, which reach them while they're still sitting in the impact zone, rather than up in the lineup. The swell direction seems congenial for a spot called Himalayas. As he's driving down the hill, Noa calls Mo and asks him to meet up there—"when it's big, you know your friends that are down to go." It's eleven o'clock. They park their trucks at Lani's, have a quick look, and then begin putting on their wetsuits and safety vests. Impact vest first, and then wetsuit over it, to prevent the vest from sliding over their heads in a wipeout or if they have to dive under a wave.

And then they see the first truly big set of waves coming in: a thirty-foot wall of water rising up, stretching from one side of the horizon to the other. As it begins to break, it looks like a tsunami wave, where the best chance of safety is to drive up high in the hills rather than going out to sea. Jet-ski riders who are in the lineup at Himalayas seem to agree, as they sprint for the beach to avoid being caught by the white water that is racing toward them like an avalanche. Mo and Noa walk down to the beach, starting to think that it may not be safe, let alone possible, to paddle out here. Also, not having a jet ski for assistance seems too dangerous. They talk to one of the lifeguards they know, and he says that this is actually the second set of waves that has broken that far out. Then he adds: "A couple of guys already tried to make it out just earlier, but got denied"—the ocean didn't allow them to get far enough out that they could try to catch waves. Noa then says, "Mo, I think we should go check out Waimea; that's a safe bet. There are lifeguards there, and we have inflatable vests." He also points out that there are a lot more people in the water there, and that the break is not so far out to sea.

As it is with every large swell, the traffic is terrible. Mo says: "It takes forever just crawling back to Waimea." Their wetsuits still on, Mo and Noa are practically frying in their car as they approach the last turn coming into Waimea Bay. Stuck in traffic that's moving slower than pedestrian speed, they have time from this higher vantage point above the Bay to have a good look at the lineup—far, far from the shore. The panoramic view here makes it a place where many photographers set up. But they see something odd and puzzling. A mile out, they notice a dark plume in the water that is getting sucked out, almost as if all the sand has been brought up from the bottom. After some thought, Noa says: "Oh, shit. It looks like a bomb just happened in the Bay; a war just happened." They eventually reach the parking lot at the church next to Phil's house. Noa tells me:

> We had just got there and the energy was scared. We pulled up and like: "Mo, the people are scared right now." At least that's how I felt. This sand was like lifted to the surface of the water in like one hundred feet of water. "This was the same set that took Kelly Slater out" (his brother says): "he tried to get out, and got *denied*." This big set took him out and I guess he said later that was the first time he's ever been denied at the Bay. He tried to get out, broke his leash and had to swim in. A whole group of guys had to do the same, so there were only ten guys out the back that survived (nervous laughter) basically that set.

They park their car, and then Mo says: "Let's just take our boards down." Then they agree that if they actually take their boards down from the back of the truck, they're going out. But is it too big? Too dangerous? Is it actually possible? They conclude that a decision needs to be made in the parking lot as to whether they will paddle out or not. The weight is more on the no-go side. But how to decide?

Mo says: "I don't know. It looks a little sketchy out there." Then they see a number of surfers just now making it back to the parking lot.

Noa says: "All these people are coming in just rattled, they got taken out by this set. They look like they got in a fist fight." Some of the surfers have broken leashes, some have had their boards broken in half, many others have both. That set must have "mopped them up," they think. Noa adds: "Up close and personal they're just walking back to their trucks and they're just *devastated*, you know? They're like: 'Whoa, I'm so glad I'm alive.' 'It's fucked up out there. I almost died.'"

"We're like: 'Oh, this is heavy.' And I'm like: 'Oh, shit.' (laughs) I don't know if . . . 'Mo, are we into this?' I don't know what happened just now, but I know the swell is rising; sometimes that's the thing, you know a swell is rising, but it's hard to predict what's going on. We just went out to Himalayas and tried to get out and it was closing out, which I've never seen." Plus, hours have passed, and it's getting late, closer to sunset.

Then they see Chris Owens, who's gearing up. Noa says: "All right, Mo, if Chris Owens is going out we're going to go out with him. Okay? That's the deal. If Chris goes out, we go out, and if he *doesn't*, then we have (laughs) an excuse to walk back up the beach with Chris Owens." Mo replies: "Okay, that's the plan."

They take down their boards, lock the truck, and then walk up to Chris. "Chris, are you thinking of going out?" Noa says. And with a hesitant cadence that sounds like a question, but with no expectation of an answer from them, Chris says, sounding like Clint Eastwood, "Kelly Slater just got denied. Yeah. You know, I'm thinking about it. I'm going to go watch it. It's looking . . . It doesn't look too doable. But I'll look at it. Let's look at it."

As they leave the parking lot and begin walking down the hill toward the beach in single file following Chris, Noa discreetly says to Mo: "Shit. Not doable by Chris Owens?" Then (shifting back to the story he's telling me), he adds: "You know, I always looked up to Chris throughout my life as one of the guys out there. He's *always* out at Waimea charging, and summertime he's always training paddle boarding. He's paddled some of the biggest channel crossings between the islands that anyone's done between here. Yeah, he's just like a *legend*, so I was like, 'If *he* goes out, *we* go out. If he doesn't, we're over it.'"

They arrive at the shore break where a number of other surfers are also waiting, holding their boards. Chris's arrival is like a beam of light coming through a dark cloud; many of those surfers also admire him. One says: "Hey Chris, you going to go out or what? What's the deal?"

Chris replies with a terser version of his comment to Noa and Mo in the parking lot: "Thinking about it." He's on edge, too, and he knows he can't afford to be distracted, as the raging sea may only offer a short window of opportunity to make it out between the sets (if it offers any opportunity at all). A brief lull may materialize, but seizing it will require both concentration and quick decision-making.

Mo and Noa are sweating. They put on their gear more than forty minutes ago. In his retelling, Noa assures me: "I definitely want to go out, but I'm hoping Chris goes out because if he *doesn't* then I'm going to be skeptical, you know?" Chris starts doing his warmup routine, signaling that he has obviously decided he's going to try to paddle out. Later on, Noa confides in me: "And I haven't really surfed out there that often. I rarely surf out there. I try to go surf other places that aren't so crowded, but that day wasn't that crowded, so I was like, 'All right. This is a good day to go.'" As Chris puts on his ankle leash, he says: "Yeah. I think it's doable. I think it's doable" (repeating the phrase perhaps to emphasize the difficulty of the circumstances, how exceptional they are, and maybe also to signal a bit of doubt). Everyone follows suit, putting on their leashes. Now they all look "kind of ready to go." But maybe, as in the previous story with Phil, some are still hoping that Chris will call off the squad, commanding them to retreat. They all keep waiting for what feels like a long time. Two surfers then strike up another conversation with Chris, trying to blow off some nervousness while also looking for cues as to what to do, whether it's actually safe to try paddling out. "What should we do?" they ask. Noa instinctively ignores this incident, again fixing his attention on the horizon. He tells me what happens next:

> I saw what I thought was going to be a really good lull. If I was making my own judgments without Chris Owens, I'd go out right now. But maybe it's not the call? It just looked like good timing. I looked over and Chris was still in conversation with these guys. I was like, "Fuck. All right. I'm going to take ten steps forward down the beach, and if Chris follows me, I'll go charge."

He remembers holding his gun and thinking to himself then:

> I feel like this is a good time to go. But, like if I go and he doesn't go? Then that's a good judgment. So I just took a few steps down (demonstrates by getting up from his chair), kind of like going. Chris saw me and he looked out (toward the horizon), and he just started running down the

beach with his board. I'm like: "Okay, now's the time! Chris approved!"
(laughing triumphantly). So I just started sprinting. We just jumped in. It
was just adrenaline (snaps fingers) from that moment on. We just *battled*
out the channel. I remember the way we got out, we were almost on the
rocks at that time.

"Wow!" I say. It's clear from this detail how far the current had moved
them toward the left side of the Bay.

Yeah, the current just took us way out to the rocks over on the other side.
That's what Chris said: "Just paddle toward the rocks." We're like: "All
right" (dubiously). "That's not what I would have done, but let's do it"
(ironically). So, we went toward the rocks and I remember we just missed
a big set that came through; we just made it over. We made it out, that
was sick and there was only like ten guys out there. Twelve guys. It wasn't
crowded. Whoever was out there was out there for a reason, but at the
same time just really appreciating the waves that were coming through.
Once we had gotten out in the back there was this crazy-like mellow feeling. I felt like it was just really relaxed. Because there was barely anybody
out. It was beautiful bomb waves that were coming through and there
wasn't that same, the normal pressure of Waimea where there's like fifty
guys battling for a wave. Where you have to worry about: "Is this guy
going to drop in on me? Am I going to get tangled up with this guy? If
I go on this one, if I miss it, is there going to be seven guys in my face?"
It was just like: these are big waves and here we are at Waimea, let's ride
them, you know? There was nothing else. It was a pretty unique feeling.

Noa then tells me about the lineup, and how he and others sat further
out than perhaps they should have if they wanted to try to take some
waves. Safety. Further out, so as to avoid having a giant wave break on
their heads. He remembers paddling over a couple of pretty large sets.
Surfers were basically trying to understand where those waves would be
breaking, and how "to get one of those things." "Where would a wave this
size begin to break? Do we go any further? Or do I hold my ground and
try to catch one of these things? But maybe it will be on my head." Then
he talks with a pro surfer who says: "You kind of got to go on *anything*.
You just got to turn around and go, I guess, on these things. Because they
all look like they're going to close out."

Then Noa tells me:

And some of them did. That evening three sets closed out [the Bay]. After he said that I was like: "That's right, kind of just got to go on anything" (accepting the strategy suggested by the older, more experienced surfer). That evening I ended up . . . this one set came and luckily I was in position, I kind of got a corner (a chip shot, as had happened for Kawika). It wasn't too crazy, but I managed to get into it. If I was a little deeper it would have been a *really* sketchy drop. But just being able, like even from wherever I caught it, was so fun. I remember holding my ground: "Okay, this one's pretty big" (self-talk). But I noticed the last few sets if I paddle out, I'm not going to catch 'em. So I wait. So I'm waiting, and actually that pro surfer ended up calling me into it because he tried to go and he couldn't get into it, and he's like: "Go! Go! Go!" I was like fifteen yards, twenty yards deep inside, deeper, and he said to go. So I went, managed to get up, and it was just this crazy feeling being like peripherals, seeing the *whole* Bay, the *whole* Bay was coming in. To the right it was like a wave, and to the left it was a wave, I was just like: "I feel like I'm just going to go straight" (laughs). You know? "That's all I can do." But uh, yeah, so I went straight (instead of riding sideways on the wall of the wave going right). It actually backed off a little bit and then I rode it for a while, and then I ended up like really relaxing and appreciating it and I fell off (laughs) right before it closed out.

Next I ask how they made it back to shore. Noa explains to me that according to Chris and other old-school guys, the trick for getting in on the big days revolves around working as a team. In between sets, if you don't manage to get one medium-size wave (potentially all together, as a "party wave"), surfers have to paddle as fast as they can toward the peak—where waves generally break—and then move toward the shore. If a big wave comes, then you should be out from the impact zone—where the wave detonates and where most of its energy is channeled—and the white water rushing toward shore will blast you in that direction, pushing you underwater, but also toward the beach and away from the breaking waves. Then he tells me: "You know, if you don't do that, you may end up waiting there forever." Stuck in the water. Waiting. Case in point: a number of surfers paddled out earlier, before the swell began rising, and stayed, stuck in the lineup as it grew. They couldn't make it back in. Hours going by. Other surfers noticing it, seeing how when each set came those guys would be trying to get out of the way, not trying to catch any waves. Their eyes filled with terror. Noa then tells me that especially when it gets to this size, it becomes a small community experience where everyone is watching out for each other.

> There's this sense of security between the group. For instance, just paddling out: knowing that there was me and Mo and Chris Owens and a couple of guys that were like: "Okay, these guys" . . . a couple guys paddled out because *we* paddled out. They weren't going to paddle out, but they saw us go out. They were like: "Okay, these guys have confidence in going out, so we're going to go out." So they went out, and they had a purpose to be out there, but they were just *unsure*, just like we were, about going out. There's a certain energy you *latch* onto out there (pauses), just of the trust and people being out there. It's like you see some waves sometimes and you're like: "That's kind of ridiculous (laughs), that's a scary wave," but then you look around and you see a couple of your friends, and you're like: "All right, we're out here. Maybe it's a ridiculous wave, but at least we're out here trying to surf it, and we'll be cautious, and we'll be safe." If something does happen, at least you know I have faith that my friend's going to at least do his best to try to help me out.

Then he gets back to explaining how they made it out of the water:

> I remember that day coming in everyone was working together. It was like groups of like five guys trying to get in at the same time: "OK, now! Now! Now! We're all going in!" Just paddling in, just trying to after a big set came through. There were a couple guys out there that, like you said, weren't meant to be out there, didn't *intend* to be out there and they were just trying to get in, you know? (slightly laughing). And those guys everyone made sure that they were kind of the black sheep that everyone was herding in. Making sure that they were okay like: "Okay we're all going in, you're coming in with us. We'll watch you, you know?" Everyone was safe because of that.

I ask him: "How did you make it back in?" He then tells me that other surfers started saying,

> "We gotta get a wave in." And then I thought: "Okay, this is my plan. This is what I'm going to do: Let's go do this as a team." Maybe not even spoken so much as a team, but it's just like, okay, this guy's committing to *this*. There's a certain level of confidence about what this guy's doing (Chris), and I trust *him*. So I'm going to do it too. Five guys go, you know?

I remember, I think I got a *party wave* in with a bunch of guys. Toward the end of the day, when it gets big, I find that common, like everyone tries to catch a wave and just comes in together, you know? Just to get in. It's nice knowing there's no one out the back that you're going to leave behind. It's like: "Okay! Let's try to get this one in!" Especially with my friends, if we're just surfing. A lot of times we'll surf out here alone. If you're coming close to the end of the day, instead of like: "Oh, I'll catch one more, see you in there," it's like, "Let's catch this one together." We know we're both coming in. We don't want to get to the beach and have to look out and see that there's this big set that smoked you, and have to go back out because we're worried. Something *could* happen.

Noa's father, Sean, who surfed Waimea decades ago, confirms: "And that's how it used to be and how it still is. Sometimes you even say: 'Party wave. Let's go!'"

Mentorship and Peer Influence

We are the groups we belong to and interact with. To play successfully and get to the "next level," as surfers say, we need *significant others*. As I will discuss further in subsequent chapters, these individuals may be mentors and friends, but also rivals. All these relationships matter, albeit in different ways and arguably at different points in our careers. What is key is that those significant others must be similarly committed to what we want to achieve, and that (in the case of friends and mentors) we get along with them. Put differently, in order to voluntarily spend considerable time with them, we need to genuinely enjoy their company and learn gradually how to tune into the same frequency—points I will touch upon in the next chapter when I discuss fun and friendship, and, more broadly, social cohesion.

As the first story in this chapter illustrates, an older, more experienced figure can help us reach our goals—and he can do so in different ways. Because of his proven competence, Phil demands respect without having to ask for it. Because of his skillful reading of interactions, based in part on his experience, he knows how to get the best out of his team while also gifting them confidence[22] and enthusiasm. Because of his social standing, he doesn't need to draw attention to himself to display his worth, which might cause him to lose sight of his crewmembers, sucking out their energy. He sets the plan, sets and maintains the interactional rhythm, and doesn't allow his group a glimpse of his doubts. His stance and demeanor exude confidence. His crew's admiration increases his own energy, and he feeds that energy back toward them, albeit at a lower intensity. When faced with questions of self-doubt, he replies shortly and firmly, often reframing the situation and making sure that his team members don't become overwhelmed by fear, but instead focus on the steps they have already accomplished. Expressions of doubt are met with subtle orders. At times he doesn't answer questions directly,[23] instead commanding members of his group to move closer to the action where he can more easily try to help them convert their feelings of fear and anxiety into forward momentum. As the leader, he also breaks the mission down into smaller tasks to get the group moving further along, and he rewards each of them for how far they've gotten.

In the second story, we find Chris functioning as a *specialized other* on which less experienced members of this social world rely to try to make sense of a critical situation. Like Phil, Chris embodies charismatic traits of successful leaders; he gives short replies and functions as a sacred object around which others gather to draw energy and to gain knowledge. Members of Chris's group mimic his behavior, as Phil's group did. For instance, when Chris puts on his leash, others near him do the same. When Chris walks down from the church parking lot to the beach, Mo and Noa follow him. When Chris and Mo and Noa decide to paddle out, they communicate their forward momentum to others on the beach, who follow them, plunging into the water.

Mine is a theory of process: in a moment when one is facing a life-changing, challenging task, a fateful moment, frozen by self-doubt and fear, interaction and identification with a charismatic mentor or peer can resolve the internal conflict, emboldening one to accept their judgments and freeing one to take a transformative step in life. Rather than a theory of interaction rituals *à la* Collins, I formulate a theory of self-transformation in the midst of a particular type of situation. This theory adds to Collins's work, which deals with creativity, solidarity, and interaction chains, a focus on particular types of situations and the internal processes within a person who is considering a life-changing commitment.

While this chapter focused on novices and mentors, chapter 3 focuses on sociability among peers. In it I discuss how a sociological conceptualization of fun can help us further understand how groups who experience intense interactions leading to *emotional energy* may also develop cohesion over time.

CHAPTER THREE
Fun and Community

Do you want to meet "Coach"? Pick any morning, don't mind the rain, and make sure to get out of bed earlier than you might want to. Then, if you're staying up the hill in Pūpūkea like I do, drive down, try not to fall over the cliffs or into a ditch because you're still only half-awake or you're gazing at the horizon to look at waves coming in from as far as you can see. From above, from the beach, and from the water, waves look, smell, taste, and feel much different. No matter how big they are, looking at them from above is deceiving; with nothing else to give you perspective, they look like miniatures. A large and stormy swell makes the whole ocean, from above, look like a raging mess—"victory at sea," as they say—while a good, big swell with light winds looks like orderly moving dunes, which from the water more closely resemble mountains. "Men riding mountains," they used to say, until about a dozen women started ascending in the sport.

At the bottom of the hill, turn right and pick any spot in Foodland's parking lot. This early, it's almost empty. And it's quiet, and also quite cold, and still dark outside. Perhaps this is why some like to experience this part of the day—at least temporarily, they don't have to deal with tourists, who mostly see the sunny side of this coastline. This overpriced supermarket is the epicenter of the social life on the North Shore. It's one of the few communal spaces where you can learn such local news as who caught the biggest wave of the day or who pulled in the best barrel of the season. The central node of the coconut wire. Stories are told and retold, and new ones are craved with anticipation and appreciated with genuine interest. Nature and human performance in nature provide opportunities to create culture in the form of oral history, as well as through film, video, and the written word. Life on land and life on the water—a significant border between two different worlds that sometimes intersect and clash. Some say that the North Shore has much culture, meaning that a lot of surfing history is anchored along these seven miles of phenomenal waves, heroic accomplishments, and tragic stories.

Some locations light up at night, and some never sleep, while others are only lived in daylight and outside, and sometimes uniquely from the water. The North Shore is decidedly the latter kind. Unlike residents, tourists live different hours of the day. They can also afford shopping here instead of taking the thirty-minute drive to Costco, which requires a state ID. Time is precious when you just have a week or so before you have to head back to reality, and then who cares if a gallon of orange juice costs eleven dollars? In what is still called "Country"—as opposed to Honolulu, which is "Town"—everything closes early. By nine p.m. you won't find anywhere to eat besides Foodland. And don't even think about night life—there is none, unless you're invited to a private party either at one of the houses on the beachfront owned by surfing companies or at the home of another tourist or a resident. By ten p.m. it's also silent. Most people, especially the residents, are asleep, and you could be reprimanded for talking on the road next to any of the thin-walled wooden houses, or sometimes even just pulling into the wrong driveway and having to turn around, which can easily happen even in daylight. Case in point: one of my friends was chased off by a notorious figure apparently for simply driving on "his" road—meaning the road in front of his house, not the driveway connected to the house. I ask Mason if he was driving too fast, and whether he stopped. Having spent more than fifteen years on the island and having embodied its slow tempo, Mason simply replies, "No," and then another "No," in monotone, as if asking me: "Are you stupid? Of course I kept driving."

The Coffee Bean is in the same building as Foodland. Every day of the winter, Chris—or as he is known by some, "Coach" or "Skippah"—is typically the first customer, and you can find him sitting by the window, forecasting mainly big waves. The young women who work there like him both because of his polite manners and because in the early morning he's like their bodyguard. They arrive at four a.m. to prepare to open the shop, and when they first open the door and it's pitch black, they don't know who's going to be walking in. With Chris there they feel safe. He's in his late fifties, lanky, lean, and still strong. In the colder winter

Chris at work in his office forecasting.

mornings he wears a beanie, a flannel hoodie, and jeans. Blue eyes, bald, a large jaw, and a skin worn out by a life spent in and on the water. Push-ups and especially pull-ups, which he embraced as a daily routine before it was fashionable to be fit, even in a place like Hawai'i where taking care of your muscles and soul takes priority over nurturing your intellect, have kept his body trim and muscular.

Be there sometime between five and seven thirty a.m. Don't be later than that, because by eight he'll be gone. That's Chris's office, those are his working hours, and that's where most of his social life on land unfolds. Even though conversation is less common than I may have implied, especially during the first part of his morning. You can feel social without being vocal: think of being at the library, for instance, or of people working on their computers at coffee shops, or even of how best friends can sit silently without feeling awkward. Chris has a job to do, and those who stop by are also eager to seize the day and get to where they need to be—many toward Honolulu, where most jobs are. While waiting for their drinks, though, each has a few minutes to spare. Fleeting relationships and recurring interactions that follow rather predictable patterns.

Chris tells me he stayed up all night forecasting, and that the swell peaked around two a.m. "From my house, it felt like they were launching a rocket or like forty Harley Davidsons." Then he shows me a text he received from Clyde Aikau replying to a notification that Chris had sent him about the potential magnitude of the swell: "GREAT. BE ON IT."

I ask Chris when he started developing his passion for forecasting and basically keeping part of the North Shore community alert to new sizeable swells. He says he's been studying it through tutorials on various websites for the last five years. He also mentions social media, hinting at the fact that when he began posting his predictions he enjoyed the attention and appreciation he received from the local community—the pleasure of belonging while contributing to the scene.

One guy I know asks me about the forecast, but he quickly corrects himself, saying that instead he should ask "the right man." Another one asks: "Hey Chris, how's the weather?" To which, after a short pause for dramatic effect, Chris replies with a smirk: "Rainy." It has been pouring since yesterday morning and it doesn't seem like it will stop anytime soon. Later on, an established big wave rider asks him too: "You think it's an Eddie Swell?" Looking at the broken screen of his computer, which displays the models, Chris says: "It's possible, but it depends on the winds. It's still too early to tell."

Coach has two jobs: one as a self-taught big wave surf forecaster, which is monetarily unpaid but compensated by the attention and recognition of some of his peers. He enjoys studying the weather patterns and making people aware through postings on Facebook not only about waves, but also about possible hurricanes, often ahead of the news. "When it comes up on the news, people report back: 'Chris, you were right!'" And even local news forecaster Guy Hagi consults his surf report.

The other job is construction work and painting, which he is particularly inclined to buckle down on when he "needs to put money in the tank." But Chris doesn't miss workdays unless the surf is big or exceptionally good. His day starts with the first vocation, and usually ends with it too—after sunset you'll find him back at his computer at the same spot, but usually for a shorter time. Occasionally he'll also be there after lunch, but don't count on it.

Chris probably gets a discount from the shaper who makes his boards, but I don't think he has more than two. He likes keeping his expenses to a bare minimum. Others who live in this capital of surfing tell me that Chris has dedicated his life to this lifestyle, perhaps suggesting that he has compromised more than they have. I can hear admiration in how most of his peers describe him. A local hero, but on a global scale, although except for the Bay or among the North Shore surfing community, he flies under the radar.

His dad pursued a successful career in the army, and when he retired he worked at Kamehameha School, training Hawaiian students in military skills. He advised Chris not to get into the military because according to him it didn't get any respect anymore—certainly not as much as when, coming back from Germany after WWII, he was welcomed as a hero. He kept in shape for a long time, jogging and being the first in his family to paddle board. And Chris inherited much of his stamina and strength from him. Long after he retired, he went back to school, mainly taking history classes and earning two master's degrees over eight years in college at UH Mānoa.

Chris's older brother is Bobby, previously known as "Mr. Sunset," a former Eddie invitee and surf prodigy who now works at a surf shop in Hale'iwa. Chris tells me that back in the 1970s he also wanted to undertake a professional career, but he had many other interests at the time. "I was more like a bad teenager," he says, while "my brother was like a perfect child: growing up straight edge, listening to mommy and daddy. He drank, but not like I did." According to Bobby, there were two more reasons why Chris might not have pursued a professional career: because he didn't like competitions, and because their family had to make a decision on which child to invest in. Back in the mid-1970s professional surfing was in its infancy. As Bobby tells me, "Chris was almost always in my shadow." When Bobby left O'ahu in 1995 to relocate temporarily to Santa Cruz, California, Chris was free to come into his own. Bobby says:

> I think he saw this as a good time for him to really become dedicated and to pour it on. I think he felt freedom. And when I came back, people were like: "You're Chris's brother" (laughing). Oh, it was like: you're not Bobby Owens anymore. "Yeah, that's cool." It felt really good. It was very cool to see him find his niche. It just came later instead of earlier. He had to go through a lot of different periods in his life, different experiences. And when he was really young he spent a lot of time in the hospitals, and all of that, eventually somehow it manifested itself in the last twenty years when he started paddle boarding and getting into Waimea, and all of a sudden he was able to let go of all these things and he kind of became someone.

Chris's younger brother is Gary, a dedicated skateboarder now in his late forties who has possibly drained more swimming pools than anyone else in the world. A few years ago a well-known company printed a T-shirt displaying a sample of them: tiny pictures fitted together in a mosaic that resembled the tiles typically found on the inside of a pool, below the edge. So many that you would have to get a closer look to understand what they are. Chris also owns a skateboard made by a local company called Hawaiian Pool Services, which Gary used to co-own. Its name was chosen as a cover-up to disguise the true purpose of their operations—draining private pools to skate them. He has a prone paddle board he uses during the waveless North Shore summers when he trains for races like the Moloka'i; a truck that he moves only when necessary; a guitar and an amp his dad gifted him on a special Christmas after his mum passed away. And in his yard is a small fishing boat he's fixing up.

The house he shares is a three-minute walk from Foodland. Next to the TV in the living room there's a stack of trophies that Chris has won paddle boarding. A certificate reads: "The Senate State of Hawai'i congratulates Chris Owens on the occasion of his successful crossing of the Kaua'i channel to O'ahu on a paddle board. On Thursday, August 18th, 2005 North Shore paddle boarder and big wave surfer Chris Owens, completed the 65-nautical-mile crossing from O'ahu to Kaua'i in a time of 22 hours and 6 minutes." Until then, the only person to complete the crossing had been Gene "Tarzan" Smith, who did it in the 1940s; years later, *Surfer Magazine* called Smith "The Greatest Ocean Paddler of the 20th century." The December following his crossing, Chris was awarded the title Quiksilver Waterman of the Year. The medal hangs next to his TV alongside a poster from an edition of The Eddie.

For the last twenty years Chris has dreamed of getting an invitation to The Eddie, and finally, in 2018, he was put on the alternate list. That same year Clyde Aikau selected him along with Ian Masterson to be the forecasting team for the event. Chris had surfed Waimea since the early 1990s, catching almost every major swell while missing only a few days, so most people on the North Shore thought the invitation was long overdue. Mark Healey thinks that Chris has probably surfed Waimea more times than anybody alive today, and that "people look up to him because he is the old wise bull."

Only a few individuals are up and about at this hour, and most of them seem to know one another, or at least to know *of* each other, or to have been close before some rupture put distance between them. And then there are the few regulars who stop by every day to share more extended conversations. Chris is a fixture on the scene, and a distinct character both here and at Waimea, where he has earned a special spot in the surfing lineup. The lighter it gets, the busier and louder the parking lot and coffee shop become, but by then Chris is long gone.

The North Shore: Waves for Waves

In Hawai'i living costs are among the highest in the country, the infra-structure and education outcomes are some of the poorest, and the home-less rate is one of the highest. For many, one job is not enough; others, no matter how hard they work, struggle to keep a solid roof over their heads. Some eventually leave the islands with memories of a long-gone dream or concerns about an unfeasible future, as for instance when they decide to raise a family. On the North Shore waves, business, love, and sexual relationships are shared, sometimes antagonistically, over a small pool of individuals comprising comparatively fewer women than men. In addition to the locals, there are many who come to visit regularly each winter season. Jobs, sexual and romantic partners, housing, money, and waves are scarce resources. They are fought over, and at least the waves are also *traded*, locally as well as internationally. As the Brazilian big wave champion Carlos Burle tells me, "waves for waves," explaining how hard it was for someone like him, coming from a country that doesn't have world-class waves, to earn a spot in the local scene. "So, Italy (knowing that I am Italian), I never went to Italy to surf," but "I have come to Hawai'i for thirty years. Why? Because this is the capital of surfing. There is power here."

As in any other small community, on the North Shore everyone knows everyone else's business, to savor gossip. What goes around comes around quickly here and seems never to leave you, with people literally watching for you to do something out of line, and willing to come find you and put you in your place when you do. Do well and everyone will know; behave poorly according to this community's norms and values, and you will be warned or even urged not to come back. Try not to take more than you can give, and give your seat to someone else before one is offered to you. And actually, even if one is offered to you, think twice before you take it. Be humble and keep a low profile. Intimidation is not uncommon here, but it's also typical that friends will try to help you if you're in need. *Kōkua*, a concept akin to altruism that means extending loving help to others without regard for personal gain, is observed here.

Aloha is a cultivated value integral to the indigenous culture based on sharing, or, as a young Hawaiian pro surfer puts it, on "Having a good spirit and a welcoming heart, welcoming people and having good vibes too." Since other surfers have told me that his manners personify the trait, I ask him where he learned it. "My parents. To be humble, let the surfing do the talking, have fun in the water, be respectful to your elders. Not being like the cocky kids talking shit."

Along with aloha, *modesty* and *respect* are as central to Hawaiian culture as "l'arte di arrangiarsi" and "bella vita" are to Italian culture. Respect is a core value both on land and in the water, because most societies in Oceania are based on reciprocal support.[1] In Hawai'i, respect has a multitude of meanings that derive in part from different kinds of behavior and operate in different contexts. In the water it can be based on fear, or spring from outstanding or heroic performances, or accrue as a recognition of particularly intense moments shared. It can be reciprocal or one-sided, and when mutual it is binding.

The cover of the April 2008 issue of *Surfer Magazine*[2] shows the perspective of a surfer tubed at Pipeline. Positioned behind the surfer, the camera looks out toward the exit, the lineup, and the shore. The caption reads: "You Belong Here: Why Hawaii Is Still the Place to Be." The issue celebrates the North Shore. Chris Mauro introduces the editorial with "No Hawaiians, No more Aloha," pointing to the fact that much of the indigenous population lives in tent villages on the east side of O'ahu. As sociologists Katherine Irwin and Karen Umemoto[3] confirm, Native Hawaiians make up a disproportionate number of the "house-less" population—a term introduced to acknowledge the history of colonial takings, implicitly asking, "Can you be homeless in your homeland?" The most short-sighted response to this tragedy has been to move them out of sight.

A local surfer elaborates on the meaning of respect by addressing visiting surfers:

> Respect when you come here. Remember that you don't own the place. You're a visitor. Be nice to me. Remember I have a real job. You are on vacation. I am not. So when you come out, let me catch my waves and do your thing and catch your waves. Don't come here and take pictures. Don't come here and try to fight me for waves. If I'm powering for a wave, guess what bro, I have to go to work tomorrow morning, you do not. You're taking a back seat. And that's kind of the way it is. It's all about sharing. And you show that respect, that same guy will hook you up with waves.

Like many others, this surfer also expresses how frustrating it became for him to fight for waves; his subtext is that surfing should be a diversion from the preoccupations of work and life on land. And he also talks about how riding big waves eventually afforded him a way to bring fun back in.

Fun in Interaction: Reverberating Intensity across Time, Space, and Place

In one of the first depictions of surfing by a European, Captain Cook's surgeon, William Anderson, observed a Tahitian riding a wave in a canoe in December 1777, and noted that "this man felt the most supreme pleasure, while he was driven on, so fast and so smoothly, by the sea; especially as, though the tents and ships were so near, he did not seem in the least to envy, or even to take notice of, the crowds of his countrymen collected to view them as objects which were rare and curious."[4] Searching for an equivalent activity in his home society, Anderson pointed to the pleasure he got from ice skating. Seeing the Tahitian paddling his canoe with such zest, though, his first thought was that he had stolen something from one of the expedition's vessels; in reality, the native was simply rushing out to catch a wave.

Laughing at how some older big wave surfers used to compare themselves to astronauts, explorers, or gladiators, Brock Little told Matt Warshaw: "You know why I surf big waves? The big secret? Because it's fuckin' fun! It's the funnest thing ever!"[5]

While surfing is certainly pleasurable, sometimes it's also fun. But what is fun? And what's the difference between fun and pleasure? In short, sociality—the tendency to associate in or form social groups, and the pleasing effects of that association. Fun is collective pleasure, group pleasure. It's active enjoyment. Historian John Beckman emphasizes: "fun is one pleasure that can't be felt. Fun, like sex, must be had."[6] It's not passive entertainment. While fun typically involves pleasure (positive feeling) for those involved, it extends beyond mere satisfaction, comforting embodiment, or agreeable affect. It results in two main outcomes: the kind of positive feeling Collins describes as *emotional energy* (drive, enthusiasm, confidence), and a sense of solidarity among those who share it—an aftermath of what Émile Durkheim, in his study of religious rituals, identified as *collective effervescence*. Put another way, fun is one pathway among others to solidarity. Shared fun, and thus social acceptance and the delight in becoming and realizing oneself within the social, as Aristotle would put it, promotes bonding among friendship groups.

While fun may appear trivial, or even benign, these designations are not accurate. Fun matters a great deal, both to those who pursue it and those affected by its consequences. Indeed, Beckman[7] argues that the history of North America is rooted in fun and in what he calls "joyous revolts," which, according to his analysis, have been key for democracy. Yet one may reasonably argue that fun could just as well threaten democracy's foundations. Fun, like creativity, has a dark side, too.

To understand fun we need to identify its basic conditions and characteristics, and then read into the social relations it activates among participants. To explain fun and what is fun in big wave surfing, I introduce several ideas and concepts from sociology and social psychology; later I illustrate these concepts through examples from my fieldwork.

There Is Risk, Danger, and Uncertainty in Fun

Fun, like play more generally, is autotelic, meaning that it depends on the willingness of participants to engage in it to no particular end other than satisfaction. Put differently, it cannot be imposed. Forced fun as a kind of forced ritual drains energy. It's a failed encounter. Doing something for fun often stands in contrast to acting with the instrumental purpose of getting something out of it besides the experience. In this sense fun is exploratory: the less predictable and surprising the experience, the more intense it's likely to be. As a kind of successful social encounter,[8] it depends on the same ingredients: there's a mutual focus among participants who grow intensely aware that each of them is maintaining the common focus, and their focus and bodily motions and vocal rhythms progressively intensify and attune. For a similar dynamic, think of laughing with others as contrasted to laughing alone, and how in the former scenario individuals may encourage one another in the production of laughter while amplifying it.[9] Fun is difficult to define, so much so that even *Ur-theorist* of play Johan Huizinga wrote that "the fun of playing . . . resists all analysis, all logical interpretation. As a concept, it cannot be reduced to any other mental category."[10]

Gary Alan Fine and I define fun as "a collaborative and unscripted sequence of action that produces—and is perceived as producing—joint hedonic satisfaction while delineating group identity and establishing boundaries to those who do not belong."[11] Fun has a sunny side resulting in group cohesion and a dark side producing division. Exclusivity and co-presence with a common focus intensify fun. Mutual awareness and recognition of the similar interpretation of the "fun experience" by participants is key, as are the ideas of spontaneity, constraint built on groups' idiosyncratic group cultures, and the elements of unpredictability and surprise. As sociologists David Snow and Dana Moss[12] emphasize, the unplanned emergence of action is triggered by certain forms of social relations. In the case of fun, these may involve preexisting trust, a shared interactional history, or a desire to build social ties. A sense of reciprocal respect facilitates fun as it enhances spontaneity (decreasing or eliminating fear of being judged), willingness to take risks, and ultimately communion. Fun depends on the active participation of those involved. In other words, individuals need to feel that their presence is needed and appreciated to successfully carry out the fun project. Feeling like bystanders, hindrances, or (metaphorically speaking) buoys in the water precludes us from having fun and may also undermine the fun others are experiencing, and thus erode the social and physical boundaries between outsiders and members of the group.

Fun relies on at least three basic conditions that support some of the characteristics I mentioned above: *structural affordances, collaborative commitment*, and *shared narrative*. First, fun requires *structural affordances* constituted by time, places, and spaces that are conducive to and appropriate for the intended activity, but that may or may not end up producing fun moments. For instance, the ocean is by definition an unpredictable[13] setting which lends itself to both surprise and excitement—the force, sound, and sudden appearance of larger waves, the necessity to improvise a course of action, and the intense focus required to do so.

It also demands that the individuals involved in it share a *collaborative commitment*, a desire to engage in action that conforms to the group's culture alongside individuals with similar interests. Activities like big wave surfing, or like an extreme form of a team sport, demand collaboration and the sharing of knowledge and skills among an elite few who nurture respect and to some degree depend on one another.

While many experiences may be memorable, they become cultural through discourse. *Shared narrative* is this cultural characteristic of fun resulting in collective identity, cohesion, and further commitment to maintaining the group. Fun creates allegiance both through its emotional engagement and, as Randall Collins and Curtis Jackson-Jacobs have also pointed out in their respective studies of violence,[14] through its subsequent narrative iterations, which provide satisfaction and memory of the satisfactions that colleagues have shared. In other words, fun has an emotional tail. The memory of fun, collectively reinterpreted, allows the emotional experience of the original fun to be experienced and re-experienced—sometimes in a lower register, a fun residue, but also as an altered experience that can at times intensify the original emotion, as when the memory becomes bigger than the event itself. As such, fun links voluntary action and emotional entrainment, becoming a form of affective recall that can solidify social relations. Fun fosters collective identity—a sense of "we-relations," as philosopher Raimo Tuomela[15] calls it—and invites what Georg Simmel calls sociability:[16] a form of interaction inviting those who partake in it to act as equals with no instrumental purpose other than the success of the sociable event.

As a form of interaction, in this case with other surfers and with the waves, surfing is social, cognitive, spiritual, and physiological. Collins argues that *emotional energy* "is bodily energy that is simultaneously mental, a process happening in your nervous system along with your muscular physiology."[17] And that bodily and mental energy rise and fall together.

Big wave surfing can be pleasurable because, like such other activities as mountaineering, chess, a great conversation, or a music session, it demands a total focus of attention that sometimes results in what psychologists call a *flow* state: facing a task that isn't too easy—boring us—or too difficult, overwhelming us. It's an optimal state that can be experienced either alone (e.g., while reading or writing) or with others (e.g., while performing collaborative tasks such as playing chess or sharing a conversation). Unlike many other activities, big wave surfing also entails what sociologist Stephen Lyng conceptualized as *edgework*—voluntarily facing situations that are not only difficult, but also potentially debilitating. For Lyng the "edge" is a line between life and death, or at least between safety and serious injury. During these situations, which demand careful planning and preparation and the acquisition and development of skills—the *work* part—individuals may experience *flow moments*.

Big wave surfing also entails a physical and physiological component, described in great detail by historian and sport scholar Douglas Booth[18] and expressed in simple terms as the adrenaline and dopamine buzz. Writer Thad Ziolkowski tracks the similarities between drug and surf addiction, and how the latter can be either a gateway toward drug addiction or a path of recovery from it. An informant's girlfriend once told me, "They're all adrenaline junkies." Intense pursuits like *edgework* involve personal development, a social component, and a physiological aspect which also varies across types of situations and physical and social environments, ultimately impacting the intensity of different situations and the level of emotional energy and solidarity they produce. According to Ziolkowski, surfing resembles other addictions in that its strong attraction is at least partly due to the unpredictability of reward (in this case, waves, and based on the nature of the setting where it's practiced) acting as "intermittent reinforcement," which intensifies the surfer's attention and contributes to his getting hooked.[19] In line with interaction ritual theory, this characteristic (if communally shared) is also likely to increase emotional energy. But the lure of this pursuit is not just tied to unpredictability; it is also rooted in the *edgework* principle that if one gets better, one increases the odds of scoring more and better waves while also improving performance.

Conceptualizing big wave surfing as *edgework* means placing it within a specific social and spatial context, and thus extending a discussion on interaction rituals by trying to understand intensity variance, and thus the different degrees of *emotional energy* and solidarity produced by different experiences—a topic to which I will return at the end of this chapter and throughout this book.

The intensity of *emotional energy* depends on various factors, some of which relate to the points identified by Collins and some of which go beyond his analysis. Let me detail a few of them. As Collins writes,[20] intensity is to be understood in contrast to previous situations in an individual's experience. I want to add that it also needs to be understood in contrast to other situations experienced by the group, as well as in relation to the objective singularity of events the group has experienced historically. Further, to discern intensity we need to contrast it to the elements that make certain rituals fall flat and fail, and in particular the possibility of boredom, which impairs the group's ability to build or maintain focus. Additionally, uncertainty and danger, either physical or psychic, lead to greater focus, which should make the experience more intense and thus more likely to generate both *emotional energy* in participants and solidarity between them. The more intense the situation—individually, collectively, and historically understood—mentally and physically, the more likely it is to provoke the two outcomes of emotional energy and group solidarity. The more authentic and potentially consequential the situation is and appears to be to partakers, the greater should be the focus it generates. If *flow* states are moments of heightened focus within ritualistic encounters, *edgework* represents a longer span of time conceptualizing those events that can be deadly or gravely debilitating. Within those encounters, and between different encounters of the same consequentiality, we find *fateful moments*—small fractions of episodes that can alter participants' lives and are thus turning points. In those moments we depend on skill, courage, creativity, and luck because the situation we face is new and vaguely defined, and as Lyng would say, "verging onto chaos" and demanding solutions that need to be implemented quickly. As Richard Mitchell writes, "Creativity requires a degree of uncertainty."[21] Referring to Csikszentmihalyi's work on *flow* and arguing that it's not possible to experience it without a certain amount of stress, Mitchell notes: "A stressful situation is one that matters, one that is real, meaningful and commanding. Stress is simply and essentially stimulation."[22] Put another way, it requires focus because of its intensity. *Flow*, which in fact is the title of one of Csikszentmihalyi's books,[23] is that optimal state above boredom and just below anxiety.

The more memorable and re-tellable the *fun moment* is—which varies according to groups' cultures—the more meaningful and bonding it will be for its members. Memory and the sharing of meaningful experiences through telling and retelling provide a reason and pretext for repeated voluntary interaction resulting in cohesion. In this sense, the success of a ritual depends not only on the situation—and the vestiges of other situations—for each participant (Collins's main focus), but on what comes before (the broader history and the group history and culture) and what comes after (how the event is talked about, and perhaps how it is reenacted).

Fighting for Waves, Breaking the Crystal

As Carlos Burle explained, fighting for waves can undermine fun in the lineup, unless you are part of the group that is claiming ownership over them. This is what Fine and I call "the dark side" of fun—how it can also serve to separate outsiders as it draws groups closer together. As Jack Katz[24] documents, there is a sensual and deeply enjoyable aspect to violence. Surfers in various parts of the world use intimidation (and, rarely, violence) to prevent others, including newcomers, from crowding their spots: throwing rocks from cliffs, waxing car windows, scratching cars, or even, as Peter Cole was telling me, shooting others with BB guns from the shore. A few years ago, two men and a teenager were shot at from the shore while surfing a remote and guarded spot in New Zealand. The shots were merely a threat. During my fieldwork I was also told of a surfer in California who apparently had a knife taped to the nose of his surfboard for taunting. And this is in addition to the occasional scuffle, slaps, punches, or more common "stink eye," yelling, and other non-physical forms of harassment. But even though it is rare, physical violence does happen. Violence is woven into the social fabric of the North Shore, and surf violence is a palpable danger in the lineup as well as in local and state institutions. Despite the state's relatively low violent crime rate, Hawai'i's police kill at a higher rate than the national average. Like others, Carlos thinks that the surfing violence on the North Shore has decreased noticeably since he first visited in 1986. Why? Media devices and the internet. "You punch someone today, and then—" "Then what?" I interrupt him. A little frustrated because I cut him off and I'm not understanding his point yet, he opens the palm of his left hand and bangs down on it quickly three times with his right fist—"You are fucked. Do you understand?"

There are, of course, instances when surfing is more collaborative, more communal, and less selfish—such as big wave surfing. Surfing is a territorial and geographically dependent activity where sharing is generally an exception to the norm, unless the number of surfers out in the lineup is considerably lower than the quantity of waves coming in, or the only surfers out are a small group of friends. One strategy surfers use to mitigate this situation of "all against all," or a strong group against everybody else, entails regularly surfing certain spots not only to get to know and be known by the people who frequent the spot, but also to understand the field, which can help in securing waves, sometimes even the better waves. In other words, one can move up the pecking order, and pecking orders in some surf spots are easier to navigate and climb than those in others.

Philosopher Aaron James[25] writes on the meaning of being an ass-hole—someone who "allows himself to enjoy special advantages in social relations out of an entrenched sense of entitlement that immunizes him against the complaints of other people." According to James, most assholes are men, and they are disproportionately from individualistic countries like North America rather than from collectivistic ones such as Japan. Many of the observations that contributed to this definition come from James's own observations surfing in California. He further argues that at every surf break there is at least one individual who encapsulates these traits particularly well.

Carlos explains:

When I first started surfing back in Brazil, it was amazing because I wanted to go in the water and have fun with friends. And we were sharing waves, screaming and clapping for my friends. Then I realized you had to travel and then you become a *haole* (as in "ghost"—in Hawai'i that is a Caucasian, but contemporarily also used to describe a tourist) and then you have to fight for waves, to fight for waves also during the competition, and then all that bad feeling it's just polluting your mind. As soon as you realize you have to fight, the whole crystal breaks. And then as people begin to get more greedy, the feeling of having fun goes away.

The limited supply of waves and the group ownership claimed by local surfers tends to protect the right by some surfers to some waves in specific locations. Besides fitness, skill, and experience, how do traveling surfers manage to surf good waves abroad in popular spots? One way is by making local friends, and one way to make friends with local surfers is by "trading waves with waves." Carlos claims to be the biggest *haole* in Hawai'i because he comes from São Paulo in Brazil, which is inland, so that growing up he did not have a local surf break. He says this factor made it harder for him than for other surfers coming to Hawai'i. Why? Because Brazil is not famous for having good waves. When he's abroad, Carlos can't offer potential visitors logistical help or a free ride to the top of his local surf break, as someone from Tahiti or Australia could. Because he doesn't have one.

Inside the Church

A different day, but a similar routine. Sitting in his usual seat at the coffee shop as the first light begins to shine, Coach can look across Foodland's parking lot and see the waves of a new swell coming in. Suddenly, three waves come in that are noticeably bigger than the small, lake-like waves of a few moments ago. He can also read and evaluate their arrival according to the models he studies on the cracked screen of his laptop. Waves near and far. The faraway waves materializing locally like an anticipated Christmas gift, still wrapped. Life on the North Shore revolves around swells: How big will it get? Will the direction be right? Will it be too windy? Will this be a good winter? Will this be a potential Eddie swell? Everyone wants to know, and pretty much everyone thinks and talks about these matters, or is indirectly affected by them even if they couldn't care less. Divorces, fights, drug and alcohol abuse, and job loss could be correlated to the quality, size, and consistency or scarcity of swells year by year, and season by season. The North Shore, for instance, goes virtually flat during the summertime, which affects the mood of local surfers, who are suddenly left without excitement or purpose. Many find themselves frustrated by not knowing where to channel their energy, and how to refuel it when it drains out.

At lunch I see Chris at the Coffee Bean. He is wearing a baseball cap, a sleeveless T-shirt, and shorts, and he's intently jotting notes on a small piece of paper. I ask him what he's doing. "My friend has invited me to give an inspirational talk at the AA meeting by the Church at Waimea." I say, "That's very cool," and I offer to practice it with him. It's a short story about his life, about how he and his family ended up in Hawai'i. His father was a marine who participated in the occupation of Berlin in World War II, then fought in both Korea and Vietnam. He served as Army infantry during the Korean War, was a Green Beret during the Vietnam War, and qualified to be part of the Special Forces. Then he was commanded to go to Iran to work for the Shah. But one day when Chris was only a few months old, he crawled into the kitchen sink, turned on the hot water, and (in a time that predated safety systems moderating household water temperature) severely scalded one of his legs. Chris's skin and confidence were permanently scarred, and it took several surgeries to repair the worst of the damage. Thereafter his father decided to relocate his whole family to Hawai'i, where hospitals at the time were presumably better than in Iran. That's how they ended up on O'ahu, and also one reason why Chris started drinking in his teenage years.

As I enter the AA meeting, Chris is sitting in the back of the room with a friend. It's cold, and Chris is dressed head to toe in thick dark clothes. His large, white smile glows in the shabby fluorescent glare of the room, and he invites me to sit next to him. He introduces me to the guy sitting next to him as his good friend from Italy, whispering: "I was born in Vicenza, Italy, and my first words were *bambino piccolino*." The organizers serve Oreo cookies on plastic plates and have everyone quickly introduce themselves by first name and status: sober or recovering, number of days of sobriety, and future plans. After briefly telling us about her family history of alcohol abuse, a blonde woman in her late twenties says, "I'm afraid to procreate (her voice trembles). It runs in my family . . . I don't think I'd make a good mother."

The total number of people at the meeting, including the organizers, is eleven. After introductions, anyone who wants to talk gets about twenty minutes to tell their story. An Australian man in his early thirties with short, dark hair and an overall clean, fit look begins his monologue. It's difficult to decipher what he says because of his strong accent, but he goes on uninterrupted for the allotted time.

Chris walks to the front of the room. He starts by narrating his childhood accident, the eighteen major surgeries he underwent before age four, his life in a hospital, the scars, getting to the islands, how he would be ashamed undressing around women, and how this factor affected his life as he reached his teenage years. He had no problems meeting girls, but any next step would be too painful to bear. Chris's mother would tell him: "You've been blessed with a beautiful face." But the problems persisted. To this day he surfs wearing wetsuit pants, even in the warm waters of the Pacific.

Then he says: "On October 13, 1995, I left behind a demon that was with me from when I was fourteen years old until I was thirty-five." He got sober with the help of a psychologist, not through an AA support group (he leaves this point implicit), and then he started a serious fitness regimen. From the back, Chris looks like a strong man in his early thirties. He told me with some amusement that up until a few years ago he would sometimes get whistles from women in their twenties who saw him from behind, but when he would turn around they would be shocked to see what to them was obviously an old man. After he got sober, he managed to turn his life around, and even won several medals and awards in paddle boarding and a few in surfing. Chris's story is clear, pertinent, and moving, but just over five minutes in, some of the organizers start waving their hands signaling him to cut it short. By ten minutes, two older participants are motioning him to wrap it up. Taken aback, but not missing more than a beat, Chris flips through his notes and manages to make it through to his conclusion with coherence and composure.

He comes and sits next to me again in the back, and he asks me: "Wasn't that weird?" I nod, feeling embarrassed, sorry for him, and quite upset. "Let's leave, Chris," I say. Without hesitation he gets to his feet. As we walk out toward the back door, the older woman leading the meeting shakes her head at us. As soon as we're outside, we feel relieved, but still annoyed. Chris tells me I'm a good friend. We get in my car and drive to Hale'iwa, where I'm hoping to find somewhere to eat, but not finding anywhere, we head back to Foodland, where we buy some fried chicken on sale. We walk across the street to sit on a picnic bench by Three Tables overlooking the ocean. It's dark. And we eat while "talking story." Chris says, "Getting sober. That was probably my biggest achievement in life, because that's what I credit everything I have done that's been a good accomplishment, it was from quitting drinking." Because his relationship with his son's mum was falling apart, he was depressed and couldn't sleep. He decided to go see a psychologist at Kaiser Hospital in Honolulu. The doctor sat Chris down at a table and in one afternoon helped him draw up a plan. Knowing that when he was in his twenties he enjoyed exercising, she told him that he needed to quit drinking, design a good exercise program, make himself super healthy, and move out of the house and as far away as possible from his ex. Since that day he hasn't

touched a drink. He was thirty-five years old. He remembers walking to
Foodland one week after he had quit drinking and people saying: "Whoa,
you look good, man." "Looking good, man." "I just fed off of that. If that's
a reward for quitting drinking, I like that. I always stuck with it. And I
also thought about my son and I wanted to be like a good role model."
From then on he also improved at surfing big waves, getting his strength
back. Or as he says, "I got my youth back. I feel like it saved my life, but it
also made me live a kind of lonely life because I wasn't going out to the
parties anymore and meeting people. It's hard to find somebody that's
just like you." Reflecting on his longevity, he says:

> I'm like an old rooster who can still do it somehow. My goal was always
> like. . . . I was thirty-five years old and I knew that forty years old was
> coming up. And I kind of trained in how I was gonna be when I was forty.
> I just told myself: "I'm gonna be a strong badass forty-year-old." And then
> the same thing when I turned forty: I focused on when I was gonna be
> fifty. And the same thing I'm doing now, keep myself in shape for . . . I'm
> approaching sixty now. And I'm planning on doing the same when I'm
> seventy. I want to be the strongest, best senior citizen big wave surfer
> in the world. For me life is about being biologically young, being able
> to do things that are young, and actually being able to hang out with
> the young, surf with them. Stay out at Backdoor and catch waves. A lot
> of them (older guys) just don't want to get in the middle of them and
> surf. Part of it is from skateboarding too. You're skateboarding with kids
> all the time.

The doctor also told him to find a partner who would be "just like him"
and to start a new family.

Looking back, Chris adds:

> It took a long time, you know? To find the right one. I went through so
> many girlfriends, they just end up crazy. A lot of times when you meet
> somebody when you're older, it's kind of either one way or the other:
> she broke up with a guy who's crazy, or she's the crazy one. Something is
> usually wrong when you meet somebody in middle age and they're not
> with anybody 'cuz a lot of times the best ones are taken. The best ones are
> keepers and they've been taken. There's only so many good fish in the sea.

From where we're sitting, the Church is on our left, not far from where
we are. And the lineup of Waimea is just below it. If you surf the Bay,
this is one of the three places where you would park your car. At these

locations no one I know of will cut Chris short. Most are eager to learn, listen, talk story, and joke with him. Inside the Church, it seemed like no one cared about him; they didn't seem to care about the time and effort he put into preparing his presentation or about what they could learn from it, let alone his status in the local surfing community.

The Fun of Surfing Big Waves

Structural Affordances

Which features of the environment contribute to making surfing—and in particular, big wave surfing—fun? Exceptionality, natural beauty, unpredictability, and danger. Good waves are rare, and big, good waves are even rarer. "So many variables have to come together." During a typical season on the North Shore, Waimea only breaks well a handful of times, and some years never provide congenial conditions. Different spots light up on different years. Elements like the strength and direction of the wind close to the shore and the alignment of the swell matter, as do broader weather patterns. Size counts, but it's not the only factor.

Particularly good swells are given specific names or are referred to by their date. For example, "The Brock Swell" honors the life of Brock Little, a famous Waimea surfer who was taken by cancer a week before The Eddie ran. And the day The Eddie didn't run in 2016 has also been recorded, and many would be able to recall it. Others remember it as the day Luke Shepardson surfed one of the largest waves ever seen at the Bay, or when pro surfers Kelly Slater and Ross Williams "got denied," pushed back onto the beach by the surf when they "mistimed their entrance" trying to paddle out to the lineup. Notable seasons are also written into the books. El Niño years like 2016 produced the memorable swells described earlier in this book, and those of 1969 and 1983, born of the same weather pattern, are also treasured. While some of these swells are publicly recorded among those who regularly surf the Bay and by the broader surfing world, there are other swells that are only remembered by smaller groups: for example, groups that have experienced exceptionally large swells at other breaks, like the Outer Reefs. Groups treasure singular swells as well as singular waves, and they remember who was there at the time. Most big wave surfers, in fact, not only strive to catch the best and biggest wave of the day or of the season, but they also talk about chasing the "wave of their life." Trevor Carlson tells me:

That's what makes big wave surfers and skydivers so similar. It's like there's some invisible goal, that even when you achieve the goal, you just want to go and do it again. You'll spend your whole life chasing it and the day you die, you'll say you were on the chase your whole life. The goal is that you've been officially chasing it your whole life as hard as you can.

Talking about fun in surfing, and introducing the elements of complexity, unpredictability, and natural beauty, he adds:

Every wave is different, so you have to be constantly changing. That's what makes it fun. The ocean is doing whatever it's going to do, whether I'm there, whether I'm not there. For you to match the ocean you have to be connected, in tune enough with yourself, your body, and your mind. To be able to see it and immediately match it. The hard part of surfing is not to surf. The hardest part of surfing is learning to understand the ocean, the way it moves. That's also the most rewarding part of surfing is when you understand the way it moves, you're in tune with the ocean, in tune with nature, in tune with something so much larger than yourself. Feeling you are at one. You build a relationship with the ocean. That's why I talk about the ocean telling me what to do. You hear me say this over and over, the wave tells me what to do. I see the wave and it's almost like we have a conversation. Mentally, I'm talking with the wave, it's telling me what to do.

And as if amplifying the fun of regular surfing, Aaron Gold mentions the rawness and the beauty of riding big waves.

It's just a crazy element of being out there. It's raw and rugged and when it's going, there's something serene about it, or it's just monster waves coming and it's beautiful. Seeing something that amazing, absolutely an amazing creation. So, from that perspective there, just being out on the water, in it and feeling it, when a wave breaks, the noise and the sound, it's exciting, it's exhilarating. It's actually fun. It just erupts and you feel the energy in the water as soon as you jump in. There's something just more than what it is. You're getting this amazing firsthand view of nature in general and that's one thing that's super fun and crazy about it.

As other surfers have, Aaron, who is a practicing Christian, alludes to the spiritual meaning of surfing big waves. But for him, being in the water is his "God time," a time to meditate as well.

Touching on the unpredictability, danger, and consequentiality of big waves, Filo, like others, also claims that some of the best and most fun rides are the ones "when you think you're going to fall, but you keep your knees bent, and you stay centered over your board and you ride out plain." Maybe the spray is also blinding you, and if you surprise yourself by eventually making it out, you're relieved and excited to have temporarily cheated death or a potential catastrophe.

Filo tells me people have suggested that he meditate, but he doesn't. Then he explains:

> When you're surfing regular waves—waves that may not have a lot of consequences—there's a lot more room for other thoughts, for everything that goes on in life. Down time. Time to wonder, it allows the noise of the world to enter your mind, and along with that, the ego.

One of Filo's favorite parts of surfing is the distraction it affords. Like others, he thinks that the more danger, and the more enjoyment, the more he can focus solely on the task at hand—surfing, recognizing the texture of the water. "Bigger waves translate into a greater ability and need to remain fixed just on the surfing," he says, and a lot of it has also to do with the people he shares these experiences with. The psychologist Mihaly Csikszentmihalyi[26] calls it *flow*: a positive mental state in which challenges closely match the level of our abilities, and thus force us to focus completely on the task at hand, blocking out distractions. In some sense, flow is a form of active meditation in which self-consciousness disappears and time perception muddles. Because things can go wrong quickly, unpredictably, and dangerously, you are compelled to maintain focus on what's in front of you, shutting out secondary thoughts.

Proximity and Cooperation

The area where surfers wait for waves is called the takeoff zone or the lineup, the latter term being a reminder, and a vestige, of the norm of sharing. At Waimea it's rather small. As Ben puts it: "The takeoff spot is about twenty meters and if you've got twenty, thirty guys, in the water, they're all bunched up. So whether you like it or not, you're going to have interactions with the people around you." This element, though, is common to many other surf spots, including those breaking at a smaller size. What is distinctive about Waimea, however, is that the wave itself (its size and shape)—and the tradition that developed and endured since the spot was pioneered in the late 1950s—allows more than one rider to fit onto the wave's wall. This means that surfers can ride alongside one another, generally not hindering each other's rides (save for the occasional but rare accidents). Surfers can also watch one another ride the wave, and can often cooperate, whether to make sure that one succeeds in catching it, or to save each other in case of a wipeout. They can also see and keep track of who has just taken a wave and who's been waiting the longest. These dynamics are in play at other big wave spots too. There is also a characteristic level of friendship and acquaintanceship, as those who ride big waves are a subset of the greater surfing community. Describing Waimea, Filo, who temporarily relocated to Hawai'i from New York City to ride big waves, says:

> The lineup at Waimea particularly is very fun and very friendly. We, the regular guys, know each other really well: we have parties together, we have barbecues together after surfing, we talk on the internet for days ahead of time before a swell. And when I paddle out I say "Hi" to about fifteen to twenty-five people before surfing, because we all know each real well. It's a wonderful, welcoming feeling when you show up and you're surrounded by your friends. Normally you might know one, two, or three people. It would be an odd coincidence if you knew more than a few in the lineup. Whenever the Bay is breaking, you can count on a good thirty people who are gonna be there if they can.

No Fun

Bypassing the question of whether we can ever really be alone, rather than just physically apart but mentally experiencing the presence of others, there is a certain component enhanced by co-presence that underlines the social aspects of fun. When I ask Chris about fun in skateboarding, he is quick to say that the camaraderie among skateboarders does not compare to surfers:

> There's nothing compared to the camaraderie with skateboarders because you don't have to be in position to grab your wave. Everybody pretty much takes turns and everybody has an equal opportunity to rip this pool or whatever you're skating. Sometimes it can get a little out of hand, I'm sure you've seen it. In general, skateboarders are a bunch of friends, they get together and go and have a good time. There's kind of nothing like it. Surfing is a lot more selfish, a lot more egos. People . . . I guess at certain

(skate) parks you go to and they have these locals that are like that, you know? It's kinda sad in a way about surfing though. Sometimes people just have the wrong attitudes when they go out.

Chris is referring to several factors that affect the social dynamics in surfing that don't apply to skateboarding, and we will see in the next part of this chapter how this logic relates to big wave surfing. The first factor is that waves, and good waves in particular, are a scarce resource. There are only so many swells each season, only so many of them hitting a specific reef depending on the direction of the swell, and an even more limited supply of best waves per session. In addition, surfers notoriously claim ownership over natural resources like waves and surfing spots. The rhetoric is often rooted in safety, respect for locals, and the claimed universalism of such norms across space and time. Sharing waves equitably is often either ignored or contested.

If you were to paddle out to a particular localized spot—meaning a spot with a group of surfers who protect the place by using various tactics of intimidation on newcomers or people who do not belong to the core group—you would be told to go back to shore, or even prevented from entering the ocean altogether. Alternatively, you might be told to move to the side, so that you would only be able to surf the lesser waves—the scraps—and not the ones breaking further out on the peak. And if you were to make a mistake, like falling while taking off on a particularly good wave or the first wave of your session, or dropping in while another surfer is already riding a wave and cutting him off, you would face some kind of confrontation, or simply have your access to the better waves confiscated. Waves should not be wasted. The first move you make in the water often determines your place in the social order of the lineup, and that place also already depends on your reputation, which is partially dependent on your proven dedication to surfing a specific spot. Any surfer anywhere, at least in the Western world, can tell stories of verbal or physical abuse over surfing: either abuse they suffered themselves or abuse they inflicted on others. Behavior is largely learned, and as the cultural anthropologist René Girard reminds us, when we suffer violence because of social hierarchy, we often emulate the same kind of behavior toward those below us as we move up the ladder.[27]

Once I was surfing a spot in Portugal, and while two other surfers were arguing in the water, I started talking with the only surfer who looked Portuguese. He quickly cut me short, saying, "I don't need to make any friends." Making friends not only means distraction, but also makes it difficult not to share, because the other surfer becomes a person. Jack Katz and Randall Collins discuss how physical distance and emotional dominance help when we try to carry out abusive behavior.[28] Carlos Burle once told me how this plays out in surfing:

> Surfers want to cruise around themselves, they want to have friends they can share with, but you can't share waves with everybody. Kelly Slater, I've known him so long, but we're not very close friends, because if you're close friends with everybody in the world, how are you going to share a wave with everybody? There aren't enough waves for everybody. There aren't enough waves for everybody in the world (raising his voice to further emphasize this point). We have to share the lineup all the time, so that feeling of fighting is a terrible feeling, it's the worst. It's different than when you do snowboard, or ski, or skateboarding, you can have fun with your friends all the time.

Kawika claims that surfers are some of the most insecure individuals you'll ever come across. Even in the parking lot many surfers are assessing one another and trying to understand who's a friend and who's a foe, who's skilled and who's a "kook" (an inexperienced or plainly bad surfer). They check out each other's equipment and style, try to figure out whether they can be aggressive and have others back them up (or not), and if they're locals or visitors. In the water, they secretly watch one another but try not to meet each other's eyes. As Phil tells me: "Surfing is so mysterious. They don't want to look at your wave. They want to block you out. In their ego they think they can do better." Both in the water and on land, surfers also use deceptive strategies to fool others—for instance, inducing them to paddle for the wrong wave or drive to another spot, or withholding useful information about surfing conditions or equipment. In general, the smaller, more crowded, and more inconsistent the waves, the more surfers fight over them. But the same logic also applies to more highly valued surf spots.[29] Conversely, the larger the surf, the more cooperative the behavior in the lineup tends to become. Big wave surfing is a game not of quantity, but of quality: the kind of wave you choose to take requires not only good judgment, but also patience, a point that I will discuss in a subsequent chapter.

Collaborative Commitment: The Last Pure Thing

While looking at photographs I shot on the day that The Eddie didn't run, Mattie says to Ebony, "Whoa, look at this thing, that thing is a bomb!" referring to the biggest wave of the day, the one Luke Shepardson caught. Then he adds: "I'm halfway to the mainland by this stage," meaning that by then he was happy to already be safely back on the beach. Matt Aldridge is a former professional longboarder from Australia who surfed on the day The Eddie didn't run, along with Chris, Noa, Mo, and Phil. Like the others, he says "these were without a doubt" the largest waves he has ever surfed. At sixteen years old, Ebony Wilson is one of the best Australian juniors. Mattie is coaching her, this is their second trip to the North Shore, and this year she also rode the biggest waves of her life "so far." Mattie says:

> That was the biggest day for me ever, and how many years have I been surfing? I'm thirty-three years old now. I was a water baby . . . I was in the water since I was three or four years old . . . let's call it around thirty years . . . it was such an amazing day. I feel so blessed to be a part of it. I was in no way chasing the bombs or anything like that. That was for someone else to do. I was just out there to reach my own limits and take the smaller ones inside (laughing)—twenty-, twenty-five-footers . . . some amazing surfing going down . . . without the lifeguard we wouldn't be able to do it . . . they know the ocean so well . . . I felt safe with the lifeguards in the water on the skis.

He continues:

> The camaraderie among the fellow big wave surfers is fantastic because it's not like going surfing anywhere else. Ninety-nine percent of the people are out there to make sure everyone is safe, and everyone really looks out for each other, and makes sure everyone is OK. And if someone gets a good one, everyone watches to see if they fall, and if they did fall, they make sure they are OK. I competed for a lot of years, and once my . . . the competition was great: I met a lot of friends, traveled around a lot, and surfed a lot of great waves. But I felt that my love for surfing is what I enjoyed the most and I don't need to put on a rashie (jersey) to find out who the best surfer is . . . I just wanted to be a part of something that *was as good and fun and why people started surfing a century ago* . . . and then the big wave thing came . . . I'm not out there to join the (Big Wave) World Tour or surf the biggest wave . . . I really want to push my own sort of limits . . . I don't need to free-fall out of a forty-foot wave . . . just pushing my limits, get the adrenaline going . . . and not on the edge of insanity either . . . that's good for me.

"So, what's the edge of insanity?" I ask. Mattie answers, laughing, "Wednesday was very close to it. Wednesday was very, very close to it. Those waves they were hands down the biggest waves I ever surfed in my life." I ask him, how does a lineup like Waimea differ from other breaks on the North Shore or elsewhere? He says:

> Waimea Bay is a lot friendlier to everyone, especially girls, over places like Pipeline . . . it's a cut-throat place . . . the mentality and the people there want to see people safe. The true essence of surfing is to have fun and enjoy it. It's supposed to put a smile on your face; we're in the ocean. We're supposed to be happy. If you're angry and you're not having fun, to me that's doing it wrong. You're not surfing right.

Then Mattie explains to me that at Waimea, and in the big wave scene in general, people don't care whether a surfer is sponsored or not, whether he has a paycheck or not. Other factors matter more. "It's a life or death situation: raw, open." This idea of equality in the face of possible death seems to enhance the fun experience. Mattie tells me that he knows some guys, maybe the best surfers, who would rather remain unknown, a statement that corroborates what I've learned during my fieldwork. To better explain this *social world*, he recalls a telling episode from the previous year, which was Ebony's first winter season on the North Shore. He says it was a fun-size, solid Waimea, and there were a lot of other surfers making sure Ebony was in the right spot and sharing other information about the break.

> And when a really good wave came through, one of the guys out there, Phil—amazing surfer, top guy, local guy—saw that Ebony was in the spot, and he turned around and said: "Go, get into this thing!" I don't know many other places in the world where that would happen. A fifteen-year-old from a top-level big wave surfer . . . that's when it really sort of came: these are the type of blokes that I belong around.

I ask Ebony what happened and why she thinks Phil pushed her to take that wave.

> I was out there trying to get a wave, trying to stay wide, trying not to be in anyone's way. Then this one came, and it was unbelievable the amount of people who were telling me to go, and it was such a nice ride. I think that he (Phil) thought I had the ability to go, and he wanted me to get a good ride for being out there. He knew I was waiting for a while to get *the* one.

Dennis Pang also tells me about the camaraderie:

> In any big wave situation, the common thing is danger: there are people you have to be looking out for in big waves, your friend, or whoever, not necessarily your friend. I think there's a little more interaction between big wave surfers, and it was like that from the beginning. More so than just in small waves: "Hey look at me, I'm ripping (lowering his voice to underline irony) compared to you, and I surf better than you." There's a difference in the mentality of a big wave surfer, the camaraderie in the big wave surfing group. There's a tight bond between those guys. When the shit hits the fan and it's big, guys are looking out for each other.

And correspondingly, Chris explains that big wave surfers operate like a platoon:

> Sometimes in small waves guys couldn't give a shit if you get hurt. They might even hurt you to make you go in. But in big waves, people will throw themselves in the lineup to save you. They'll risk their life to save you. It's camaraderie. That's where it changes, you know? When you get out there, especially on an outer reef, you're dependent on one another. All of a sudden, you're unconscious and you're under. You need people that will come in and help you.

I ask Chris to comment on a quote I read in a photographic book about big wave surfers of Hawai'i that said "big wave surfing is like a family within a family":[30]

> It's kinda like our crew at Waimea. We're kinda like a family. We hang out and we have parties and stuff together. Have a big party once a month, you invite the family over. Compared to surfing other places, Waimea brings you close to one another. Big wave surfing in general. Compared to a lot of guys I surf with on a general basis on small waves. The guys I surf with on big waves, those are the kind of people you want, they will have your back. If they saw me on the street getting beat up, those are the people that would jump in, because we're just like that. I compare us more a bit like the military, we won't leave anyone behind. We'll risk ourselves to save somebody and we're always watching over each other. When someone takes a big wave, we're concerned that he made it a lot of the time. Sometimes you can't see them and those are the scary times. Some breaks are so far out that when you take off on a wave it's: "Okay, I'll see

you in twenty minutes." He's gone, just making his way back out, it takes a long time. The ride might be so long, you know what worry is, and you have to focus in the lineup at the same time.

"Buddy system?" I comment. And Chris continues:

The friends I meet in small waves, that's always a vague friendship, but when you see the guys you surf big waves with, you shake their hands and give them a hug. We're way closer. Even the youngsters too. The youngsters in normal surfing, they don't really care about you. They look at your eyes, old man surfer. But in big wave surfing the young guys grow up with guys my age. I have kids that are twenty years old, they like going surfing with me. With the shortboarders, it's not gonna happen. It's different in that way. It's like you said, a lot of big wave surfers will spread the knowledge and stuff. Being a waterman, giving you a lot of tips. Whereas in the small days, they'll tell you to figure it out yourself, maybe.

Sharing and Cooperation

On a day when an outer reef named Phantoms was breaking well, it took Trevor close to an hour to find two friends to paddle out with. He tells me he uses this strategy to increase safety. For example, when a surfer takes off on a wave, there is at least one other person who holds a position in the lineup to prevent others from ending up in a bad spot and potentially getting caught inside by a large set.

A guy from Maui further explains the dynamics at the outer reefs, where the danger is greater than at Waimea, and where the basic skill level and physical preparation required are also greater:

Surfing has lost so much of its purity. The last pure thing in surfing is big waves. When I go and surf an outer reef I know I'm not going to be hassled by another guy for waves. I know that the guys I'm surfing with, or the girls, if there's girls out there, are looking at each other and they imply, "I got your back, man." Because the consequence of failure is so extreme. You go to the outer reefs, a crowd at the outer reefs is ten guys. And those ten guys are locked into a tight-knit crew and they're trading waves. It's like: "You going?" and it's a legitimate question. It's not "I'm taking this wave." When you surf any of these outer reefs it's heavy and everybody knows. Just to get out to some of these waves takes a lot of training. There's no lifeguards at the outer reefs. That's what I love about it. I'm so glad I was never good enough to be a pro surfer. There are very few things in the

world that are pure, and the world is so screwed up. . . . I got so sick of the
hassle, I got so sick of the "I've been here for thirty years and I can drop in
on anybody I want." And people just getting aggressive over the waves you
don't need to be aggressive over. Taking the fun out of it. I had a real job
and I didn't want to come home from my real job and go and do something that was just going to create more stress. And the first time I started
surfing big waves, I was like, this is stress release. This is me getting away
from the rest of the world and finding out what really matters. Air, food,
water, shelter. You go surfing on a twenty-foot day at Phantoms, those
four things take on a whole new meaning. I go surfing to get rid of my
ego. That's what big wave surfing is to me. You go surfing on a big day at
Phantoms, that wave will surgically remove your ego from you.

The enjoyment and fun includes pushing others into big waves, either
by helping them understand when they are in the correct position, or by
enticing them to take one when they might otherwise have hesitated—a
reciprocal dynamic I will discuss further in subsequent chapters. Along
this line, Garrett McNamara says: "Yeah, in big waves you're doubly hoot-
ing and hollering for your friends to go. Sometimes it's a catastrophe too,
because you don't want to push too hard and they might not have gone
and you are yelling 'go, go!' I catch myself yelling at the top of my lungs
whenever I see somebody paddling and I think they can make it and I
try to encourage them."

Aaron explains the pleasure that comes with seeing your friends succeed, a point which further highlights the complexity and collaborative
dimension of this sport, as well as the mutual respect among fellow
surfers.

Watching your friends get a good wave, it's so rad. It's just as much fun as
you catching your wave. To see someone take off and put themselves in a
critical situation, it's just exhilarating because you understand how much
effort it took. How everything had to come together in that moment of
timing. It's like the best show in the world and you're right there, front
row seats. I love it: it's actually an amazing feeling when you see your
friend get a great wave and kick out, and likewise when you get a wave.

Party Waves

Filo tells me about a chat board that some of his friends have created
called Pinballs Masters, as a parody of the prestigious surfing competition taking place at Pipeline called Pipeline Masters. In the chat, as in

Party wave!

the lineup, regulars have nicknames to augment the fun. Pinballs is the smaller wave breaking closer to shore than Waimea. Its name derives from the number of rocks a surfer needs to be aware of and potentially dodge while riding it or getting back to land. Filo says it's an inside joke by the regulars because "the best guys don't call it Waimea unless it's twenty feet. It's pretending to be humble and funny." He tells me that if there's enough room on the wave, then it's not "burning"—"if your line isn't obstructing someone else's, and there's enough space for more than one surfer, then we share a ride. Sometimes new people don't know this rule, and if someone is deeper, closer to the curl, then they don't go, especially if the surfer seems to be known by everyone else in the lineup."

Filo says that sometimes on smaller days he and his friends play games in the lineup. The Sandwich Game, for instance, involves several surfers taking off together on a wave, and earning different points depending on their position in relation to the others. The scoring system varies by session. "Do you know how a sandwich is? Two pieces of bread and then there's the meat," says Filo. One could get points by being on the shoulder, in the middle between other surfers, or deeper on the wave, depending on the rules of the day. "It's not complicated, and it's all friendly and everyone is accepting"—meaning that it's very easy to join the game, given its simplicity. He also tells me that when the "big guns"—meaning the sponsored guys—are out, his group doesn't play the game, and they tend to be subtler to avoid looking like "dorks."

Another joke they often make—"understanding they are all ego-maniacs"—is asking what time it is after a ride, so that later on they can rewind the webcam and hopefully find a recorded memory of it. An additional inside joke is "squat for the shot," which references the idea that bending your knees while riding will make your wave look bigger in any photo that gets taken. At the end of the session there's often hugging—which also sometimes happens when a surfer is going in to shore while another is about to paddle out—and high-fives, to celebrate a good game like soccer players would, and perhaps also to emphasize the teamwork it took and the group's overall accomplishment.

Stevo expands on the mutual respect among fellow big wave surfers and sharing rides:

> You're sitting right there in proximity with so many people, maybe somebody's from Brazil and somebody's from Australia or California, Hawaiians from right here or from another island, and we're all sharing the most intense moments of our lives. Why not make it about friendship? What can I share about this moment? I have to admire the spirit of people from around the world that come here to make a passion of surfing like this. . . . They come here, and especially if they're already over twenty years old, to try to learn to surf bigger waves in Hawai'i it's not easy. It will break your heart to see these guys struggle, but some of them get it. It's really impressive. You really have to show up year after year.
>
> I really just got to love and respect everybody because they're out there dealing with it on their own level and trying to have a good time too. Everybody is trying to have a good time and it's kinda weird because it's extreme. We don't get ahead by stepping on somebody else or each other. It's all about cooperating, especially if you're sharing waves.

Shared Narrative

"Tell me about my wave," Stevo says. And then he quickly adds: "We almost prefer the other guy to tell our story. Sometimes we have evenings just full of that. My former wife used to say: 'Oh gosh, you just got out of the water and you're going to talk about what happened in the water?'" For big wave surfers, catching outstandingly large waves is a life achievement that has demanded much time, effort, and sacrifice. And it can also result in serious consequences. But it's an elusive goal, because there's almost always a bigger and better wave to look forward to, a better ride. And while some talk about the wave of their life, I know of only one surfer who, after claiming to have caught that one wave, quit. And it's arguable that that wasn't part of a marketing strategy. The sharing among surfers of what Stevo calls the "most intense moments" of their lives is both a reason and a means to forge friendships. As he says:

> You only remember your last wave. You walk in the store and you see the guy that saw you on that wave. And he's like: "Right on," and he's patting you on the back and going again over the story of how tall that wave was that you got. And it's like: "Cool, thanks." It's not really why we do it, it's a reflection of the fun we have and it's those moments with those people. I don't get to choose who's going to be in there, they choose. And I wish some people could be there, and they're not. And there are others there, and maybe you wish they weren't. That's the thing . . . we're the ones that are here today. We're sharing this experience with each other. Today is a bonding experience, and that's the human connection. Sometimes it's so intense it's hard to find words. There are only certain moments of images of a wave that had a certain angle and a situation. There are only so many things I can recall all at once. So many years of the same wave, doing the same thing in the same place. Sort of the same. You take off on this wave and you don't remember. If it was a good one . . . if it was one out of five or ten waves, it's almost like this traumatic stress thing, fight or flight syndrome thing where you kinda remember it, but after a few hours maybe you don't remember. He's going to tell me if it was good. And I'm going to tell him: "Hey, your wave was good."

Stories are central to group life: they draw the contours, colors, and depth of group culture, cement informal roles among members, forge friendships, and draw boundaries. They affix badges of personal and group identity and weave in expectations, both reciprocal and toward oneself. Stories retold periodically become classics, while others don't stick and are forgotten. Group stories relate to episodes that can be particularly funny, or epic, or tragic in the moment, or a combination of these traits. And in retrospect, even a potentially dreadful event can become fun in the retelling. Likewise, a stressful situation, or one that was not fun as it unfolded, can become fun in the retelling, where laughter is channeled and amplified perhaps through the feeling of having temporarily cheated disaster or death.

Chris tells me about a situation that could have been tragic, but became fun in the immediate aftermath and in the retellings, and thus brought a group of friends and acquaintances closer. The ability to witness, record, and narrate becomes crucial to the initiation, continuation, and strengthening of bonds among members of a group. Chris describes being "caught inside" by an exceptionally large wave at Waimea during a swell in November 1996—a *fateful moment* shared among those who experienced it, but also publicly recorded. Recalling the episode, he says:

> I'm claiming it was about an eighty-footer. It was such a heavy experience for all of us out there. Everybody thought they were going to die when this wave broke in front of us. It was a real rogue wave. The waves were twenty-five feet this day, and then this wave came in more than double the size. It was crazy. It could have almost been a hundred-foot wave. I saw this wave feathering. It wanted to break, it looked like five miles out. It was trying to break out there . . . whatever it was, it was looking for a reef, and it wanted to break already. I knew it was giant and I told everybody: "There's a huge wave coming at us right now. Everybody follow me." We must have paddled for three or four minutes, and we just kept paddling, and we paddle a hundred and fifty yards further than we normally sit . . . We went over a couple of waves . . . and all of a sudden we looked over and this thing was already breaking . . . it broke top to bottom right in front of us. I can't believe we even *lived through it*. It just looks (switching to present tense) so enormous. And then after it happened, when I came up, when I lived through it, we were laughing (laughing). It's just what it does to you. Whenever you survive it, you start laughing sometimes. The wave was so big it made both *Surfer* and *Surfing Magazine* with a story behind it. There was only about like fifteen of us. And the same people, if we see each other, we go back to talking about that day. It's almost like we're stoked to have experienced that . . . you know what I mean? When we see each other, those certain people, we always talk about it.

"Are those some of your closest friends?" I ask. "A lot of them became better friends from that day because we were out there, and what happened to us," he answers.

On occasions that are particularly stressful and intense, like those described above, individual group members may have difficulty recalling in detail what happened, and their partners can help to articulate the event, which sometimes only becomes fun afterward.

It's not just a narrative focus about one moment, though. To affect the group, fun requires a diachronic component. Stories are continually referenced, and community members, even those who were not present for the events, learn the appropriate response to the narrative. Filo tells me about seeing a big wave approaching. As two of his friends, Mark and Orzo, begin to paddle to take it, he screams to the one in the most critical position on the wave: "Go, Mark! Go!" As the wave abruptly steepens, Filo starts thinking to himself: "Oh, no, Mark isn't gonna make it. There's no way he can do this." But instead, he says: "Yeah, Mark, go!" Both Mark and Orzo attempt to take the wave, and both fall. Twenty seconds later, both of them are in the white water "tombstoning"—being held under water while parts of their boards stand out above the surface. Eventually, they both paddle back to the lineup, and Mark says to the others: "Filo, what a guy. He calls me into a wave, and then when he sees it's too steep and I can't make it, he starts laughing at me." Then Filo tells me: "I thought I was holding in the laughter. It was embarrassing. So now anytime we see one of our friends going for such a wave we say: 'Oh, guaranteed it's a good one!' which really means you shouldn't go for it." Anthropologist Clifford Geertz writes that "to be teased is to be accepted,"[31] but we might as well add that acceptance also depends on one's willingness to be teased.

I ask Aaron Gold if stories bind the community together and, if so, how. He says:

> And that's the best time of the day, when everyone's come in safe. Other times you're beat up, tired or didn't get the best waves, but everybody was there and had the same experiences. It's great when you get to share and talk, and everybody is sitting around and . . . "Oh, did you see that? And he went, and this and that happened." It's not always about the waves, it's about being out there in general. There's guys out there on the boats, and the boats get caught. There have been times when the jet skis have been coming over and almost hit someone. All kinds of little dynamics, but it's all part of the day. If you're dealing with such raw elements, and everybody comes together and is talking about it, and talking it up, it's super rad. It's cool because nobody's going: "Oh yeah, did you see that amazing wave that I got?" But you're talking about the experiences they have and super fun and everybody else is there, saw it, and shared it with you. I grew up spending a lot of time on the outer reefs and I'd surf by myself and get good waves. I'd pull in and get a good barrel and there's no one to see it. You'd be hoping that one of the guys would come out and would have seen it so you'd have something to share. It's almost like: "Did it really happen?" Because there's no one to share it with. That's part of that kind of surfing which is funny because it's an independent sport, but

at the same time it's not. There's camaraderie and the nature of it: that's sharing your joy of what you love to do. And having someone to share that with you is what's special.

Embodied Pleasures

Black and White, Simple and Raw

The historical period we're living in is marked by an ever faster pace of life, as well as an overflow of information and mental stimulation, even distraction, which constitutes noise. And it's also distinguished by how much we value excitement as an emotion,[32] and by a longing to experience intense sensations, as Gerda Reith[33] and David Le Breton[34] contend. Concomitantly, it's also characterized by two kinds of boredom: one, defined by Leo Tolstoy as "the desire for desires"; and another, referred to by Peter Toohey[35] as existential boredom, and denoted by a feeling of emptiness and alienation that spans a longer time. And while silence causes us distress, it is also a commodity, and various forms of meditation such as yoga have experienced a massive upsurge over the last decade. While it has arguably become increasingly hard to stop thinking, to empty your mind and reset, activities that put us in close contact with nature are becoming increasingly popular. Those involved with the commercialization of various forms of surfing are capitalizing on the broader trend of adventure tourism, spirituality, and the cult of wellness. But besides the social aspect of fun, what does surfing big waves provide mentally and physiologically? Lyng writes that "those who venture close to the edge are attracted by embodied pleasures of such high intensity that they often have addictive consequences."[36] Confirming this point, twenty-eight-year-old professional big wave surfer Billy Kemper tells me that:

> The feeling of overcoming fear is a complete addiction, and I can't get enough of it. And breaking that mindset when you're thinking that you're scared and overcoming it to get an adrenaline rush to where you conquered something at that size and ability is like what we live for.

So far this chapter has addressed the connection between fun and cohesion, fun and risk, considering an audience made up mostly of *significant others*. This section highlights the *embodied pleasures* related to risk-taking.

Surfing big waves provides more than just group cohesion, excitement, and meaning for those involved. As theorized by Lyng in relation to other *edgework* pursuits, it also provides a hyperreality. As Jeff Kidder writes, "In such moments there is a feeling of veridicality absent in ordinary existence."[37] In those situations nothing else matters, because the potential for injury or death is so high as to prevent you from being distracted by other thoughts. And as in other autotelic activities, the feedback is straightforward, reducing anxieties both existential and associated with the quality of performance. Put differently: Did you survive the session? If you did, well, then you did most of it right. The activity is purposeful because it requires your effort to maintain your own physical existence. And while complex, big wave surfing is also simple. The task is unambiguous, the feedback immediate, and once you enter the ocean, unless you're overtaken by panic, you cannot afford to be thinking of anything other than the task at hand. By experiencing *flow*, big wave surfers can access the positive feelings associated with relaxation. In these situations participants also experience a temporary annihilation of the ego, and once the activity is completed they walk away feeling stronger about themselves, more centered. As Lyng writes: "The hyperreal quality of *edgework* lifts participants out of the mundane reality of rational meditations and transports them to a world of sensual immediacy."[38]

The Buzz

Big wave surfer Garrett McNamara tells me that the biggest rush he has ever experienced, coupled with the most intense fear, was when he surfed a wave generated by the breaking of an iceberg in Alaska. Wearing grey sweatpants and lying flat on his back on the grass of his home in Mokulēʻia, he fully looks his age—fifty years old and in pain. This is a side of daredevils like him we seldom, if ever, get to see, and I cannot help feeling empathy for his suffering. He is healing from a serious surfing injury he sustained in a wipeout at Mavericks in California. During our talk, he says:

> For me, that was pivotal. It made me realize how comfortable I was in the ocean. Doing things for the rush isn't worth it. I was doing things for the rush. That's why I rode big waves, looking for the rush. From the Glacier Project forward, I didn't get the rush anymore. I don't get scared in the ocean anymore after that. I still have fun on the waves, though.

Then, echoing what other surfers his age have told me, he describes the situations when he can, sometimes, still feel the rush.

> It's more of a rush putting somebody on a wave and then going to rescue them. You're responsible, it's more life and death. That's the time I will probably get a rush these days, is putting someone on a huge wave that I know is super dangerous for them. Then I feel more alive than when I'm actually riding a wave.

A competent surfer from Maui who is at the beginning of his journey tells me:

> The adrenaline in big waves is so much more (than in other kinds of surfing). When you are coming down the face of a bomb at Waimea, you think you're gonna die. I don't know if it gets easier as time goes on. If the guys that have been doing it for years don't get that rush, but like you have to, for me at least, I had to come to grips beforehand that I may die. This may kill me. It's a good day to die. When it's bombing, when it's monstrous and you catch one over the bowl, it slabs up so hard. It's so hard to make that drop. And it looks like a wall and it's so thick. It's just this massive steep death pit, and fuck, it's the heaviest. I know there are heavier waves in the world, but I haven't surfed them yet.

Stuart describes to me how surfing big waves helped him find a way out of alcoholism and drug abuse. He also tells me about the social aspects of big wave surfing, the cooperation involved, the sharing of narratives, and the existential meaning it has provided him.

> For me it boils down to the simplest form: drugs and alcohol. I was either gonna kill myself, kill somebody else, or get incarcerated. . . . It's the drugs, dude. People don't understand, adrenaline man, it's the most addictive thing. Way better than coke.

> "Why is it better? I've never done coke," I say.

> (After a pause, as I've thrown him off track) Ohh . . . ah . . . because . . . I guess it depends on where you get your coke (laughing), but the initial rush, that initial high is very similar. The difference is when you get that high off of adrenaline there's no down, really. When you get that high off cocaine you come down and it's like you're depressed, your nose is all . . .

you can't think straight, you got a headache, dehydrated. But when you're coming down off of an adrenaline high, you're all smiles. You're a little fatigued from the experience you just had, but when you're coming down off drugs that's no fun. It's not like the next morning you wake and call your friends and: "Man, you remember that great line we did last night?" You're depressed . . . but like the next morning after that experience, after a swell that big and you were out surfing, you call your friends the next day and you're like: "Do you remember this wave, and that wave?" And you're looking up stills, and footage . . . that's why it's way better.

Fun: Sociality and Thrills

In this chapter I've introduced Chris and life on the North Shore. And I've discussed the characteristics of big wave surfing that make it fun. Surfing big waves entails core elements of the successful interaction rituals described by Randall Collins, above all the mechanism of converting an initial emotion provided it's strong enough, via focus and rhythm entrainment, into another emotion, the confidence and drive of *emotional energy* (EE). Unlike ordinary surfing, which is largely an individual sport undertaken for pleasure and personal enjoyment, big wave surfing is a team sport requiring coordination and interdependence among participants. Especially in the most dangerous and unpredictable situations, and at remote areas such as at the outer reefs that are miles from shore, one's fellow surfers are no longer opponents, as in regular surfing; instead they become assets for one another. This dynamic creates interdependence among individuals whose common goals are surviving and not getting hurt, and then performing. Those who are capable and willing to put themselves in such situations nurture respect for one another. This mutual respect contributes to feelings of exclusivity, nourishing equality and thus encouraging similar participation rather than the alienation or boredom that comes with being a bystander.

During these sessions, surfers tend to be more aware of each other's rhythms, from paddling out, to catching waves, to coming in. They focus intensely on the horizon, but also on one another, especially as the action unfolds. They're also more aware and willing to share the experiences, either by riding a wave together or by letting someone else take it because it's their turn or because they're not as well positioned. And ultimately, they're dependent on one another to witness and retell, to one another and to the community, the stories of their epic feats.

Experiencing the ocean in such heightened states leads surfers not only to try to be in rhythm with one another—because of the increased danger and difficulty—but also to be in rhythm and almost in interaction with the ocean. It's almost as though one synchronizes oneself with how the ocean moves and how each wave wants to be ridden, rather than forcing one's will on it, as seems often to be the case in modern surfing. The environment and the slow pace of big waves during a session—often only a few sets per hour—and the interval between each wave of a set allow surfers to interact in the lineup almost as they would at a party. In smaller surf the pace *tends* to be more hectic, and surfers are generally more silent and intent on out-maneuvering one another rather than helping each other. In a conversation with scholar and writer Andy Martin, Matt Warshaw says that "surfing is devalued by all the inflated talk of gods and heroes: it is nothing but a 'rhythm,' a 'pulse,' an alternating tension and relaxation—and this is grand enough, I don't need all the religion too."[39]

The rarity of good, large swells has also an impact on the intensity of such experiences. Group members and communities remember and re-experience through retellings the uniqueness of certain feats. The more intense the situation, and the more consequential it is for surfers and for their community, the more binding the experience and the more *emotional energy* it is likely to produce.

But there is also an embodied dimension to these kinds of interaction rituals. The high danger of the activity produces high adrenaline and high excitement, and thus pleasure. This can be socially converted into a successful interaction ritual, and hence to the shaping of oneself around the *emotional energy* (EE) that comes from the experience, which can lead to getting hooked on this particular kind of emotional and physiological transformation. Additionally, high danger leads to intense focus on the task at hand, another ingredient of a successful interaction ritual; in big wave surfing, this focus is social in the cluster that's waiting for the right wave, assessing each wave together, and sometimes even riding the wave together. To get the interaction ritual ingredients (strong emotion and focus of attention) to extremely high levels, a surfer has to seek out dangerous waves in the presence of like-minded surfers.

According to Collins's theory, specific interactions with mentors, rivals, and allies generate emotional energy (EE), enhance self-esteem, and provide motivation to do creative work.[40] But in my theory EE is also an end in itself to motivate action, more generally. The search for situations generating EE can also become, as in my case, an addiction, motivating flow and a search for more interaction rituals that lead to EE.

While the term addiction carries a negative connotation—a temporary escape from traumas and troubles in one's ordinary life—my description of big wave surfing suggests a kind of positive-attraction theory, rather than a negative-escaping theory.

Fun kinds of interaction play a crucial role in building commitment to a group, affirming a group's boundaries, and giving narrative form to a group's identity. Big wave surfing offers intrinsically gratifying group interactions aimed at achieving rather difficult goals under highly stressful and dangerous conditions. The interactions are entrained in a series of interdependent acts requiring members' attention and skills. They are the kind of interaction that ends with the participants giving one another a "high five," hugging, or shaking each other's hands and saying "good job" when surfers manage to get back to the beach safely after a session, amazed that they have survived it. In general, people do this when they have executed a complex, interdependent chain of interactions that accomplishes a goal—all have done their part and performed well, and they know it. These kinds of interactions generate experiences that the group preserves in narrative form. The narrations provide the group with an image of who they are, or maybe who they aspire to be. The stories can be brought out and retold, like a family album, and the roles they have played in the stories become an essential component of each person's identity.

Chapter 4 focuses on wiping out, and how an apparent failure can be reframed as an intense interaction ritual signifying a turning point in a surfer's life.

CHAPTER FOUR

Failing to Succeed, Failing to Become

Jamie Sterling is a thirty-nine-year-old professional big wave surfer from the North Shore of Oʻahu, and like most big wave surfers he has to juggle different jobs to earn a living and chase large swells across the world. By 2019 he had lost all of his sponsors, was no longer on the Tour, and couldn't seem to be able to get back on it. Yet he thought he was physically stronger and technically more knowledgeable than he had ever been. Some argued that he wasn't investing enough in his career by paying for his own travel to chase swells. I couldn't have missed his frustration. "I have a hundred percent less money," he says. "I feel like a dog on a leash that wants to go play with the other dogs in the neighborhood and run around, travel, surf, be on every swell. But I can't because I don't have the cash to do it." "It's a catch-22" he expands: "to get on Tour you have to travel, chasing swells wherever they pop up, but unless you have sponsors, a rich family to back you up, or a lucrative business you can rely on, you can't travel."

Despite winning the world championship in 2011 and finishing second two years later, Jamie was overlooked by the organizers of the 2019 Big Wave Tour annual award ceremony. "How could they forget?" one of his friends remarks. After all, this is a small world. And while Jamie isn't the kind of guy who would make a fuss about it, this episode is indicative of how the broader surf industry works: it largely depends on who you know, how you look, what your media presence is, and how you consistently perform. Age matters too, and gender even more. Jamie ponders whether he has gotten too old. And even for those who were well known at one point, being left behind or replaced happens routinely, and quite fast too.

Big wave surfing operates much like other creative industries, and is largely held by a media company. And the supply of athletes clearly exceeds the demand. That's how this industry works, and why highly successful athletes like Garrett McNamara and Laird Hamilton strategically opted, as they aged through the middle of their career, to get more involved with non-surfing-related sponsors. Jamie knows that too. But I will discuss the professionalization of the sport in chapter 6. For now, I want to focus on Jamie's beginnings, because they resemble every big wave surfer's. In this sport, wiping out is not only a major and constant element, but also potentially a turning point in an athlete's career. It's another *fateful moment* without which a surfer may not even become a professional.

When I first meet him in 2016, Jamie wears a thin mustache and a buzz-cut, and drives an old black and orange Toyota pickup truck. He connects sentences with ease, like a surfer linking turns on a good ride or a yoga teacher transitioning from one asana to the next. And Jamie certainly undertakes a fair amount of both, each informing the other. Teaching surfing is also a way to supplement his income and fuel his surfing career, or at least allow him to keep surfing big waves while also providing for his family. As big wave surfers know, this is an "expensive occupation," meaning that except for a very few at the very top, most of the surfers in this subdiscipline spend more than they earn or break even, and must devise different strategies to make ends meet.

Jamie is rather short—or maybe it just looks that way since he seems more broad than tall. Gentle yet opinionated, he talks in a high pitch and is almost as prone to laughter as his close friend, Mark Healey. When he does laugh, his voice tends to squeak a little. But make no mistake: Jamie Sterling is a beast. The kind of guy who values and protects his integrity, and can get quite openly vocal about it too. But only if you ask him. His upper body is exceptionally wide, and his arms look unusually long. "You don't want to get in a paddle battle with him," a few of his peers tell me. When I hug him goodbye, I feel stronger, calmer, and more confident too, almost as if I can hear him saying, "Everything's going to be OK. We're going to make it. Let's do this" (without exclamation).

This chapter describes how overcoming a bad experience, a serious failure that almost kills you, can be the turning point on the path to becoming truly expert, and truly committed—emotional-energy committed. In his study on Olympic swimmers and the mundanity of excellence, Daniel Chambliss finds that true champions distinguish themselves from others of similar ability by their cool-headedness under the pressure of competition. As he writes: "excellence is accomplished through the doing of actions, ordinary in themselves, performed consistently and carefully, habitualized, compounded together, added up over time."[1] While part of the process of turning points concerns getting oneself to dare, to try and fail, the fateful moments I will describe have more to do with the decision to *retry*.

From interaction ritual theory we know that exceptionally successful individuals, regardless of field, manage to produce much more than they ultimately become known for. And this entails that each success at what they try to accomplish is preceded (and followed) by failures of one kind or another. Indeed, when we look at their careers, we are often impressed by how much these individuals have been able to create, and how long they've been able to do so. One key to their success is how they manage to initiate and sustain positive and emotionally charging internal thoughts, coupled with positive interactions with groups they belong to. Building on Norbert Wiley's research,[2] Collins refers to the former as internal interaction rituals, to distinguish them from those that take place physically between interacting actors.[3]

The last part of this chapter analyzes how lifeguards police the edge. In their research on risk and social control in skydiving, Jason Laurendeau and Erin Gibbs Van Brunschot[4] write that we shouldn't be surprised if those who voluntarily practice risky activities resist social control. After all, much of what drives them toward these activities is their desire for freedom and personal autonomy. Yet as the authors argue, we should pay attention to where edgework activities take place and how practitioners interact to monitor one another's pursuits and to mitigate accidents. I will discuss here how lifeguards' performance, and the safety devices introduced to the sport, impact the quality and character of *edgework*, not least in terms of who practices it, how it is practiced, and how the practice is being changed by innovation. Almost all surfing lifeguards are also big wave surfers, and my interest will be to analyze how they exercise social control over their peers, the techniques and technology they use to protect them, and how those techniques and technologies have evolved since the beginning of lifeguarding in Hawai'i.

Falling to Become

I ask Jamie if, like the other surfers I've met, he's ever found himself in a critical situation that required him to do his best to remain calm because doing so would increase his odds of surviving it. "Has there been one pivotal moment in your career?" The answer hangs thirty feet away from us. From where we sit on the couch of his home, he points toward the opposite end of the living room next to the kitchen. On the wall a poster-size photograph shows a large wave and a surfer who seems to be doing a wheelie that maybe, just maybe, he might be able to pull off. His feet are spread wide in what some would call a survival stance. Some would think of old-timers who had to desperately hold on for dear life trying to make every wave they chose, because they wore no leashes. His arms are stretched wide. He looks in control. His gaze is fixed ahead at the nose of his red board which, like its ten-inch yellow fin, has been caught momentarily free of the surface of the water. I wonder about his facial expression, but his figure is too dark. Approaching the picture, he says:

> That's from Waimea, from when I was seventeen years old, so, junior in high school. And I ate shit on that wave really hard. And that was the biggest wave of my life at that moment. I never felt the power of a fifty-foot (face) wave at Waimea up until that moment. It hit me like a ton of bricks and I almost drowned.

Yet, as a blessing in disguise, that wave changed his life. His biggest wave so far, but also his heaviest wipeout. An "Eddie-like kind of wave," and for him just as consequential. No invitation needed, though. Only skill, luck, and desire. Even for *just* wiping out and surviving that thing. A will to stay alive, and a will to get back at it and keep on paddling. Keep on pushing on. Twenty-one years later Jamie recalls not only the date—December 8, 1997—but also that it was about ten in the morning, and that he was feeling exceptionally confident. He also remembers that all he was wearing were his boardshorts and a rash guard, and that there weren't any rescue jet skis in the lineup—safety devices of various kinds and knowledge about rescue techniques were only just beginning to be introduced to the sport. Not an average day to skip school to begin with. Back then, in the late 1990s, only a handful of teenagers surfed Waimea, or even Sunset for that matter. And oftentimes those were only two: Jamie and his best friend, Mark Healey, in what the latter called a "two-man show—bing, bing, bing," to emphasize how each played a key part in the development of the other.

Clark Abbey, who was then at the top of Waimea's pecking order, had just a few weeks earlier jokingly asked him in the lineup, "Do your parents know you're here?" Underlining the obvious, but also illustrating

Jamie: A dark moment leading to a bright future.

that those who surfed the Bay back then were a small, tight-knit group of older regulars.

Jamie has already been in the water for about two hours, during which time his confidence has kept building, one good wave after another. Surfers describe this inner state as being in a good rhythm, as if what they do resembles a jazz session, but one where the notes from which you fashion your contribution come from the ocean, which leads the music, and not from an ensemble relying on conventions. Extraordinary, deadly circumstances rather than preexisting arrangements to which one can add improvisation. Feeling particularly valiant, Jamie decides to paddle further out from everybody else. I don't know what possessed him, but youth and feeling especially strong on that day and in tune with the ocean certainly played a part. Other surfers probably thought he was out of position—forecasting then was rudimentary, nothing close to the real-time data surfers can monitor now. No one knew exactly what to expect, and surfers often got caught off guard by an occasional larger wave. On that day the waves were coming two or three to a set. The pack sat as closely together as it normally does. While waves at Waimea tend to break in the same small area, you can still be sitting further in toward the inside trying to catch the smaller ones, or further out waiting for a larger set that may or may not arrive. Wisely, Jamie lets the first wave of the new, bigger set go by. As others say, if you make a mistake by falling on the first one, or failing to catch it, then you have to deal with the rest of the set from the "impact zone"—a position where you can't escape either the waves about to crash on you or other surfers' boards. Making a mistake on the first wave of a set puts you in one of the worst-case scenarios—"getting drilled" by that big set. But after the set of waves is through, you might be waiting for twenty or thirty minutes or more for another one. This sport entails patience: attentively monitoring the horizon and the water's texture and bumps. One's ability to read the ocean grows with experience, as does knowledge of how your body reacts under critical conditions; both of these are key aspects of the sport. When asked about how to spot the best surfer in the lineup on any given day, a surfer tells me: "the one who is there"—meaning in position to take off on the wave, "six seconds before the others."

If you look at the photograph you can see that the first wave has already come through because of the white water on the flats—a residue of the first wave's explosion, like the white foam after you open a bottle of champagne. When Jamie paddles to catch the wave, everything feels routine, it looks perfect, and it looks like he's in the right spot to successfully take off. But as he gets to his feet he starts feeling a different kind of magnitude than any other wave he's ridden before.

Jamie recounts getting to his feet and the water picking him up, but without letting him go forward. As the wave steepens, the ten-inch-fin of his board comes out of the water, and he becomes airborne for a few seconds. He keeps his feet, looking for a way to land and make the wave, but instead of bringing his board down flat on the surface of the wave he lands on his board's rail, and then falls on his back.

His older friend Mags recalls the action:

> I remember a big set coming in, I was too far inside, and as I was paddling over the wave looking down watching him. And I saw him fall after the sky and wipeout. It was one of those waves where I don't care who you are, you question yourself about taking off, and he didn't think twice, he just wiped it and went.

Lying upside down like a helpless cockroach, Jamie watches the wave barreling over him. It feels surreal. Time slows down, but then the impact drives him deep under water—so much so that he has to equalize the pressure in his ears. His twelve-foot leash stretches, and the nose of his board begins doing "the tombstone" as if waving left and right for an SOS on the water's surface. The turning is violent, chaotic, painful. Spinning/tumbling, spinning/tumbling—repeat. He tells me: "That's the most I've ever felt, the fastest spinning out of control by the force of the wave." The violence eventually begins to slow down, but by that point Jamie's oxygen reserves are about used up and he's close to blacking out. Recollecting this point, he says:

> I started to get a weird taste in in my mouth, kind of like a bio taste. I started to see white dots and black dots—the sign of an imminent blackout. And I started to become dizzy, and then I somehow just found myself at the top. I don't recall swimming or struggling. I just somehow feel like I almost blacked out for a few seconds, but then I was at the top and I'm looking, right when I came to the top another wave of that size is barreling down on me . . . this must have been the fourth wave in a set, probably the biggest set of the morning, and it came with a lot of waves, right when I came out for the first breath there was just a wave right there.

His friend Mags tells me:

I was in fear for his life. He ate it on the first wave, was underwater for a very long time, and when he came up I was yelling at him: "Just relax! Just relax! Take a breath!"

His eyes were huge. I saw the fear and I was just telling him to relax as I was paddling over another twenty-foot wave.

I was very concerned for him, I thought he was going to drown *actually*, but I was telling him just to relax, don't panic 'cuz when you panic, when a human needs air it's natural to take a breath of air, but when you're underwater that's not a good thing, it kinda turns out really tragic.

Then the next wave hits Jamie and he goes underwater again. Jamie remembers:

> . . . and it blows me up and I go back down, and then the same thing happens again: I don't have much oxygen, black dots, white dots. I started to black out again and I remember coming up and seeing the whole crowd of people looking at me to see if I'm okay. And my friend Mags almost coaching me from a distance. Watching me, but also making sure I'm OK. Encouraging me to relax.

Mags, who had paddled into the impact zone and put his own life at risk to save Jamie, remembers thinking:

> I'm not gonna let this kid drown, I knew his mum and dad, and I would just feel really bad if something bad happened to him and I didn't do anything . . .
>
> The people before me, the legends, I'm fortunate enough to have grown up with them—Brock Little, Todd Chesser, they coached me. They got me and Shane Dorian and Kelly Slater into big waves, and I feel like I had to live up to it, own it, and help the next generation coming up, which I still do. I just feel it's my duty.
>
> So, I paddled over to Jamie and he was fine. He was scared, but he was OK: it was very heavy, very, very life-threatening.

Reaching Jamie, Mags tells him, shaking his head, "That was crazy, you're taps, kid! Are you OK?"

Jamie replies: "I'm fine!"

And then Jamie gets pushed aside and somehow finds himself in the channel, trying to make sense of what just happened and coughing up blood.

Getting Back on the Horse

By this time Jamie feels like he has two voices arguing in his head: "Go in. Go back out. Get back on the horse and keep going, or retire . . . go in." Then, lying on his board close to shore, he reflects further:

> If I go in, I probably never want to do this again because this was terrifying, but at the same time I was kind of motivated by the experiences in that moment because, well . . . I kind of handled it, even though somehow I almost blacked . . . didn't really black out, because I didn't need any resuscitation, and no one had touched me. No one had rescued me except a little bit of that verbal communication from my friend. I should go back out. I survived. That's probably the worst that's gonna happen to me.

In that moment he decides to paddle back out and catch a few more waves before calling it a day. And that moment not only propels him toward continuing to push in big waves, but puts him on the map beyond the North Shore. The experience also helps him realize that to try to make a career in surfing he doesn't have to compete in organized, regular surfing events, as he had been doing. Like his close friend Mark, he wasn't very good at it anyway, and he knew that. He could follow a different path, a path that at the time barely existed. Focusing on big waves could perhaps become a reality.

In 1997, when this event unfolded, there were only a couple of big wave competitions, and no World Tour had been put together yet. Few at the time thought of big wave surfing as a viable career alternative to regular surfing. The photo of that incident, the one on Jamie's wall, was used on many publications, as well as in advertisements for some of the sponsors he had back then. It was a turning point in his career. The experience and its documentation catapulted him into the spotlight of the surf industry, but it also gave him the motivation and the desire to keep surfing big waves because of the strong rush he felt and the camaraderie and respect he earned from other surfers, and from the North Shore community more broadly. And he recognized that he had now gone through one of the worst experiences a surfer could have had, and certainly the worst he had had up to that point. More than two decades later, that's still one of the heaviest wipeouts of his life.

Surviving that wipeout, and the intense interactions he shared with Mags in the impact zone, infused Jamie with confidence to paddle back out. Back in the lineup he was cheered by the older crowd, who were congratulating him. The senior guys like Clark Abbey and the other regulars were impressed that Jamie went for the wave, handled it, and had the bravado to come back for more. "That was nuts!" "That was crazy." "That was huge!" Jamie felt as proud as if he had won the world championship, a contest, or a prize. All he earned was a feeling of respect and support from his peers. "Like a ying yang," Jamie says to me, "a negative turned into a positive" that ended well and launched him forward, consolidating his life trajectory. Jamie recalls that after being greeted by his peers, he decided to catch a few more waves to make sure that his heart and his intentions were pure. That was the moment when he said to himself: "OK, cool. I like surfing big waves. That was really heavy. I almost died, but that was the most alive I ever felt."

When I ask Mags to help me understand why Jamie paddled back out to the lineup, he tells me:

He had just been in the worst predicament you can put yourself into ever. And once you survive something like this, it makes you more comfortable, not getting cocky, *but just knowing what you should do*. It was very heavy. At that age I would have went in.

Remembering Jamie paddling back out to the lineup, Mags tells me he was in disbelief:

This kid took off on the biggest wave that came out that day, just had a horrendous wipeout, and just shook it off? At this point, the look on his face wasn't even scared. His look was nonchalant. That wipeout at such a young age was insane. I thought: "Wow, this kid's gonna be the next world-renowned big wave rider," because he was just fearless.

When I ask Mark Healey why most kids their age didn't want to have anything to do with big waves, he says: "Because it's fucking scary!" And then he explains that along with the psychology of it, the safety aspect is completely different nowadays:

When one person does something, then just everyone else's psychology changes. It's like the first . . . how long did it take for somebody to run a mile under four minutes? And then as soon as they did it, within a year like I think five other people did it.

To underline the significance of Jamie's feat, Mags says: "Nobody at the time at that age was doing that. Kids back then were into performance surfing, not into big wave surf. That day Jamie set the standard for teenagers to surf big waves."

A Negative into a Positive

Jamie's wipeout can be read through the lens of interaction ritual theory. Jamie feels strong because he's in a good rhythm that day. Then, filled with confidence, he decides to take off on a wave that's much larger than anything he's ridden before, but he wipes out. Many of his peers in the lineup are focusing on his attempt, and when it fails, they look to see if Jamie is coming back to the surface OK or not. This dynamic unfolds in this way because he's taking off further out from where everyone is sitting, and because of the norm of watching out for one another in large surf. While he's alone under the water, he knows his friends are watching him. He heard them yell when he was trying to catch the wave. As he resurfaces, his peers are staring at him, and one of them, Mags, coaches him from a distance at first, and then paddles to the impact zone for rescue, telling him again to keep it together, that he's going to be fine even though there are more waves from that set about to fall on him. The interaction with his older friend is a powerful ritual. During these parts of the experience—his interactions with Mags and the other surfers—he has become the sacred object around which his community focuses its attention, which refills him with energy. Every surfer wants to be part of the action. Jamie then gets pounded by those other waves. Once he's washed in the channel, he ponders whether he should go in or paddle back out to the lineup. The attraction of wanting to go back and be with his peers, and also to take another wave, is too strong to resist.[5] Once he reaches his peers, his role within the community is not only solidified because he's proven himself in an extraordinary situation, but it's boosted up the social order. His friends and even some of his heroes focus their attention on him again, lauding him. His energy increases further, and that *fateful moment* propels him toward wanting to have more such experiences. The collective effervescence and solidarity he's contributed to generating among his peers is almost as powerful as the emotional energy he has received himself.

Consider this other illustration, which took place years prior but, unlike Jamie's, wasn't documented. Professional surfer Shane Dorian recounts a pivotal wipeout in his career when he was teenager. Two mentors he idolized, Todd Chesser and Brock Little, want to surf an outer reef called Himalayas. Shane and two friends his age reluctantly follow. Once in the water, Shane is the only one besides Todd and Brock to make it past the shore break and out to the lineup. He's scared. Waves are about twenty-five feet. He sees his mentors catching waves, and he begins feeling embarrassed for not having caught one yet. Eventually a wave he describes as "monstrous" approaches him. And even though he's paddling up the face of the wave to escape it, seeing Brock further toward the shoulder turning around to take the wave, he decides to try taking it. Years later he says: "I was so pissed and ramped up in the moment that I just turned around and put my head down and just went for it." Shane suffers a dramatic wipeout, and after the last wave of the set has passed and he is back on the water surface, he sees Todd and Brock looking at him. He is vomiting and then begins crying. He gets washed back onto the beach by the following waves, and later on that day Brock has a serious talk with him about the gravity of the situation and big wave surfing's perils. Remembering the experience, he says:[6]

> I had this crazy connection with Brock and Todd Chesser after that. They became like big brothers to me, and I became one of them that day. I felt like I came up a level to like I wasn't a little kid anymore, like I got jumped in the gang that day.

These illustrations show that an apparently negative experience, a wipeout, can have strong positive effects and thus be turned into a series of successful interaction rituals. What matters is the intensity of the initial emotions, in this case fear and excitement, and how they are shared among participants. The strong emotions Jamie—and Shane, and their friends—feel are converted and reinterpreted by the individual and by the group as a bonding experience and reframed as a success. From the moment Jamie takes off, through the wipeout, for the rest of the session, and during the retellings in the following days, weeks, and years, he steps into the leading role others, like Chris Owens or Phil Owen, have played. Because his feat stands out in terms of intensity from others of his, and in the history of the community, it becomes a turning point—*a fateful moment* in his life. Similarly, Shane's account provides a concrete illustration of "growth," being recognized by the masters, being included, measuring himself in their eyes, seeking their approval. This *fateful moment* provided entree into the mentors' circle, and opened the door to sustained mentoring that carried Shane to a higher level of performance. These are not just two nasty wipeouts on two large waves; they are attempts at this activity made by teenagers who are at the beginning of their journey.

In the rest of this chapter I look at how big wave surfers discuss their pursuit by focusing on wiping out. I also show how their quest can build their confidence while also verging on becoming an obsession. I describe how top performers separate themselves from their competitors by employing techniques that help them remain calm during wipeouts. And I talk about lifeguarding and how it has changed since the late 1960s, reflecting broader changes in the sport.

Wanting It

Surfers often say "you have to want it," because it can take everything from you (including your life), and it will take much from you: injuries, time, money, social relationships, and jobs. So much so that if you were doing it for the "wrong reasons" (another topic frequently discussed), then you would likely regret getting into it in the first place, and possibly quit. Or at least seriously question your decisions. As consistent as it is with the idea of surfing as a hedonistic and selfish pursuit, the rhetoric is that you have to chase it because you love it. Otherwise, you'd be doing it for the wrong reasons.

"If you surf big waves for long enough, you'll eventually learn why you're doing it," Trevor says. "You'll be tested. You'll be humbled. Over and over again," Polly adds. "Some days you'll conquer, some days you'll be conquered," Clark says. "You'll learn who you are," Kevin tells me. Yet, your perspective on the sport as an extension of your life will also inevitably evolve. It will make you and break you both. But hopefully it won't kill you; hopefully when you walk away, you'll be just like Clark: "a survivor." But you will get hurt, many times over. And then one of the biggest challenges will be getting back in shape and keeping on despite the lasting impacts of your injuries. Getting back on the horse after a major wipeout is a challenge you will face early on, and one that typically will impact whether you want to continue or not. Put differently, a first major wipeout is a turning point, a consequential moment: a way out or a way deeper in.

If you pass this test, much of your subsequent life will reflect that; your own appreciation of living will depend on surviving the experiences and feelings derived from chasing and riding big waves. And on the thrills, the feelings of accomplishment, and the camaraderie. Your whole life (at least the part of it you devote to this pursuit)—your year, your occupation, your social relationships—will be organized and reorganized around it: not to miss a day when large waves materialize, not to miss a contest when it's suddenly on.

Confidence Building

Mark Healey is not alone in thinking that big wave surfers are a bit different from other surfers to begin with because of genetics, and also because of their upbringing. "At some point," he says, "every one of those surfers were sitting around fifty other people in the lineup and said: 'I think I want to surf out there where it's bigger,'" just like Jamie Sterling did twenty-something years ago. Besides the adrenaline rush, the excitement, fun, and camaraderie discussed in chapter 3, how else does one get pulled in? For Mark, and for other elders I met, there is a "people element"; many of those individuals "don't feel as comfortable socially" in their normal lives on land. Even Uncle Phil says he's not a people person, which is obvious in how he shies away from taking the spotlight and prefers to communicate through his actions. Some big wave surfers may be reserved on land, or even feel that the world they normally inhabit has an oppressive social structure. The lure and satisfaction of the wild environment, on the other hand, derives from taking a direct, single authorship—what some social psychologists call the "I," the spontaneity of an imminent present that overtakes the socialized "me" that has been imbued with societal expectations. As Gary Alan Fine puts it: "The charm of nature is that it is an 'authentic reality,'"[7] one that reminds us of its proximity, urgency, and materiality. Mark continues:

> There's a big draw to be in a wild environment and being a part of it and surviving. And it doesn't matter how big you are. It doesn't matter your skin color. It doesn't matter how much money you have, the ocean doesn't give a shit about any of this. The ocean will murder Mother Teresa just as fast as it murders Hitler. There is this sense of straight-up accomplishment that you can get, and I don't think you can ever get from an organized sport because there is always that human factor. Was that the right referee call? Whatever it is . . . to me that's pure. It's like climbing. I think surfers and mountain climbers and those big mountain snowboarders have a lot in common. I think it's the same personalities.

Solving Puzzles

Surfer/journalist Matt Rode tells me that the satisfaction derived from the pursuit of this sport is similar to that of rock climbing, a sport in which he is just as proficient. Besides the adrenaline, he also experiences a feeling of accomplishment. He tells me it's about identifying a problem—how to successfully select a wave and ride it—and then completing the task. What makes surfing so complicated, and big wave surfing even more so, has to do with the endless variations offered by the environment. He points at a rock he has been climbing at Waimea beach and tells me that if he doesn't complete the route he planned, he can come back next year. That rock will probably be in the same spot for the next thousand years. But no wave is the same as another. Next, he shows me a different route on the rock that he masters. It took him five months, but he could practice it over and over again until he succeeded. With surfing you simply cannot approach a problem with the same kind of repetitive approach. This means that when you solve it on the spot, you feel rewarded not only for your exploit, but also by the difficulty of replicating the experience. An addiction of sorts, some say, while scholars like Robert Dubin[8] would call it a central life interest: a source of meaning indicating a life trajectory.

Obsession

When I talk with Clark Abbey—who, even though he stopped surfing the Bay more than ten years ago, is still referred to as the "ambassador"—he says: "Ugo, I was willing to die." Not seeing as much of a reaction from me as he expected, he takes off his sunglasses. The sight of his creole light-green eyes contrasting with his brown skin takes me aback. And then he reiterates:

> You don't understand: I was completely willing to die for the Bay. If it was breaking, I *had* to be there. It nearly killed me. It almost broke my marriage four times (until he eventually stopped riding the Bay at fifty to save his marriage), and it negatively impacted my work.

Lifeguards wondered if he even had a job. His dedication was reflected in his high position within the spot's social hierarchy, which is forged in the memory of the community.

Recalling a collision he had with Ricardo when the latter was still learning to surf the Bay, he tells me about how he busted one of his eardrums, causing him vertigo. He rushed back to shore, and yet despite the pain, the blood running down his face, and an injured shoulder, he paddled right back out, ignoring the pleas of a lifeguard who was trying to dissuade him.

Back in the lineup, he noticed he could barely move one of his arms, so he paddled back to shore and called it a day. Many others also talk about the bad decision, made in the heat of the moment, of paddling right back out after an injury, how concussions may lead to depression, and how most often they remain undetected while inflicting permanent damage.

Sense of Achievement

The idea of success, as sociologist Joel Best[9] describes it, dominates much of our current thinking in Western societies. "Everybody is a winner," he writes, adding that many—too many of us?—want to feel prized as a winner regardless of our performance. Prize for participation or prize for standing apart from the other competitors? The point is that winning, succeeding, is both an expectation and the goal. But if everybody wins, what's the value of winning and of preparation? And if we're made to feel like winners even when we're not, what happens when we inevitably lose or when we realize that we never truly won? And if competitions are unfair, what is their worth? To be seen and recognized seems to matter more than it did in earlier times simply because it's more attainable with the proliferation of social media and inexpensive photo and video recording devices.

When I ask if he still surfs Waimea, North Shore shaper "JC" tells me: "Everyone wants to be famous nowadays," referring to the increasing popularity of surfing big waves at the Bay, which contributes to making it crowded and dangerous. Waimea is on the bucket list of many surfers who want to say they surfed it at least once.

But how does one distinguish between succeeding and failing? How easy is it to draw the line? And how much does it depend on the complexity of the task we're performing or the goal we're trying to reach? Even though riding big waves should not be regarded as a simple task—requiring as it does intimate knowledge of the ocean and all of its moods, the waves, their personalities, the seabed, and the myriad other factors that influence their rise, strength, and shape—as an activity it is both straightforward and elusively complex.

In surfing, in spite of how good your ride may have been you most often feel as if it could have been better; but replicating the experience, some would say, is impossible since no wave is quite like any other. The environment you play in is constantly changing. This quality of waves and of surfing—their singularity and the excitement they provide—influences how addictive[10] and fun the activity is; we can never get quite enough, and the more we have of it, and the better we get at it, the more we generally want to experience it. While the challenge is endless and elusive, the rewards are immediate.

To an extent, success in riding big waves is fairly clear: "Did you survive?" Not many would quibble with such a result. "Life on land stresses me out," a surfer tells me while comparing it to her life on the water and how relaxing and comparatively unproblematic that is. Everything else either is forgotten or becomes secondary. There's no time to think of anything else—or sometimes, to even think at all—in extreme situations. You just have to react. You can freeze and be overtaken by panic. You can yell for help, overtaken by fear. Or you can just do what you practiced to be doing in such situations.

We must ask, though, how one gets to the point of being able to enjoy surfing big waves. How can a surfer get to where he can enjoy purposely getting himself in situations that are obviously dangerous, potentially life-threatening, and unpredictably stressful? What are some of the key moments in the making of a big wave surfer? Whether or not it causes physical or mental injury, a major wipeout is certainly one of them.

Garrett McNamara says that before surfing large waves, a candidate should be dropped off in the impact zone to see if he enjoys getting "pounded." This is akin to saying that if you want to pursue a career in academia or in any creative industry, you have to get used to being rejected. Yet there is a process in learning how to fail properly. Some surfers also believe there is a particular genetic makeup that determines who will pursue the activity and who will not, or will eventually drop off. It is an unsettled argument that is obviously much larger than this small social world. Nature or nurture, or a combination of the two and the interaction between them? Scientific research in the psychology of risk-taking supports the idea of a risk gene, while the sociology and social psychology of risk-taking emphasize that behavior is learned and fine-tuned in groups. Legendary Maui tow-in surfer Dave Kalama is renowned for his skills in the progression of tow-in surfing at Jaws. But he is also loved for his humor. More than once he has argued that the reason he took risks had to do with hanging out with "stupid peers." Interacting with friends who influence one another for an extended period, daring one another to ride larger and larger waves, up to the point of riding waves so large that no one at the time had ridden anything like them before.

Trevor says that for many who go through a first near-death expe-

rience, it comes down to a simple "Been there, done that, fuck that."
But how do some surfers keep going despite having been exposed to the
sport in the first place and having been in dangerous and potentially
debilitating situations?

Wiping Out

Big wave surfers talk about the importance and meaning of the first
"really bad" wipeout, a "pounding"—the first fall, the first time a wave
breaks on your head and "squashes you like a bug," or when the white
water "mows you over" like you're a leaf scratched up by a rake. The water
holding you under the surface, moving you long distances in a span of
time you cannot know in advance. Hopefully, pulling you away from the
"impact zone" where large waves are breaking and where most of their
energy is concentrated.

When big waves break, they detonate. Guns are both much thicker and
much stronger than either a regular surfboard or a human spine, and yet
they snap in two like chopsticks, and quite often too, when they're hit
by the lip of a breaking big wave. Yet these boards are heavy and strong
enough that when they strike your body, they can also severely damage
you. Fins are the equivalent of dulled knives. In big wave surfing, and in
surfing in general, the greatest danger is being hit by a board, either your

Getting caught inside and preparing to be mowed over.

own or someone else's. Being hit is statistically much more likely than any other hazard, such as drowning or hitting the reef.

Phil warns me that the worst-case scenario is probably being hit by your board, blacking out, and having your leash snap. Finding you in time to try to revive you—or finding you at all, even if only to bring some peace to your loved ones, then becomes a nearly impossible task. The depth and expanse of the ocean swallows you. As Tom Farber writes: "Drowning, death from submersion in water. Swallowing the sea, being swallowed by the sea."[11] The majority of drowned bodies are never found, which makes closure difficult while adding mystique. Eddie Aikau is only one name among a long list of surfers who died this way, not counting the many others whose bodies were never found. Phil adds that a good thing about wearing a flotation vest is that your family can have your body back, and can have an open-casket funeral. "It's huge for having closure," a lifeguard confirms. Phil says he has seen all sorts of freak accidents, the bottom line being that as soon as you enter the ocean anything can happen. Your leash can get tangled on a submerged rock, causing you to drown, and some argue that this probably contributed to the death of the Hawaiian big wave surfer Mark Foo while visiting Mavericks in California. Foo's last wave, as documented by a sequence of photographs, was not particularly large. Certainly nothing out of the ordinary for him in terms of size. But it was a wave somewhere other than Waimea, and in colder water too. Foo was tired from a red-eye flight, true, and the cold water probably magnified the impact of that factor. There were of course many other surfers and photographers there; but there wasn't any explicit rescue plan in place, and no strong community norm of surfers working together to enhance and ensure safety.

Before the formation of the Big Wave Risk Assessment Group (BWRAG) in 2011, and other similar groups, "people would get desperate, or wouldn't pay enough attention, while now everyone knows what to do. They have life-saving eyes," a founder of the group says. A handful of surfers established BWRAG because of the drowning at Mavericks of their friend Sion Milosky. The group holds a yearly four-day workshop before the start of the winter season, including presentations by paramedics, lifeguards, and other specialists teaching apnea, jet-ski training, breath-holding, and forecasting. One topic that is discussed is the exit plan at each surfing spot: what will you do when things go wrong? "Everyone needs to be on the same page," the same guy tells me.

Big wave surfing has progressed and changed much in the last decade, and understanding the evolution of safety procedures and technologies is certainly key to understanding risk-taking in this social world.

I haven't experienced a truly bad wipeout surfing Waimea, but I almost drowned while surfing Jockos on a double-overhead day when I got caught inside by a larger set. Some waves can hold you down more than you would expect, while others may "release" you quicker than you were anticipating. "You just never know," Phil says. Standing by the food trucks at Sharks Cove, I ask Chris how it feels to be caught by the white water at Waimea. He points toward Foodland and says: "You see that fence (eighty yards away from our position)? You get pushed that far real quick."

Stevo describes wiping out like this:

> It's like being in the amusement park. First you're in the bumper cars and you get a little crash, you flip over. And then you're in the Ferris wheel, you go all the way around. You splash down and it hits you, you go in a giant circle and then you go straight down and then it's like the cliff hanger. The roller coaster that goes straight down, then it's the Ferris wheel one more time, then it's straight down. And the real tumbling begins, then you're forty feet underwater. It's like the whole football team kicked your ass under water. And you have to relax.

Wiping out is key to success. Failing without too much physical and psychological damage—or preferably none at all—can be one of the major factors in building a surfer's confidence, or permanently breaking it. It's a turning point, a truth moment. Another *fateful moment* within an unpredictable environment, but one where the odds, at least in personal terms, are not random: some factors, and increasingly so with the development of the activity, should be held constant. Thought out. Planned. Calculated. At least, as much as one can prepare for the unpredictable. And that's how the professional surfers justify some of the danger they face: they take to the water having done all they could, as they say, "to get back home to our families safe."

When wiping out, which is a general category that includes a number of things that can go wrong, you may be held beneath the surface long enough that you think you might die, or black out when you exhaust the oxygen that fuels your muscles, your organs, and finally, your brain functions. Ricardo, who teaches an apnea course for big wave surfers that Chris Owens and I took, tells me that blacking out often starts with a tingling feeling in your fingers, arms, or legs; but as others have told me, it may also be preceded by an uncontrollable feeling of euphoria. The "black dots, white dots" mentioned by Jamie. That's how some divers die: by simply deciding to stay at the bottom of the sea. In an ecstatic state where everyday problems gradually wash away, leaving you in a blissful state that some don't want to leave.

Then surfers discuss how to mentally and physically deal with wipeouts and other critical situations like those described above. And each of them devises different coping strategies, which sometimes clash with one another, because truly, no one right answer applies to the contingencies of every situation. Perhaps some strategies apply only in hindsight. But even then. One apnea instructor, for example, told me that part of his training program involves getting as close as possible to blacking out, to understand the indicators. But another one holds that you should avoid it at all costs, because "once it's in your head, it's very hard to get it out," and the experience may result in fear that would hold you back or make you hesitate. Good judgment, skill, preparation, and ultimately commitment and luck are some of the factors that align whenever a surfer successfully navigates the boundary between making it and not. And probably a certain amount of foolishness and recklessness too. As an informant tells me: "At one point, you just got to commit and hope for the best and be ready to accept the consequences, whatever they are." But too much commitment when the odds are clearly against you can also undermine your reputation. You can be a *charger*, someone who pushes the limits; but you can also be reckless, someone who pushes more than is necessary—especially without enough mental and physical preparation—sometimes also endangering others.

Busying Your Mind and Preparation

Surfers think about how to control fear in these situations, and also how to use it to their advantage to mitigate risks. How to get your mind to think about something else to make time go faster or to avoid being overtaken by panic. Phil, for instance, used his own tricks, getting me or Kawika to enjoy the view once we managed the paddle out at Waimea. Chris, however, talks about "getting your mind off the beast":

> Say if you're a fighter and you're going to fight some guy that's way bigger than you, but on the other hand just still have the chance to beat this guy up because you're tough. But that guy looks so big and intimidating. You look at him, but that can put the stress on you and make you not be able

to win that fight. If you go into that fight not even looking at him, thinking about something else maybe, like a form of meditation. Not thinking about that person's size, but of what you're going to do instead. So with the apnea training, when a big wave breaks in front of me, like those closeouts at Waimea, I know the situation of the waves coming at me, but I look down at my board, try not to look at the thing and see how big it is. You just gotta realize it's big and you're gonna get a little hold down, but you have confidence in yourself and you realize you have the strength to get through it.

When Randall Collins[12] discusses interaction—and more specifically, violent situations—he points out that emotional dominance precedes physical violence. In this sense Chris and others I talked to try not to let a wave disrupt their own rhythm. For instance, as a big wave is about to crash on him, Robbie stretches his arms toward the sky and tells himself: "You're not five-eleven, you're a hundred feet tall!" And even though they know that they can't be in control of the environment they're facing, they decide to be in control of their own training and reactions, which helps them maintain a confident stand. This strategy leads them to fight at the peak of their ability and thus increases their chances of surviving a major hold down as well as surfing to the best of their abilities.

Others also tell me their own strategies during a wipeout: "I think about what I have to do when I get home. What do I need to get at the grocery store?" "I play dead," Mo tells me. "Turn into a dolphin!" Robbie says to himself. Another talks about imagining rolling cigarettes, while yet another tells me he shuts his eyes and envisions a little fish coming to check him out. If you panic, not only are you more likely to make the wrong decisions, but your heart rate speeds up and you waste precious oxygen. Slowing down your heartbeat through specific breathing techniques and relaxation is one way to deal with critical situations. Ricardo tells us that he uses these same breathing techniques both in the water, while waiting for waves as many others do, and on land anytime he feels stressed out.

Recent years have seen the increased availability of courses on apnea and survival in extreme surfing conditions like the one Chris and I took from Ricardo, as well as information and courses on how to train best, which includes diet. Additionally, some talk about how their approach to risk changes as they age and, for those pursuing the activity professionally, as their careers progress. Which risks are worth taking? What could be the potential reward? Am I willing to risk losing my life for just *this one* wave? Would it be the "wave of my life?" more than a few ponder.

Preparing by Simulating: Finding the Bathroom in the Dark

In addition to these techniques for how to enter and exit specific spots, how to oxygenate your body with certain breathing exercises, and how to get mentally and physically stronger to prepare for the worst, Mark Healey provides me with one of the clearest explanations of how to survive an essentially unpredictable situation.

He tells me that when he wipes out, he mentally goes to his place. He laughs softly, before adding: "I go to work there. I free-dive so much I have that space pretty well figured out in my head usually, and yeah, just hibernation time." His preparation involves simulating being in a highly stressful environment where you not only have to make quick consequential decisions, but you also have to operate with a large amount of adrenaline going through your body. He tells me to think about my house. "If it suddenly gets pitch black, can you still find the bathroom? What if it's another house instead?" Asked by her young daughter the meaning of fear, the anthropologist Margaret Mead[13] told her: "It's a dark hallway." Part of Mark's idea of preparation is making that place of discomfort *your* house where you don't even have to see because you already know where everything is. The idea is to establish a familiarity with the feeling of being tossed and turned and becoming oxygen deprived, yet still making the right decisions without panicking or losing additional oxygen. And that familiarity is achieved by free-diving, exercises in the pool, and experience in the ocean.

> You have to visit that place beforehand. You have to . . . you don't want any surprises of how you act when that pressure is applied to you. You have to go and make that place your home. So instead of it being a house I never been in, I make the dark house my house. I don't even have to see. I know where things are already. It's so that if I visited it, I have a familiarity with that feeling and situation. I go there in a controlled way before I get forced there by outside circumstances. I know how to move around in it.

Mark's idea revolves around "pushing yourself beyond what you feel your breaking point is a lot of times and realizing that you can go past it."

The idea of familiarity with uncomfortable and unpredictable situations is also emphasized by people like Ricardo and implemented by lifeguards who train by simulating possible scenarios.

Dying to Live

Erving Goffman[14] begins his 1967 essay "Where the Action Is" with a quote attributed to the German American high-wire artist Karl Wallenda, who often performed his stunts without a safety net: "To be on the wire is life, the rest is waiting." Much of our existence is (or appears to be, to those who cannot perceive its potential fatefulness) inconsequential, both to us and to others. Some of us search for and crave being in *action*, perhaps more so once we've had a good taste of it. Living through intense situations satisfies our appetite for adventure, yet it also gives us a taste of what life could be like—or, as surfer Mark Healey notes, what life used to be like for our ancestors.

Mark is fascinated by the concepts of time and risk, from both a psychological and an evolutionary perspective. "What is time, but a perception? How can we define risk if we don't know how it feels to get the reward?" While acknowledging that since the introduction of life vests and other safety devices no one has died practicing the sport—but being cognizant that undiagnosed concussions and mechanical injuries have probably risen along with the sport's popularity—he thinks that "the ratio of risk, honestly, is lower than people think." Yet he also tells me that surfers get "close calls" often enough. Then, as an example, he mentions drugs like DMT and "tripping hard" for about ten minutes but feeling like you just lived a hundred years. Perhaps understanding that I can't relate, or just wanting to be clearer, he says: "Do you ever do that? You fall asleep for five minutes, but you have a full, long dream? Time is our most valuable asset, yet it is constructed in our brains." He explains this point in relation to surfing big waves:

> Money ain't gonna buy you fucking time. If you can have one moment
> that lasted ten to fifteen seconds that is so much more meaningful
> than the next three months of your life—you will forget all the shit that
> happened in the three months of your life preceding and following that
> fifteen-second time window . . . you'll forget all that, it's just white noise,
> it's in history somewhere, but you'll remember that fifteen-second time
> window of riding that wave so vividly and you'll remember the feel-
> ing until the day you die. That fifteen seconds is more powerful to your

overall life than months of your life are, in the end. So, what's the value of
that? What kind of risk are you willing to take for those kinds of things
that you can't just make happen? You can't fucking take a pill when it
happens, you can't buy it. What's meaningful to you? That's kind of the
way I look at it. And I think it's a healthy thing.

For Mark and other surfers I talked to, those experiences are not only
meaningful, but also to some extent more predictable, and thus less
risky—or more worth the risk—than other hazards we also willingly
expose ourselves to. But how can you weigh the worth of a fifteen-second
phenomenal ride against a permanent and potentially debilitating injury,
or (in the worst case) death?

Mark's next example is driving to a job that you detest, or even just
driving to work whether you enjoy the job or not. How can you calculate
and predict that your trip there will be safe enough if you can't account
for the fact that a number of drivers may, for example, be texting? How
many variables you are not even aware of?

When I'm driving on a freeway, I can't calculate what that person who is
texting behind me at 70 miles per hour is doing. I have no control over
that. Yes, I have less control over variables driving down the freeway, yet
people who are driving to their job that they hate are exposing themselves to this probably an hour and a half a day.

"Multiply that," I say.

Exactly! Pick your poison. Everything is like medicine. Everything is toxic
at certain levels. You drink enough water and it will kill you, but you need
water to live.

Mark seems to imply that he needs those experiences to live a meaningful life. Ultimately, life is risky and finite, so it's up to you to "choose your
poison." Like Carlos and others, Mark also thinks that

We are rewarded for those moments because we are wired. Our ancestors for a long, long time had to make life and death decisions every day.
Like real, calculated life-and-death decisions living in nature. So, what it
looks like to me, is that most of our evolution to create these brains and
bodies is based in those settings. And all of a sudden we're padded away
from it. Why are people seeking more, then? Because we're supposed to

be in environments like that? Why is depression going through the roof even though our lives are more comfortable and on paper better than ever? It's that addiction to comfort. It's like a heroin addict. It's hard for the heroin addict to put the needle down, it's hard for us to get rid of comfort.

Carlos says: "If you don't take risks in life, you don't evolve. Tell me something in life that made a huge difference for humanity that didn't involve risk. It doesn't exist. Everything related to evolution, to surviving, takes risk."

But how has the safety equipment changed the risks taken by the big wave surfers who ultimately practice the sport? And how has the work of lifeguards changed along with technological improvements? The last part of this chapter introduces you to lifeguarding at Waimea Bay; I will expand on this in chapter 6, on the professionalization and commercialization of big wave surfing.

Guarding Patients on the Beach and in the Ocean

In 1975 Mark Dombroski was working on the military base of Schofield Barracks in Wahiawā, a few miles inland from the North Shore. When his job ended, he went on unemployment. Not a reason to sweat when you're in your early twenties. Eddie Aikau, who in 1967 had become the first lifeguard at Waimea Bay, suggested that Mark apply for a job to work alongside him, his brother Clyde, and a handful of others.

What Mark enjoyed the most about his job was its unpredictability and the instant adrenaline rush he would get during rescues. He enjoyed the variety of scenarios and characters he would encounter on any given day. "That's what kept me busy and kept me here." Mentally and physically busy. "At other beaches you could fall into the doldrums because sometimes there's no people on the beach. Not literally fall asleep, but fall asleep in your head," he specifies, as if to preserve the respectable image of his occupation and to avoid misunderstandings.

You see, it's about the unexpected: whether it's with humans or the ocean, or it's *in* the ocean—the sea life. It keeps you on your toes and it's fascinating, and people are fascinating in their own way too, you know what I mean? (Pause) "Dude (getting louder to signal showmanship), you just made my day, in a weird way because you're so weird." You run into the trippiest people.

And he explains to me that while it may seem that lifeguards are often inactive, there is more that goes on undetected by the untrained eye. Besides physical fitness, there is a mental side to the job, too, that requires some of the same skills and qualities it takes to surf big waves.

> You have to have confidence in your abilities. There's no time for second-guessing yourself and what you have to do. It's just like a split-second thing, you have to react. It's all reactionary. There's nothing to do about being smart, it's about having common sense and experience, and certain factors like that you know where the rip is, you know how to get out there. I don't have a problem with doing it right now, even though it's twenty feet; it's the risk factor: you're taking calculated risks. And you're not calculating in your mind, you already know what to do: you know where to go because you're prepared, and there's gonna be certain things that you've never experienced, but you know how to get yourself out of it. Because you've been in similar situations—not the exact same situation, but you understand the ocean enough and your capabilities and stuff like that . . . but when you throw another person in there that you know nothing about, now your strategy has to change again: How to get this person in? Or how to get them out?

Mark never surfed the Bay. It wasn't his passion. Because it's one of the most notorious beaches in Hawai'i, and because of its wave, I wonder how hard it is to end up working here. Different guys like working different places for all sorts of reasons, just like surfers end up gravitating toward certain beaches and avoiding others. But here there's a quick turnaround: many think they want to work at the Bay, but when they start they realize that the responsibility almost overwhelms them. They ask to be moved, or they may stick to only one day a week instead of five like he did—and he's stuck around for four decades. Requests for assignments are mostly accepted, because you want guys who are emotionally invested in working at a specific spot. They perform better when well matched with other crew members and with the surroundings.

Dombro retired in 2016 after working for forty-one years as a lifeguard at the Bay. By then he had become one of the most skilled jet-ski operators around, pulling off legendary rescues. In the second part of his career, being around guys even thirty years younger helped him stay young, and his relationships with them built his own confidence and theirs, and ultimately improved their performance. From this occupational vantage point, Dombro has seen big wave surfing change over four

decades, and has witnessed key technological developments that profoundly affected the sport: the invention of the leash, the introduction of
jet skis as safety devices and as a means to tow surfers in to large waves,
the use of mobile patrol, the improvement of forecasting science, and the
development and popularization of padded and inflation vests.

The first guys who surfed Waimea can be traced back to the late 1950s;
pictures from that era depict surfers at the mercy of nature, just wearing
boardshorts, and oftentimes wiping out with their boards spinning into
the air unattached to their ankles. Back then, and actually up until the
1980s, surfing entailed a lot more swimming, as most times you wiped
out—which happened mainly because of the rudimentary surfboards
available at the time—you had to swim to retrieve your board or to make
it back to shore. Leg-ropes connecting a surfer's ankle to the tail of his
board either hadn't been invented or weren't popular yet, especially in
big wave surfing.

From a Reactive to a Proactive Approach

I ask Dombro about the Bay and about the ways his job has changed since
he started. First of all, he says, there were no four-wheel-drive ATVs until
at least 1989—no mobile patrol on this side of the island to help you,
only the fire department less than a mile away—and no jet skis. In critical situations you could rely on a helicopter with a hoist, but that took
time to make happen, and it cost a lot. All lifeguards had was fin tubes,
a rescue board, a megaphone, and a radio.

Crowd Control

Anywhere you had to go, you had to run, you didn't drive there, so lifeguards would be running up and down the beach with a megaphone
warning people: "Get back away from the ocean!" "Don't get near the
shore!" "Don't go where there are no footsteps, where the sand is flat
and smooth!" Beachgoers who drown on this side of the island mostly
get swept off while just walking on the shoreline. "People don't realize
how far the surge goes up and how fast and hard. It's almost impossible
to fight it." There could be a lull and it looks flat, and then you look at
the horizon and see it gets dark. It can be really chaotic at times unless
you take control of it early, which is a strategy that lifeguards couldn't
implement until the 1990s, when technological advances allowed them
to move beyond being *reactive* and to become *proactive*.

Back then lifeguards mostly assisted beachgoers, but not the surfers. In the 1970s and 1980s there were only about fifteen to twenty-five people regularly surfing the Bay, and because they didn't wear a leash and couldn't rely on other safety devices that would be introduced to the sport later—"crutches," as he calls them—they were all strong swimmers who knew how to get themselves out of bad situations. Nowadays one can easily spot fifty or even sixty surfers at the Bay, a minority of them locals and a good portion of them traveling surfers. Remarkably, only a third of them truly knows the craft, catching most of the waves.

Dombro tells me that during the 1970s, he doesn't remember having to help any surfer unless they got hurt. He and the other lifeguards knew all of them, and all were capable of getting in and out of the water by themselves. Brendan Shea, who is now one of the more experienced active lifeguards, adds that in the 1980s and even into the early 1990s, between all the lifeguards on duty they could name every single surfer and describe each one's capabilities.

Today the situation is strikingly different: lifeguards can recognize maybe only about a third of the surfers, and many of the surfers rely heavily on safety equipment and personnel rather than on their own strength and skills. Now part of the lifeguards' job is preventative and covers both beachgoers and surfers: it entails spotting those surfers who look like they might not be capable, and then talking to them and suggesting that it may not be their day. Ultimately, though, the lifeguards can't stop anyone from going into the water unless the beach is closed, which rarely happens. Dombro says that nowadays some guys start waving for help from a lifeguard on a jet ski as soon as they wipe out, not even trying to make it back to shore on their own. Then he scolds: "If you can't swim in, you shouldn't be out there."

One might think that a bay would be easier to patrol than other areas, but it's not. All that water coming in has nowhere to go. Its volume— ferociously massive. On the right side of the Bay you have the keyhole, just below Phil's house, the only place where you should both paddle out and get back in. Next to it, you find the river flowing into the ocean. And at the opposite end, you have the jump rock and other rocks that give that area the nickname "coffin corner." Did I mention the average number of people who visit the Bay each year? Waimea Bay is one of the most popular beaches in Hawai'i, and at times there were only two lifeguards on duty to patrol an area about five hundred yards long that attracts thousands of tourists and local people every year.

Think about forecasting. As I described earlier, and will discuss further in chapter 6, today's surfers have at their disposal real data from buoys that are placed miles offshore and communicate via satellite swell height, intensity, and direction, so that surfers know even when the first waves of the new swell will arrive. While back in the day surfers were amateur forecasters, now they can easily rely on experts—yet the best surfers have also augmented their skills to increase their chances of scoring particularly exceptional waves.

But in the 1970s, 1980s, and even a large part of the 1990s, there was no way to know what was going to happen; instead "you were watching it happen." The North Shore of Hawai'i is one of those rare places where the surf can grow from two feet to twenty feet within an eight-hour period. "You don't know it's going to happen, but you can see it happening, and then it's a matter of how big it's going to get."

Early in 2002 the lifeguard tower was refurbished, and that renovation included adding a two-speaker system that, along with the ATVs, impacted how lifeguards did their job, allowing their approach to become more proactive. They could reach more people, more quickly and more effectively. Since then, on big days you will typically find three guys in the tower and two guys on a ski in the channel of the Bay, and the members of the group will switch positions throughout the day. The new strategy is based on helping people by talking to them about risks they might not be aware of, rather than waiting until they get in trouble to take action.

"Pick 'Em Up, Bring 'Em In"

Dennis Pang recalls the first Eddie competition in 1986, when for the first time a jet ski was used for safety. Waves were about twenty feet, but it wasn't good, it was windy. A lifeguard named Squiddy was on the ski. Dennis says: "It made me feel so comfortable he was there. I didn't know if he was gonna rescue us, but I knew he could rapidly get us out of a bad situation." In the late 1980s and early 1990s a group of lifeguards from the west side of O'ahu began experimenting with using jet skis in lifeguarding. One of them had wiped out on a major wave at Waimea, and a friend who had been out on his jet ski riding waves at an outer reef asked him if he was doing OK. A lightbulb turned on, so to speak, and Brian Keaulana bought his own ski and decided to develop it for rescue, eventually involving others like Mark Dombroski. Fast forward thirty years and you will find lifeguards in many parts of the world using this craft for lifesaving, and surfers using it both to be launched into big waves—

tow-in—and to save one another in critical situations. At Waimea, ever since the early 1990s, a ski has been kept on the beach on a trailer, ready to be launched in case of an emergency. By 2010, every time the surf rose to fifteen feet or higher, a ski would be in the lineup, and on average lifeguards would be making twenty to thirty rescues a day.

Think of another pivotal safety innovation—inflatable floating vests—and you'll think of Shane Dorian, who, while flying back from Northern California after nearly drowning in the surf at Mavericks, took the idea of the oxygen masks and life vests from the flight attendants' routine safety presentation and imagined applying the same idea in surfing. With the help of project developers from one of his sponsors, he engineered an inflatable vest that, when activated, could bring you up to the surface like a balloon, dramatically minimizing the risk of drowning. Those vests, and positive flotation vests like the one I used at Waimea, have had three main impacts:

First, they have helped professional big wave surfers to ride waves of unprecedented height and to place themselves in ever more critical positions on the wave—e.g., closer and closer to the curl, getting barreled and essentially trying to ride giant waves like regular waves, turning rather than riding straight. Dombro sounds certain when he says that without such devices surfers would die.

Second, like the leash, they have greatly contributed to the popularization of the sport by enabling those who haven't properly trained to venture to places they normally wouldn't and perhaps shouldn't.

And third, the vests and jet skis have negatively impacted how some surfers, even in competition, approach riding waves. Jamie Sterling calls this new style "Go straight and inflate," referring to the fact that some surfers now deliberately take off in positions where they have essentially little to no chance of successfully riding out the wave. Yet surprisingly, they often get rewarded, winning prizes even when not completing their rides. Safety devices have changed how big waves are ridden and who rides them—points I will continue to address throughout this book, and particularly in chapter 6.

All the Gear but No Idea

When Aaron Gold wanted to start surfing the Bay back in the late 1980s, his shaper, Wade Tokoro, refused to make him a board. Being a big wave surfer himself, Tokoro understood the danger and didn't want to take on the responsibility. Aaron's uncle, Tony Moniz, at the time an Eddie invitee, had to vouch for him, arguing that the kid would go out anyway, so it was safer to provide him with the right equipment. Recalling those early days, Aaron says: "Back then you would never even have attempted it unless you were a hundred percent confident in what you were doing. You wouldn't have even started surfing a big wave to begin with, because it was outside your bubble. Or you would have had someone taking you or mentoring you to that point. Whereas now it's readily accessible."

Anyone can buy a gun; even I did, and I ended up firing it, too. The lure was too powerful to resist. Provided you have enough money, today you can walk into a shop and buy a gun, the right leash, and any kind of vest. No questions asked. Anyone can decide to be, look like, or try to become a big wave surfer without first taking the necessary preparatory steps. Lifeguards face a challenge: How do you spot a novice? And with no legal authority, how do you try to prevent those you deem at risk from entering the water? How do you minimize the risks and damages? Recalling a time when he was driving his ski after a cleanup set, Dombro talks about "picking up the pieces."

Surfers can have too small a board, or even try to paddle out somewhere other than by "the keyhole." "Anybody that's even a question mark, we talk to them," Brendan says. It's a smarter approach than acting only when someone is already in trouble. And if the people in question are already in the water, lifeguards try to dissuade them with a megaphone. Brendan tells me he usually starts with a quick check Dombro calls the "donkey test": "What's your plan? (and right after) What's your float plan?" (Meaning: what's your strategy for getting in and out of the water, if something goes wrong?) If the first answers are appropriate, but the lifeguard is still unconvinced, they may be followed by more specific questions: "What happens if your leash breaks? Can you swim in with all that extra wetsuit padding?" Brendan continues: "Keep in mind that the more flotation you have, the harder it is to move through the water . . . a lot more resistance. You're more susceptible to the currents, the white water, even to some degree to the wind, depending on the kind of windy day it is." When I probe further, he says: "I shouldn't be telling you, but here's a little secret that I pull out every once in a while when nothing else works: (lowering his voice as if he's talking to the surfer in question) 'I didn't want to tell you, but I saw a shark earlier.'" And he adds: "Shark always works. Everybody's afraid of sharks. Water is murky, the river broke . . . it's a little sharky . . . They weren't afraid of the water, but as soon as you mention shark . . . maybe I can talk someone out who's really on the fence, but those who have already made up their mind, there's nothing I can do about it. 'You have been warned.' Then I walk away."

Safety devices are a double-edged sword: they've made the sport safer, heavily impacted its progression, but also made it more dangerous. They've given a false sense of security to those who rely on them instead of using them as a backup plan—for example, to protect them and bring them back to the surface if they should be knocked unconscious by their boards. Yet that wouldn't prevent them from getting in the way of other surfers, or getting hurt, or needing to be rescued.

Failing Productively

As the economist and philosopher Kenneth Boulding said: "Nothing fails like success because we don't learn from it. We learn only from failure." But how can failure be motivating? Research on creativity by psychologists like Keith Sawyer[15] has found that innovation works by building on a series of small sparks of inspiration over time and through collaboration. But this doesn't explain how successful individuals manage to produce so many sparks across their careers, and how they overcome failure, and the power of failure to undermine confidence, to continue producing. How do they manage to stay motivated, and from where do they get the information that will potentially lead to successful recombinations of ideas?[16] Interaction theory focuses on both the social networks creators are embedded in and the social interactions they partake of, whether face to face with others or alone, thinking, and thus imagining past and future interactions. Herein lies the importance of regular contact with those who are at the center of a field, where the action is, and also time spent alone envisioning future interactions that will generate emotional energy and provide the cultural capital—information—that forms the building blocks from which creative ideas are made.

This chapter has focused on wiping out in surfing conceptualized as a metaphor for failing. It started by analyzing a wipeout that propelled Jamie Sterling's career as a big wave surfer who later became world champion. It went on to discuss how lifeguards police the edge, as well as the impact of technology and techniques on risk-taking in this sport.

When Jamie wipes out and gets disoriented in deep water, he doesn't know which way to go to reach the surface. The impossibility of swimming in a boil of bubbles, and the need to wait until the water regains enough resistance to swim in, underlines how essential the ability to focus on such technical details is in getting you through difficult situations, and shows the importance of maintaining calm under heavy pressure. Like other examples I presented, this episode also emphasizes the significance of practicing failure in controlled environments—following North American pragmatism, *habituating* oneself to failing—to getting "pounded."

As Jamie resurfaces, he engages in a successful interaction ritual based on two processes, both of which motivate him to go back out in the lineup and surf a few more waves before concluding his session. Both his self-talk and his interactions with his peers work to generate emotional energy. The fateful moment is not the wipeout, but the decision to *retry*. His motivation to return to the group after his major wipeout is the outcome of thoughtful reflection, emotional processes, and external interaction with the group in the moment—for instance, his friend Mags coaching him from a distance and letting him know that he's not alone, and prospectively, his own desire to get back out, to become the center of attention or the sacred object of interactions that produce emotional energy. In this light, Jamie's example is not only about failing, but more precisely about failing productively: about turning a potentially debilitating event into an occasion that propels you forward by generating emotional energy in the moment, and fun in the aftermath—a bonding experience that strengthens ties and bolsters both your self-confidence and your status within the group; and about learning from it.

Collins writes that "thinking is a fantasy play of membership inside one's mind";[17] in other words, "imaginary internal conversations" constitute interaction rituals taking place in the mind.[18] The kind of thinking Jamie does as he is debating with himself about whether to paddle back to shore or back out represents a mental simulation that reflects the kind of person he is and presages the one he could become. For this reason the wipeout is a turning point, while the decision to retry is a fateful moment.

I will continue discussing different kinds of interactions that produce emotional energy in chapter 5 and delve more deeply into the functions and varieties of self-talk techniques.

CHAPTER FIVE
Reciprocal Influence

Two days before Jamie Sterling fell off that beast of a wave at Waimea in early December, Mark Healey ruptured one of his eardrums. Since he couldn't be in the water, he was fishing out at sea with his uncle. Meanwhile his best friend was catching the largest wave of their lives during what would have been their first "proper twenty-foot day." Thirty miles out, feeling their little boat rising and then descending on the huge swells moving toward shore, Mark turned to his uncle and cried out: "Jamie is at Waimea right now. *I know* he's at Waimea!" What he couldn't know was exactly what Jamie had accomplished, and how meaningful that feat would be for both of them.

For several years Jamie spent as many as five nights a week at Mark's house, which was next door to his own. More than best friends, more like brothers who played a strong role in each other's development. The same age, from the same modest economic means, each growing up without a brother of his own, and both gravitating toward surfing larger waves at a time when teenagers just didn't. Both of them weren't very good at surfing regular waves either—they "sucked at contests," as they admit— and that's partly why they decided to prove themselves with their courage rather than their skills alone. Bravado and courage filling in the gap. They'd go to contests every weekend, and they'd eventually lose. But if one of them did a little better, the other stayed quiet on the ride home. The competition wasn't limited to themselves, or even confined to surfing: arm wrestling, ping-pong, and soccer were included, too. Competitive teenagers, with time on their hands and only their future ahead, at arm's length from each other while growing up in the wild as wild kids.

Jamie's exploit became the talk of the North Shore. "For a kid at that age, that was a big deal," Mark confirms. But back then there were no cell phones, internet, or digital photography. Information took time to spread, and depended mainly on verbal storytelling and imagination. A multivocal story. When he reached land, Mark heard the stories being told at Foodland and tried to picture it: "How big was it? What kind of wave did he catch?" Weeks went by before he eventually saw a photo. "Shit! That's a good one!" he instantly knew. Recalling how he felt, he mentions that his first reaction was being stoked for his friend, but then also feeling like the feat opened a huge gap between the two. "I felt like I just got left so far behind. I was so mad at myself for breaking my eardrum and missing it. And I was like: 'OK, next time I'm going big. I have to catch up.'" That winter, though, didn't produce any other large swells. The next big day arrived the following winter season. Then he clarifies: "for [Jamie] to just like set the bar so much higher in one day, I was like . . . I just felt like I was blowing it (laughing), but it just made me more hungry."

Jamie also recalls how important it was having someone like Mark, of the same age and so emotionally and physically close, and possessing the same desire. It made him feel comfortable having Mark pushing and encouraging him to start to surf bigger waves when they were younger— "we both gravitated toward the outside when our other friends went to stay on the inside, and that was their limit, while Mark and I would go to the outside and so I had someone to compare myself to."

As Mark also admits, the influence was reciprocal. Each set the goal of going up in size each winter. Jamie elaborates on this dynamic:

> It was kind of like a little bit jealousy too, when you're younger, like: "Hey! I surfed 6 feet at Sunset today!" "Oh, OK, cool." And then I would want to go and surf it the next day because he told me he surfed it. We pushed each other. We vibed off each other between jealousy and encourage-ment. And you know, just being kids and the competitiveness . . . all those factors combining, and where I live is one of the meccas for big waves. I grew up watching it. I grew up around it. I'm very much in the thick of the whole culture out here. It was something I really liked doing, and I'm still not burned out on it. I'm still very much stoked to wake up every day and go surfing.

Mark agrees that jealousy was a part of the dynamic between them:

> [I was] good friends with Jamie since we were babies. And you know, we were best friends and hung out all the time, surfed together all the time but we're also still super competitive too. If one guy does something, the other guy has to do it, or try to do it better or bigger, so that plays a huge role, I think.
>
> If we were on our own we might not have pushed . . . we definitely would have not pushed as hard, I don't think. And because there was none of our friends who wanted to do what we wanted to do. Yeah, like we would have been off alone trying to figure it out (laughing).

But the partnership surfers develop in big wave surfing is more than just a desire to impress one another and dare each other to go further. It's also tied to the trust of knowing your friends' abilities to potentially save you, and to know how to help you select the right wave. And it's linked to fighting to carve out a space among those who are already established. It entails not only meaningful interactions, successful encounters, and the reinterpretation of failures—wipeouts into successes—but also effective self-talk.

Leveling Up and Pushing Against

Risk and creative action are two inherently connected concepts that are essential for human evolution. Creative work is both fundamentally deviant[1] and governed by uncertainty.[2] The American pragmatists developed some of the most comprehensive theories of creativity, arguing that breaches in habitual patterns of action can lead to the creation of new ideas and new modes of action.[3] As creativity is based on uncertainty of outcomes and on novel and useful combinations of ideas, it's also essentially based on taking risks. Creative action demands courage, daring, and building on previous knowledge while departing from experience when facing novel contexts. Besides psychological and physiological traits and timing, it requires participating in certain situations and being deeply embedded in certain kinds of relationships and networks.

In his research on audaciously creative groups in science, art, and politics, sociologist Michael Farrell asserts that under conditions of unusually high trust and idealization, members can sustain one another emotionally, cognitively, and materially for long periods of their careers, and in some cases produce outstandingly creative work. Farrell finds that the

in general.[9] All of a sudden big wave surfing became hip and approachable, provided you could afford a jet ski and find a partner. And surfing big waves in general became much safer than it had ever been. The elite, underground sport of big wave surfing was now seemingly open to those without the decades of experience and training that had previously been necessary. Plus, it made surfing lineups like Jaws crowded as tow teams clashed—sometimes literally crashing into one another.

But this new discipline also inspired surfers to paddle into larger and larger waves, and provided an opportunity to paddlers to transition to tow-in, some of whom eventually went back to paddling. Tow-in revitalized and popularized big wave surfing. But it planted seeds of animosity between those who practiced it and the purists who preferred paddling into waves rather than motoring into them.

While Jaws had been paddled at least since 2007 (especially through the concerted effort of three Brazilian surfers nicknamed "Mad Dogs"), it hadn't been ridden close to its full potential until the two large swells of early 2011. For close to twenty years, tow-in surfers argued that paddling it was an impossible mission. And if there were a handful of paddle surfers along with the tow surfers on those bigger days, they weren't given the opportunity to try riding any of the larger waves. As big wave surfer Shane Dorian tells me: "There was always at least fifteen jet skis out there, always. And that winter there was a bunch of us that were like, 'Oh, you know what, we should actually try to paddle it this year.'"

In 2011, Shane was eager to try paddling Jaws. One year earlier he had suffered a near-death experience surfing Mavericks, and on his way back to Hawai'i he got the idea for a flotation device like the inflation vests on airplanes, one that would help surfers get to the surface quicker. Armed with a brand-new gun specifically shaped for that spot, and the new flotation device he had created with one of his sponsors, he flew to Maui to try to surf his first giant day at Jaws. He tells me that he was frustrated at having missed a big surf session at the same spot a few weeks earlier because he was on another trip. He remembers waking up very early and not knowing what to expect. What he thought was that there would be a window of only two hours when conditions would be glassy, after which the wind would pick up. His plan was to take it slowly and just sit in the channel and wait, watching waves.

He sits on the jet ski, puts his fins and leash on, and waxes his board. He starts getting the feeling that he's going to get nauseous or tired on the jet ski as it's rocking. He gets off the jet ski merely to get off, and as the wind is offshore, he ends up drifting out, getting closer and closer to the waves, toward the lineup. A big set approaches and he starts paddling toward the shoulder to get away from the waves. There are boats there, and about fifteen jet skis, and he hears people starting to whistle for a big set because they know he's not on a jet ski and they seem to think he's in danger. They're whistling: "Hey! There's a big set!" So Shane starts paddling out, to get out far enough so that he's not going to get caught inside. The first wave is big, and there's no way he can catch it because he's too far out already. He goes over it. The next is much bigger. He sees a tow team driving to catch it, but the surfer being towed hasn't let go of the rope he's being pulled with. Shane tells me:

> As soon as they saw me, they instantly were like: "Oh, there's a paddler! There's a guy paddling!" And they looked right at me and said: "Go! Go! Go!" And they pulled off. They didn't ask me if I was going to go, or any-thing. They just: "Go! Go! Go!" and they pulled right off, and so (pauses) I was like: "Shit," you know? I sort of have to try if they didn't go on that wave. And I realized I sort of—it looked like I was in the right place, but I never caught a wave at Jaws before. So I just turned around and started paddling. Next thing I know I look around and was like: "Well, I think I might be able to catch this thing." Next thing I know my board just started picking up speed and it was just surreal, man. I had surfed a lot of big waves at that point but nothing like . . . Jaws is just a different kind of place. It's its own animal. I just remember looking down . . . looking at my board, looking at my hands, just tripping on—it's like going down a mountain, it really was. It was an insane ride, and it has this really just steep, fast drop and my board felt perfect. Immediately I just felt confi-dent and I put on this bottom turn. I tried to wash off my speed and I got a really good pocket ride, like kind of in the barrel but not deep. I made it cleanly, and I could not believe it, I felt like electrified . . . this energy through my body. I was so excited, it was just like . . . I had this moment, this moment like everything had changed, just right there in the last seven seconds, for me. Not like for big wave surfing, nothing like that, but for me I knew: "Okay, this is it. Now I know what my focus is going to be. From now on this is it, for me."

Recalling his decision to paddle into that wave, which would lead to him winning "The Biggest Paddle of the Year" award in 2011 and increase his devotion to paddling into big waves and surfing Jaws, Shane says:

I kind of felt obliged, a little bit, like I don't want to waste the wave that they gave me. The wave was good, and I knew right away when I saw it, this is the one. It was a really good wave. I just kind of felt I was in the right spot, and that was what I was there to do. I had everything, I was ready—I had the energy and I had the board. It was early in the morning and everything was right. I felt like: "Hey, this is the time. I guess this is it."

After the ride, members of the tow team asked him about his wave. Shane replied that it had been the best wave of his life up to that point. They were happy for him. Many of his friends also paddled into giant waves that day, albeit all smaller than Shane's. And while on the big day Shane had missed weeks earlier there weren't any tow teams alongside the paddlers, on the second day there were many of them in the lineup. After Shane's wave all the tow teams just sat outside watching paddlers surf, "giving them respect." That session changed the dynamic between the two types of surfers, while also igniting others' interest in paddling Jaws and other spots. As Shane clarifies: "On some of the waves we were eating shit. And we were blowing a lot of waves: pulling back . . . wasting a lot of waves. But we did catch a few that were really big and rode them pretty good. So yeah, it definitely felt good to be able to ride it successfully, and not 12- to 15-feet Jaws, but the real deal: all the waves that guys were towing into." From that session on, a new norm was informally established: if even one paddler is out surfing at a big wave break, then tow-in crews must stay away. Underlying the importance of that session in relation to the dynamics between paddlers and tow surfers, Shane says: "That one day changed it. For sure."

Over the Ledge

I ask Jamie Sterling to describe Waimea as a wave.

Waves are like people. Certain waves are inviting, like some people are welcoming—come to my house; other waves are like jerks, you know? Assholes (laughing). Every wave has a different characteristic. Waimea is sort of like: here I am and here I am not, kind of aloof. You got to wait, let it come to you and sit in the impact zone, sort of. It shows you I'm coming, but you can't be too excited to go see it. You have to kind of let it come to you.

Surfing Waimea requires surfers to sit in position waiting for the wave to come to them, with only the possibility of being caught up by it at last. A veteran tells me about how many "dirty lickins" he got at Waimea throughout his life, how much he got his ass kicked by holding his position trying to catch a "bomb." Some, like Chris Owens, say that one of the hardest parts about surfing it is "forcing yourself" to sit in the right spot, while others may be panicking and paddling offshore.

But surfing big waves is also about taking chances. What usually happens is that some people get scared when they see a big set approaching. They start paddling for the horizon to avoid even the possibility of getting caught inside. And sometimes running is the smart decision to make. Other times it's borderline: you can run, or you sit. And usually the most timid people in the lineup, the most scared, the most inexperienced, are the first to run. Conversely, the most experienced are usually the last to run—or they're the first to run when there's a clear threat. Experience also plays a part in knowing whether you're sitting in the right spot or not; when they see a big set of waves approaching, experienced surfers may know that they're already positioned far enough out, and there's no need to go further out. It's about triangulating your position, and at Waimea, some estimate that two-thirds of the people just look at the ones who are triangulating and decide on the basis of where those surfers are.

What many do, especially at the beginning of their journey, is shadow more experienced surfers to soak up their knowledge. Young Ken Bradshaw, for instance, remembers how the older James Jones at one point asked him to introduce himself because Ken kept following him.

Pushing Against: Keala Kennelly

Wonderfully shaped overhead waves start rolling through at Rocky Point on the North Shore. If the wind drops, as it's supposed to in a little over an hour, the spot will turn into a skateboard park made up of perfect watery transitions. With her peroxide-bleached-blonde spiky hair, Keala could be taken for a '90s raver, but she's more like the roaring panther pictured on her tank top captioned "High on Rebellion."

A forty-five-year-old professional big wave surfer asks forty-one-year-old Keala: "How does it feel to be getting older as a woman? Because as a guy it fucking sucks."

"I was already considered old in my twenties," Keala quickly replies in an ironic and sturdy tone, as if to imply "you have no idea."

Keala: Just as edgy in the water as DJing in a club. Here she is wearing compression sleeves to protect her knee ligaments in the surf.

The two chat and laugh for about half an hour before the male surfer decides to be the first to jump in. What she meant, she later tells me, is that the industry tries to get rid of you, age you, cycle you out, much earlier than men. "They want the younger ones to take your place faster because they are cuter and more fuckable" ("sorry to be blunt," she apologizes). While for the guys it's like: "You're cool, bro, just hang on a little longer" until they get "a little crustier." But that's only part of the story; Keala has faced many more obstacles throughout her career as a female surfer.

Keala is one of the most accomplished women in this specialty. In 2016 she won the "best barrel" award in a category that included both genders for a wave she was towed-in to at Teahupo'o in Tahiti. In the local language this spot's name means broken skulls, and in 2011 she hit the reef here so hard after a wipeout that she suffered gruesome cuts on the right side of her face, earning her thirty stitches, plus another ten on her skull, and PTSD besides. In 2018, after the Jaws competition on Maui, she was crowned big wave world champion.

Recalling a key moment in her life, Keala tells me of a dream she had when she was six years old. She kept being told that doing sports was for boys, even though she was already excelling at surfing, so her mother tried to comfort her by saying that women could have babies. That didn't do it. "Being a woman is so shitty," she thought. In the dream she contemplates suicide, hoping that she can come back as a man. But with a little more thinking, she decides it isn't worth the gamble: "What if there's no heaven? What if I actually don't come back?"

Keala's story stands as both an example and a refutation of the discrimination and struggles women still face, in this sport and in society at large. It represents another way surfers can find the motivation to excel: drawing energy from facing their opponents and defying their expectations. But the place and the people among whom she grew up also provided her with an opportunity to hone skills she might otherwise never have acquired, or at least not to the same extent. Closely interacting from an early age with some of the best surfers in the world in Kaua'i, an island renowned for powerful waves, may have hurt (as she says), but it certainly helped her, too.

I wanted to do all the stuff that guys were doing and everybody kept telling me I couldn't. And I was like: well, first of all, yes I can because I already am (laughing) . . . but for all this stuff that I haven't done that you tell me I can't do, we'll see about that.

Some say there still aren't many women surfing big waves because of the lack of monetary and social incentives, but their number is growing, and it will continue to swell. Before Keala and her peers' generation, women also lacked female role models to emulate. A surfer's wife tells me: "They didn't grow up with idols they could envision themselves becoming. They didn't have heroes of their generation," because surfing, and big waves in particular, is a male-dominated sport. In contrast, think of Keala's male contemporaries.

Various characters like Trevor Carlson and his friend Matt Rode, for instance, tell me how pivotal it was to grow up watching and idolizing Mark Healey, while also recognizing their similarities to him. During his early development Trevor thought:

> What's the difference between him and me? He's driven. I'm driven. He's in shape. I'm in shape. He's a good surfer. I'm a good surfer. What is there that he can do that I can't do?

Similarly, Matt explains how he decided to get into big waves around 2010, when paddling was beginning to supplant tow-in but the sport wasn't as performance oriented as it would become years later:

> At that time Healey was one of the best because he's crazy, and I was like: he's a good surfer, better surfer than me, but what he's doing, he's just going straight down a wave and I'm like: "Why do you need to be that good of a surfer? I'm not as good as him, but I think I can surf big waves," and one of my friends told me he can hold his breath for five minutes. So I went home that night and I held my breath for five minutes, and I was like: "OK, I'm gonna start surfing big waves." Like bigger . . . I was already surfing big slabs, but I meant like big, big waves.

On the economic side, there aren't as many sponsorship opportunities for women, and until recently there hadn't been as many competitions. The top women professionals sustain themselves by working one or two other jobs, whereas the top men are paid full-time and can therefore focus exclusively on their training and surfing. Keala, for example, DJs and bartends, while Bianca Valenti works at her family's restaurant. Even at the top level, women in big wave surfing have to hustle.

Together with three other female surfers, Keala formed the Committee for Equity in Women's Surfing, and the group achieved, among other goals, getting women the same prize money as the men, which drew international coverage to their cause. But it also generated antagonism from a number of male big wave surfers who thought the women weren't good enough to be paid as much as the men.

Cruel Influence and Style

As Peter Westwick and Peter Neushul write, the revival of surfing in the 1900s took place in the context of American Victorian values, not Hawaiian culture. This means that "cultural expectations confined women to the sidelines for many sports and when they did enter the game [referring to surfing and swimming] current fashions constrained them further."[10] Between the 1960s and the 1990s there weren't many competitions for women surfing regular waves, and only a few of those were held at bigger wave spots like Sunset Beach on the North Shore of Oʻahu. Most competitions women entered were men's competitions, whereas in pre-contact Hawaiʻi all competitions were mixed. As Keala and other women tell me, men consider surfing their territory, and sometimes even feel threatened if a woman is performing well. But in ancient Hawaiʻi men and women of all ages and classes surfed, and legends tell of women's prowess in the surf. According to archeologist Ian Masterson,[11] women were considered better surfers than men, and the practice of this activity offered them an opportunity to overturn (at least in the water) the male hegemonies present in Hawaiian society. Thomas Thrum[12] writes that in traditional surfing competitions, "the gentler sex carried off the highest honors." And for Masterson, surfing's archetypical style in this era found embodiment in women's gracefulness: "The goal then was to surf as gracefully as a woman, like an albatross soaring across the face of a wave." Indeed, women defined the Hawaiian style of surfing.

Historian Douglas Booth[13] describes how the Hawaiian style was based on flowing seamlessly with a wave in a dance. And in ancient and early modern contests women fared particularly well, as the judging criteria were based on "timing, balance and poise" rather than strength. In the 1960s this way of surfing was supplanted by the Californian style, which involved enhancing the beauty of a wave through turns. The next style to take hold and define the criteria for regular competitions was that of the Australians and South Africans, who adopted a more aggressive style that encouraged attacking waves from all angles to shred them to pieces. This translated into favoring men's comparative strength. An "aggro" style. Even more interestingly, Booth notes, these three different styles represented "distinct philosophies based on beliefs about mankind's relationship with nature." Is it men in nature? Or men over nature? Is surfing about dancing *with* the waves, *on* the waves, or against them? And is surfing mostly for men?

When Keala started to compete on the Women's Championship Tour for regular waves, the event was run jointly with the guys' tour and men made the women feel like they were lucky simply to be there. And typically, as competitions unfolded throughout the day, women would be asked to surf during the worst conditions—for example, when it was too windy, or waves too small, or both. And as the conditions improved, event organizers would switch to the guys.

Growing up in Kaua'i, Keala remembers going surfing with her friends, who happened to become some of the very best surfers in the world. One of them recently reminded Keala of when the group used to surf a very shallow reef break wave called Heroins and they would tell her to take off on waves she had no chance of making—"just for entertainment." "And paddling back out to the lineup Keala would ask him: 'Are you really trying to hurt me? Do you really want me to get badly hurt?'" "Those fuckers," she says, then tells me that she forgives them now, in part because she recognizes that surfing "with all those talented boys back in Kaua'i" played a significant role in getting her into bigger and more powerful waves early on.

Referring to surfers she grew up with, Keala tells me: "They make a sport out of putting each other down,"[14] by which she means that the cruelty she describes was not reserved only for her. A friend of mine, who is not surprised by Keala's description and who knows surfers from that generation in Kaua'i, dismisses my surprise and my initial interpretation of the dynamic as a gender issue, stating that "it's cavemen mentality. It's about human frailty: focusing on differences. It's broader. It's a human issue."

Early Female Confidence in Big Surf: Practicing in Adverse Conditions

In spring 2019, sixty-three-year-old Lynne asks me: "Can you imagine if I got to practice out there like the guys did? I probably would have done even better." Lynne Boyer was twice women's world champion, in 1978 and 1979. Along with other women like Margo Oberg, she belonged to the first generation of professional surfers.

Back in the 1970s there were only a few women surfing the North Shore, and even fewer who could surf large waves. Recalling this period in surfing history, Lynne tells me: "We were considered 'less than,' and I gave in to men's dominance. I didn't have the confidence because I was a woman. At the time there were hardly any women that could surf." The surfers she looked up to were guys.

Thinking of one of her best performances, during a contest at Sunset Beach with waves around ten to twelve feet Hawaiian, she tells me that her only competition was her rival, Margo Oberg, because all the other women were sitting in the channel afraid to try.

Practicing for competitions, though, was hard. If she would try to surf prime spots like Sunset, Laniākea, or Pipeline, guys would regularly overpower her to get to the right wave position. She could be out in the water for hours and only catch a handful of waves, most of them no good at all. It was very frustrating, she admits.

What helped her improve her skills was paddling out at secondary spots like Chuns or Hale'iwa during stormy days. In these conditions she could catch waves without any competition, as only a handful of others would be out in the water. A positive side effect of this strategy is that she got accustomed to big surf.

She never surfed Waimea—partly because she was scared of it, and partly because there were no other women surfing it at the time—but one of her worst wipeouts was in 1974 at Mākaha. She may have been fourteen or fifteen, and she wanted to catch the biggest wave any girl had caught. All of a sudden Lynne noticed the horizon going black, so she started to paddle offshore, but she was caught inside by a larger set of three waves. There weren't any lifeguards then, and no leashes. After diving under the last wave of the set, she saw her small board floating in the channel. She swam to it and paddled back to shore swearing she'd never surf big waves again. But that changed when she started performing and winning at Sunset.

You Don't Belong Out Here

During kids' competitions, which at the time were mixed, Keala sometimes beat male surfers who would go on to become champions. Some of them didn't take it very well, and wouldn't speak to her for a month. Other guys she won more consistently against took it more seriously. One of them quit surfing for a while because of it. But he wasn't the only one calling her "bitch" or "transvestite," or asking, "If you want to be a boy so much, why don't you go grow a dick?"

When as a teenager she started surfing Pipeline on the North Shore of O'ahu, she felt like she didn't belong out there. Guys would harass her in the water and tell her to paddle back in, just as had happened decades earlier to other female surfers. Keala tells me of the many beatings she took when she'd fall from waves because someone would suddenly drop in in front of her expecting she'd either pull out or wouldn't make the wave. And talking about Pipeline, she says: "I'd get my ass kicked and paddle back out and have to do it again, and again, and again, and again before they finally started giving me the respect. So, it took a long time." "Surfing," she adds, "is a very homophobic sport."

Growing up, she also faced another form of discrimination. As a white kid with blonde hair and fair skin, she was picked on mercilessly by boys her age at her school who wanted to fight her. Plus, "in surfing," she says, "as a woman you're constantly treated as a second-class citizen."

Regarding big wave surfing, she says: "It is super manly to be able to catch a really big wave. It's very respected. A man can beat his chest like Tarzan, 'Arggg!' but then if a little girl my size—I'm like half the size of most of these guys—if I can go out and ride the same size of waves or maybe even bigger than that guy . . . it's almost emasculating to them."

Reflecting on her painful experiences, she says: "And I just took all that pain and then later when I was out charging big waves, I'd use it." Surfing thus became an outlet for her suffering. Looking back on the "name-calling," she tells me that she couldn't get emotional about it and instead had to just bury it. "'Cuz you can't cry in front of a boy. If you do, you're screwed, you're a cry baby. You have to hold it in even though you want to cry. *Sssss* (as if inhaling air to hold your breath), suck it up, push it down."

Carrying Women on Your Shoulders

When she began pioneering surfing big waves in places like Tahiti, Keala again felt like she didn't belong. And she also felt pressure that she had to prove herself, to perform; but at this stage of her career, the pressure was larger than herself. As a woman, she couldn't have a bad day, like everyone has, without having guys blame it on her gender instead. In a time when there were only a handful of other women surfing big waves, she felt that if she didn't do well, it would reflect poorly on all women. But this pressure also translated into making her really nervous, and thus more likely to make mistakes. She says:

> They were always looking for you to fall so they could have a reason to tell you you didn't belong out there. So, I always felt like people were waiting for me to fail, just hoping that they could see me crash and burn,

which motivated me to perform, but also made me very nervous. It felt
like you had a lot of eyes on you. Feeling like every time I go surf I have to
do incredibly well, otherwise they'll blame it on my gender.

The Barrel at Teahupo'o in 2016 and Women's Contests

Unlike the top guys, Keala didn't have enough money to afford water
safety and a jet ski for towing. So at Teahupo'o she sits in the water all
geared up on the channel for about four hours waiting for the boys to
get tired, to see if she can borrow a driver. During this time her body gets
stiff, while her energy rides an emotional rollercoaster—from getting
amped up to charge, to getting scared because of the horrible wipeouts
she's seeing, and then to talking herself again into pulling her stunt.
Later, during her acceptance award for best barrel overall, she says: "Who
I really want to thank is everyone in my life that told me: 'You can't do
that because you're a woman,' because that drove me to dedicate my life
to proving you wrong. And it's been so damn fun."

She explains to me why women want their competition to run on the
same day as the guys: it's too expensive to run them separately. Permits
are hard to obtain and are usually given for a specific period—within
which organizers hope waves of an appropriate size will materialize—so
the two groups compete against each other when their waiting periods
overlap. Since waiting periods are scheduled in accordance with seasonal
swells related to each spot, this conflict often arises.

Keala mentions two events in which organizers were trying to have
women compete in the part of the day when the waves would be smaller,
but the conditions turned out to be the biggest and most challenging.

> The event in Jaws, they were trying to send us out first because it was
> going to get bigger all day, and it ended up pulsing right then. And the
> women's final, it was probably one of the gnarliest conditions of all
> time . . . they were trying to do the opposite, and they gave us the worse
> conditions.
>
> In Puerto Escondido the same thing happened . . . the swell peaked
> during the women's final. . . . If you're gonna have it on the same day,
> anybody can get the gnarliest conditions.

It's likely that her barrel of the year award at Tahiti—on one of the
largest waves ever ridden there—brought more women into surfing by

inspiring them, but it also provided the rationale for including women in the Jaws competition.

The 2018 Jaws Contest

Keala assures me that if they hadn't called the contest on, she wouldn't have gone out, because it looked suicidal. Waves were sixty feet and the wind was howling, making it very difficult to get into them early enough to successfully complete a ride. During the final, as it got bigger, there were many cleanup sets—larger waves breaking far off from where surfers were sitting waiting for them. Those waves caught female competitors by surprise, overwhelming them. A number of guys wanted to call off the competition, thinking it was too dangerous. She tells me, laughing, that she knew that 99 percent of those waves weren't rideable, and decided to go for the 1 percent. Because it was the first competition in which women and men were going to win equal prize amounts, she says that if she hadn't performed by taking exceptional risks, "the guys would have just roasted us," writing them off. "I felt the responsibility to go out and charge really hard just to show them that we deserve it." Her strategy implied sitting in the same spot the guys would have, which means "deeper"—closer to the curl of the wave and thus in a more critical position—rather than on the "shoulder."

Leaving her heart on the floor, Keala didn't complete any ride. All of them resulted in wipeouts, and she almost drowned. She had to be revived on the lifeguard boat. After the women's final, it was the men's competition. Keala says: "I felt pretty bad after my heat because we got pretty smoked. We got destroyed." But then the guys who got out and surfed also started cartwheeling. One of them, back on the boat after a wipeout, was coughing up blood. Most of the guys didn't successfully complete any ride during the event either. Then the organizers called the contest off because conditions were too dangerous.

Because of the increasing number of women surfing big waves and their improved performance, Keala no longer feels as much pressure as she used to. She says:

> I can actually go and have a bad day and it doesn't reflect horribly on every woman, because I'll go out and have a bad day, but Paige will have a good day. Maybe I have a bad day, but Andrea or Bianca or somebody else will be there. I don't have to carry all the weight, which is nice. I

don't like to have bad days, but if I do it's not like: "Oh my god, I failed all women today."

Inner Speech and Self-Talk

What we say out loud to others constitutes only a minute fraction of the conversations we have each day. Most of our talk is internalized and directed toward ourselves, in what scholars refer to as inner speech. In rare cases, we speak to ourselves out loud (self-talk). This kind of language is important for many reasons, including sense-making, controlling attention, and decision-making. Talking to ourselves matters for cognition, focus, and motivation toward action. By listening to the thoughts inside our heads, and recollecting feelings and interactions we have had or anticipate having in the future, we try to make sense of who we are, what's happening in the world, and which course of action we should take. The voices in our heads can represent different parts of ourselves, or other individuals. But they can also reflect aspects of the environment: for instance, sounds, images, smells, or specific feelings we may recollect. Often they represent different points of view on the same scene, like different photographic frames do. By talking to ourselves we construct and partake in mental simulations that help us gauge the consequences of different courses of action. We retrieve data from our consciousness, integrate them into story lines, and then edit them in different cuts. Basically, we construct narratives with alternate endings.

Sociologist Norbert Wiley compares inner speech to dreams, both of which take place deep in our consciousness and are hard to observe, study, and explain. Yet, as he writes: "dreams happen *to* us, whereas inner speech is an active process, often quite deliberately used *by* us and aimed at important goals."[15] Inner speech can be conceptualized as a directed dream state in the sense that it is partially willed, imaginary, open to discovery—that is, not fully predictable and controllable—and challenging to recollect. Another difference is that dreams take place regularly when we sleep and are confined to relatively short periods, while we talk to ourselves throughout most of our waking hours. Indeed, the moments when we just act without deliberation are rare. When facing a particularly demanding task, we may become more aware of this linguistic capacity, and may actually try to employ it to a greater extent to identify solutions and augment the concentration required to devise them and carry them out.

Along similar lines, psychologist Charles Fernyhough argues that the thinking related to inner speech is both conscious and active, and that as philosophers have argued for centuries, there is an intimate relationship between language and thinking. Often we think in words. And as he writes, "Thoughts are typically coherent: they fit into chains of ideas which, in no matter how haphazard a fashion, are connected to what has come before."[16] Yet one characteristic of inner speech is its abbreviated nature, which makes it a coded language—meant for ourselves rather than directed toward an interlocutor—whose full meaning is not always completely clear even to us.

As Wiley[17] remarks, there are two key characteristics of inner speech: its dialogical style (welcoming questions) and its conversational style ("the self speaking to another aspect of itself" about what to do). As Fernyhough puts it: "When you talk to yourself, you step out of yourself for a moment and get some perspective on what you are doing."[18] Similarly, philosopher Charles Sanders Peirce conceptualizes thinking as an inner dialogue between different parts of the self: the "I" acting in the present and the "you" that is the future self. In Peirce's theory the "me" is the past self. Collins writes that "Peirce casts the 'you' as interlocutor because he conceives of the internal dialogue as addressing oneself as 'you.'"[19]

In George Herbert Mead's theory the mind is constituted by three interacting parts where the "I" is spontaneous action and the origin of creativity, the "me" is a self-image derived from the attitudes of others toward us that responds to conformity,[20] and the "Generalized Other" represents a reference point comprising an abstract audience.

By combining elements from Peirce's and Mead's theories, Wiley suggests that we need a tripartite model composed by the I-you-me: "I-present-sign, you-future-interpretant, and me-past-object."[21] In his words: "Humans consist of present, future, and past. . . . They are . . . three-legged, with one leg in the present, a second in the future, and a third in the past."[22] The ability to blend different temporal frames by conversing with different aspects of the self underlines the difficulties humans have in understanding time.

For Peirce, as noted by Wiley, "inner speech is a means of choice and self-control."[23] More specifically, Wiley says that according to Peirce we can regulate ourselves "by analyzing our personal problems, particularly bad habits, in our minds and using inner speech to map out and practice solutions."[24] Margaret Archer[25] writes that "The key feature of reflexive inner dialogue is silently to pose questions to ourselves and to answer them, to speculate about ourselves, any aspect of our environment and, above all, about the relationship between them."

Collins,[26] on the other hand, conceptualizes inner dialogue as a form of ritual in which we imagine having an energizing interaction, sometimes with different parts of ourselves, but mainly with other people. When successful these interaction rituals inside the mind increase solidarity with our fellows—rather than among different parts of the self, as Wiley puts it—and result in self-drive, *emotional energy*. These rituals are energizing because one is so closely embedded in the community within which he or she works to anticipate which ideas will be successful, and by extension can foresee his/her validation by others. As Collins puts it: "If the process is often accompanied by a feeling of exultation, it is because these are not merely any ideas but *ideas that feel successful*."[27] To put this another way, besides its functions in relation to cognition—reflecting on and sometimes devising different courses of action—one of the purposes of inner speech and self-talk is to motivate yourself to pay attention and urge yourself to act while trying to predict the best course of action in relation to your community.

To summarize, we have at least four main and interconnected functions of inner speech. First: it can be used to conceptualize, play out, and evaluate different courses of action. This is a form of anticipatory thinking also employed to guide practical action related, for example, to athletes' bodily movements.[28] Second: we can use it to reflect on whether "bad habits," as Peirce would say, are forcing us into the same sort of mistakes we have made in the past, or we can break away from them and strike out toward something new. Third: it can help us to develop and maintain concentration. And fourth: it can have the ritualistic function of building internal solidarity, solidarity among group members, and confidence. By all these means, inner speech, as well as self-talk, can help us generate the emotional energy we especially need when embarking on a creative course of action that departs from how we behaved earlier.

In this last section I will discuss different kinds of inner speech, and also self-talk, that surfers engage in at key moments within *fateful situations*. The section is organized in a sequence, from when surfers are on the beach thinking about paddling out, to when they're sitting on their boards waiting for the right wave, to when they reflect on their experience after having wiped out. My aim is to show how the functions of this type of dialogue listed above are at play in both risk-taking and interactional ritual theory.

On the Beach and in the Lineup

In the story I presented in chapter 2, Kawika was talking aloud to himself to find the motivation for paddling out, as well as trying to provoke a response from his friends who were too focused to reply. And while he didn't fully hear and comprehend Kawika's words, Phil understood that if the wait for the right moment to paddle out lasted much longer, he might "lose his crew." Kawika's talk was both self-motivational and evaluative—he was testing whether or not it was a good idea to paddle out—much like my own nonverbal interaction on the day before, when I first went out at the Bay.

> When I was doing the self-talk, you know what I was saying? And I know it's going to sound weird. I was telling myself: "This is your destiny. This is your identity. This is where you're supposed to be. This is meant to be." I had to tell myself that. I went through a big transition out there. Huge. I went from light-headed, almost ready to throw up, wanting the jet skis to take me in immediately, to actually being able to breathe, looking around, thinking maybe I'll catch a wave (laughing nervously).

This overt self-talk is meant both to be heard by those around him, to stimulate a reaction, and to get Kawika into a rhythm, to calm himself and gather strength. That's why he's repeating the same phrase twice, and adding only a slight modification on the third repetition. It's a mantra which, as he told me, he uttered several more times during the action. This strategy ultimately works in helping him to paddle out, and once he's in the lineup, to take a wave. Collins writes of this motivational function of self-talk that "it tends to be repetitive, using the same formulas over and over again; the intonation itself is a kind of incantation, a rhythmic entrainment in one's own words, which operates to focus one's attention, to 'pull oneself together.'"[29]

Out in the Lineup

The older, better, and more successful surfers become, the fewer waves they tend to take during a year, or even within a specific session. Among other things, this strategy means that surfers often wait for long periods out at sea for the right wave, as well as for a long time for the right kind of swell, which may or may not materialize. Trevor Carlson told me of a conversation he was having with himself in the lineup at Jaws on Maui. After hours waiting outside from most other surfers for the right wave, which hadn't come yet, he started to feel bored and restless. Boredom drains energy, scatters one's focus as one feels more and more disengaged, and it can lead to agitation. At one point he said to himself: "Look around yourself. Where are you right now? Like stop being jaded by the fact that you're just sitting here for two hours. Remember, you're at Jaws, surfing Jaws. This is a big deal (ending in a high intonation for emphasis)! Don't let yourself get complacent."

In this example Trevor takes an external position to try to help a different part of himself understand and appreciate the situation he's in, and thus make the most out of it and "stay with it." By telling himself that this is a "big deal," he's looking back at all the hard work it took him over several years to get there, as if his past self (the "me") could wonder at and appreciate how far he has progressed (the "I" as present self). But we can argue that he is also (perhaps to a lesser extent) trying to see his current position with his future self ("you") in mind, perhaps painstakingly waiting for another rare Jaws swell. Don't take this situation for granted, he is saying, because it may or may not repeat itself, and even if it does, you'll probably have to wait a long time for it.

Underlying the importance and ubiquity of self-talk in his sport, Trevor says:

> The best big wave surfers are the best at tricking yourself. The best big wave surfers are the ones who have these complicated, inside-your-head conversations, that you're able to talk yourself into going over the ledge.

Among his peers, Mark Healey is well known for talking to himself, both silently and out loud. He tells me that "There's a lot of one-man motivational talk speeches out there." When I ask him to expand on this topic, he says:

> I'll start cussing myself out, yelling at myself, being off by myself. Usually it's like: "OK, you've been thinking about it. You said you wanted to do it. (This is me talking with my mind). You said you wanted it. It's fucking here. What are you going to do? Are you going to do it or are you just gonna talk about it and you gonna spend the next six months waiting for another opportunity and regretting every fucking decision you made right now?" I'll just keep doing that: "Are you gonna do it? Are you gonna do it? Are you serious about this? Because if you're not, you just shouldn't even be out" (laughing).

In this illustration, which is clearly dialogical, Mark is having an internal conversation with different parts of himself: his present self is talking to his past self to help him realize the situation he's in and how he got there. More clearly than in the previous illustration, his present self is forecasting how his future self will feel if in this moment he doesn't capitalize on the opportunity he's given.

Then, explaining to me his risk-reward assessments and the inherent uncertainty and motivation related to this activity, he says:

> It's such a strange line between calculation and stupidity (laughing out loud), because all the best waves, everything your body is telling you is "no," usually. "No, no, no!" and you just override that, and you go, and it works. And then it just kind of messes with your head, because you're like: "That was probably a good decision not going, but was it?" You never know unless you try. Period. There's no way around that. That's why not a lot of people are into it. You're always at the edge of the abyss.

Trevor explains his reasoning when, the night before the Jaws competition in 2018, one of the organizers unexpectedly called him to check on whether he wanted to participate in the event. He remembers thinking, as he was agreeing: "OK. I need to do something special. I need to like prove that I earned my spot. They're giving me an opportunity everybody in the world wants." The next day, while he's out in the lineup during the first heat of the contest, Trevor remembers telling himself:

> If a wave comes that looks approachable, I'm going no matter what. I'm just going. I kind of told myself: I'm going in this direction (pointing toward the shore) whether I go over the falls, whether I wipe out . . . go . . . I'm now putting my head down, turning, and I'm going in this direction no matter what. And this big set came which is the biggest set I saw the whole heat, biggest wave I've seen in a very long time. At first I was like running for my life because I thought we were going to get caught inside, and then like five strokes into running for my life I realized I'm kind of in the bowl like . . . I was like: (self-talk) "But this is kind of the moment like that you talk about, you dream about, like you wake up at nighttime and you're upset you didn't go, this is the moment that like—(this happens in like point two seconds). This is that moment that you are going to hate yourself for the rest of your life if you don't like try, *and I've done that before, and I'm not gonna do it again,* and here we go," and no matter what at this point I'm going to put my head down and give it like three to five

of the hardest strokes I can possibly give it, and then I'm going to put my head down and I'm going in this direction no matter what. And I fell, and that was my wipeout nomination. And that was a very large wave . . . and I landed on my side and my neck went like sideways, and my spine was curved like a solid two weeks. It was fucked up, I might have broken my neck. I had a chiropractor work on my neck a week later and then that night after that happened I was extremely sore, but then I got on a plane and flew to Mavericks and surfed Mavericks the next day.

And I comment: "Man, that's obsessive! (nervously laughing) Maybe that wasn't a smart move . . . was it?"

Maybe not, but these are the moments when you prove what you're made of. Do you want to get on Tour next year? OK, you don't make the contest, fucking surf Mavs the next day, that's how you get on Tour. Then you blow people's minds. When people see this: "How the fuck do you do this? This is unhealthy, you shouldn't even be doing this much."

Throwing yourself over the edge, as Trevor puts it—and as others have told me, using the same expression—requires as much courage and determination as jumping out of a plane. Once you jump, or you paddle for it, there's no rewinding. No turning back. No second chance. And if you second-guess yourself in action, your chances of success slip away like water sliding out of the palms of your hands. "You have to be totally committed," many say. Your decision must be definitive, and you must stick to it, maintaining composure, until you either make it or you're certain you didn't make it. In this instance Trevor is not only reflecting on how he got himself into this situation, but also trying to break a pattern of backing off from committing to take a very large wave, a big risk whose outcome is unknown. A mistake he has made before.

Before taking off on a wave, Keala tries to imagine how it would feel after she has successfully completed a good ride. Her "I" acting in the present is projecting toward her (possible) "you-future-interpretant" by recalling her past self (the "me"). Talking about Teahupo'o in Tahiti, and remembering her award-winning barrel wave, she tells me about how she tries to get into a peaceful state of mind by anticipating the rewards derived from the experience and recalling past experiences she's had:

Because I've had such amazing waves there, I just like try to remember those. "If you get a good one it's going to feel like this, and you know how it feels, and it feels so good. You're gonna come spitting out of the barrel and feel so stoked." And then when I go out, when you actually . . . somebody finally gives you a rope—after so many hours you've waited and you're really nervous and whatever, and you go out way out past the break—we're way in the ocean, and you're so far out away from all the boats and everything, and you look back and you see all the mountains, and it's so beautiful. And then I just get this overwhelming good feeling, like your heart expands because it's so beautiful. And I try to hold on to that when I go for the wave because I feel like if I can be in that space I just feel so much like love—like your heart is so expanding because everything is so beautiful around you. *If I can be in that kind of a pure place when I actually let go of the rope, I feel like I'm going to be all right.*

In this case, Keala calls to mind a feeling she has experienced in the past, and she tries to imagine herself deriving the same pleasures if she once again takes this risk, commits, and succeeds. She's looking back while projecting herself forward, justifying and finding motivation for the decision she's about to make—which in this instance proved to be extraordinarily rewarding for her and for her community.

After the Wave

As you will recall from chapter 4, after his major wipeout, Jamie had two competing voices arguing in his head: "Go in. Go back out." Ultimately, the second voice won the argument, and Jamie reasoned that since that wipeout had been exceptional and he survived it on his own, that was probably the worst that could have happened to him. Having faced the worst and won, there was little else he could fear, and so much he could gain by "getting back on the horse." Here Jamie displays the dialogic essence of inner speech: two voices advocating conflicting points of view, from which he's able to derive an informed decision.

Interaction Rituals among Peers, Mentors, Rivals, and Inside Your Head

As I have shown in this chapter, meaningful and potentially consequential interactions can take place between different kinds of individuals who are in different types of relationships. But they can also unfold in our minds as inner speech and self-talk. One type of interaction does not exclude the other. Indeed, if we partake of a physical interaction in

co-presence, we certainly also experience one in our minds, both simultaneously in the context and after we leave the encounter.

The function of these rituals is related to exchanging information,
but it's also reflected in the generation of solidarity among participants
and among different parts of the self,[30] and in the production of *emotional energy*. Each of us makes use of each of these everyday rituals, yet
we do so to different degrees, more or less consciously, and with varying
degrees of success. Each of them matters a great deal, and affects us differently at different points in our careers and our life course; yet their
importance is particularly salient during *fateful moments* that are highly
consequential in our own trajectories.

Not all kinds of inner speech, self-talk, and interactions have positive
consequences. Some kinds of self-talk or inner speech, for instance, are
characterized by obsessively finding fault in ourselves. These thoughts
generate depression and reduce self-confidence. Interaction with peers
and mentors can have the same negative effects. As with the filtering
process in collaborative circles, these kinds of peer and mentor interactions may, by providing too much positive interaction, produce the
kind of echo chamber that is a hallmark of groupthink,[31] and can ultimately lead to inappropriately risky behavior.

Chapter 6 moves on to address the commercialization and partial professionalization of this activity. It addresses how athletes modify their
approach to risk as they acquire status and age, accumulate injuries, and
mature, and as the sport progresses. It also analyzes how they are judged
and the strategies they use to make a livelihood from their passion.

CHAPTER SIX

From Adventure to Entertainment and toward Sport

Big wave surfing's frontline no longer relates only to size (how big the wave is), or positioning (how close to the curl a surfer is, typically before he starts riding it), but also to barreling, and doing turns as you would be riding a regular wave. In essence, performance in this subdiscipline now means tube riding, which is generally considered the climax of the surf experience as well as one of its most dangerous and transcendent aspects. The sport's evolution can be summarized as having gone "from surviving to performing," yet the underlying main variable remains risk. Put another way, performing means heightening the risk when it counts. But there are differences in approach to risk that depend on the career phase of an athlete, and his or her individuation; there is also a generational difference, and others related to the popularization, commercialization, and innovations of surfing. Many of those variations lie between taking calculated risks to grow the sport and the bravado (or foolishness) rooted in over-reliance on safety devices.

This chapter examines the professional and commercial aspects of the sport while also addressing reputation, status, risk-taking, and risk assessment. As surfers progress and establish themselves professionally, as they age and accumulate injuries, and as the sport and its technology evolve, how does the individual surfer's approach to risk change? Which challenges do they face? How does a big wave surfer acquire respect, accolades, and endorsements? How are big wave surfers judged, and by whom? More broadly, what does it take to make it in this occupation?

While Stephen Lyng's concept of *edgework* has proven useful to explain risk-taking that requires the acquisition and practice of skills in situations that could seriously injure or kill a participant, it hasn't been clear on two related aspects. First, how does risk-taking unfold interactionally?—a topic introduced in previous chapters. And second, how does it vary over the life course of an individual and the evolution of a field? This chapter and the next address these points.

Sociologist Howard Becker is renowned for his idea of *art worlds* as depending on collective action: the balancing of cooperation and conflict among different social actors that ultimately, if successful, leads to a production being disseminated and received. Regardless of how simple or complex an activity may appear—say, poetry versus opera—each art practice and each production depends on, and is affected by, a complex and interrelated set of relationships among different individuals carrying out different tasks while holding different interests. These individuals determine how a field is created (if it's new) and maintained, and occasionally can also govern the incorporation of innovations that modify it. Even though one probably shouldn't label big wave surfing an art, no one can deny that as a social world it depends on a fairly large and complex set of relationships. Besides the invention, production, distribution, and improvement of the various kinds of technologies (e.g., forecasting) and equipment (e.g., surfboards and safety devices), think of the planning and staging of an event and its related logistics: the making of an Eddie or the launching of a big wave surfing tour are no easy endeavors.

Previous chapters have focused on the surfers—and, to a lesser extent, on the lifeguards. This chapter brings into the conversation the judges who, like critics and juries in the art world, shape the reputations of the surfers. Along with the editors of surfing magazines and the sponsors of surfing events, the judges mediate between the surfers and the audience. As Gary Alan Fine defines it, a reputation is a "socially recognized persona." Whatever we might personally think of another individual, a reputation is broader—it is "a shared, established image" within a community, group, or field. Judges, magazine editors, and sponsorship entrepreneurs are *aestheticians* who evaluate performances. In a sense they are the gatekeepers who confer legitimacy on an aspiring big wave surfer. They determine who gets an invitation to various competitions, and who deserves to receive prize money and endorsements. Judgments regarding media visibility, sponsorship deals, invitations to competitions, and performance and placement within those competitions produce reputation, which can in turn translate into monetary rewards and prestige. Their evaluations affect a surfer's status among peers and various members of the audience of the field, ranging from expert connoisseurs to the general public.

Because the field of big wave surfing is relatively new—the first Eddie was organized in 1985, and since then it has only run nine times, and the Big Wave World Tour didn't even start until 2009—criteria for evaluating performances are still being fine-tuned. Additionally, technological advancements have led to innovations within the sport, necessitating changes in judging criteria, which in turn have driven innovations in the sport's practice—how waves are ridden. For instance, if judges reward high risk-taking versus more conservative, safer approaches (e.g., completing rides—see below), this can lead athletes to modify their approach, resulting in potentially more injuries but also greater chances of eventually changing the sport (see the Jaws competition I describe below, in which Keala and Billy win by wiping out). Furthermore, as in any lifestyle sport where subjective evaluations rather than rigorous standards of evaluation determine the outcome of competitions, judging is still mutable, and therefore a source of disagreement.

I begin by focusing on four main concepts: career, risk-taking approaches and assessment, reputation, and status.

In sociology the concept of career can be understood in two different ways: first, as an occupational path; and second (and less intuitively), as Everett Hughes defined it, as a moving perspective in someone's life. I use the first definition of the term in discussing two types of careers and reputations in this field: one that is subcultural and primarily related to the social world within which an individual performs, and one that is broader, entailing a celebrity-like status that reaches a broader audience. When I use the second understanding of career, I refer to the different ways risk-taking changes across the life course of an individual. In this context, I identify two approaches: charging (a folk term) and *sharpshooting*.

In an early career phase, a surfer needs to get noticed by peers and gatekeepers by showing a desire to access opportunities to perform, sometimes by funding his travel to competitions out of his own pocket, and then taking high risks that are often quite indiscriminate. Trevor Carlson represents one among many who have successfully taken this approach. Surfers in this career phase are typically younger and may be labeled *chargers*: someone who is willing to take great risks for the love of the sport, for the buzz derived from feel-good neurochemicals released by having novel and exciting experiences, and for recognition and acceptance within the community.

Should the surfer successfully move on to a second phase, then he'd be more selective about the risks he takes. I label these types of surfers *sharpshooters*[1] to designate someone who is consistent in his outstanding performances. At this point in his career, Shane Dorian is an archetype of the sharpshooter: surfers who fire their guns less often than chargers, are less likely to miss meaningful opportunities and targets, and try to fire only when they think it truly matters. Also, and as I will continue to discuss in chapter 7, they rely less on their strength, youthful enthusiasm, recklessness, and courage, and more on their experience. In this career stage, surfers have already built their reputations in their social world and don't need to continually prove their worth. Instead, they pursue fewer goals, and those they pursue are higher risk/higher reward. Also, their self-concept is more stable than that of the chargers, which leads surfers in this career phase to select risks that are less driven by external pressures, and more based on personal will.

In surfing, one's reputation depends on photography and records. The photographs and videos are the marketable commodities in the field, equivalent to the canvases of painters or the recordings of musicians. Digital and social media have changed the sport in multiple ways, one being that individuals who are not connected to the center of this social world can show their exploits and potentially also earn some sort of media visibility, although often that visibility is short-lived. The proliferation of media devices has also incentivized the establishment of awards of various kinds related to singular waves, which can temporarily advance an athlete's career and garner and maintain audience interest in the sport. Because the big wave surfing world requires many resources in order to function, there is an underlying incentive among those running the show to invest in and give more opportunities, visibility, and other advantages to those surfers they think will further the sport.

* * *

At forty-four years old, and after twenty-eight years of being paid to surf, Shane Dorian is one of the most respected surfers in the world—from regular surfing to riding big waves. According to my taxonomy, at this point in his career Shane classifies as a *sharpshooter*. Many, including his competitors, think he's the best in big surf, even though he seldom performs exceptionally well at competitions and has never won a world title. Indeed, he says he prefers not having external pressures, such as the heat during a competition, limit or influence his decisions about the waves he takes. His exploits are often memorable, displaying his technical competence and bringing him a great many awards related to singular waves or consistently outstanding performances over a year of chasing big waves across the planet. His surfing exhibits finesse and skills acquired from decades of surfing at the top level on regular waves and smaller boards, carried over into riding big waves on much bigger boards—longer, thicker, and while easier to paddle on, harder to steer. This gives him an edge over many who only excel when the surf truly roars, the ground shakes, and operating perfectly in a fight or flight mode and keeping your heart rate down becomes a requirement. Put another way, his surfing is more well-rounded than most. Shane is a phenomenal surfer in any conditions.

He is firm when he says that while he competed in the Men's Championship Tour (CT)—regular surfing—for eleven consecutive years, and that was certainly a sport, what he is doing now, big wave surfing, "is not a sport at all"; at least, not yet, as others explain to me.

Endemic and Non-Endemic Sponsors

Most big wave surfers are struggling to make ends meet, and pursue the costly sport only in between their paid work. "There's just really not very much money in it. The sponsors really aren't that interested. There's only very few guys who are making decent livings surfing, and it's too specialized in big waves," Shane says. "And surf companies usually only sponsor one big wave rider. That's all they need, if they even need one. And how many companies do we have? Five?" A handful of guys, not yet any women, can make a living out of it, but it is anything but a wise career choice at this point. Every big wave surfer will tell you that.

The overarching organization behind big wave surfing events for the World Tour is the World Surf League (WSL), which a number of my informants describe as a media company rather than a sport organization. The Eddie is a separate event, not part of the Tour. Because of the meager earnings available to them, and because many, perhaps the majority, feel that the competitions and awards are unfairly judged, big wave surfers have been discussing since 2019 the prospect of forming a union spearheaded by the athletes. One surfer tells me that "right now we're just like puppets for them (the WSL)," basically saying that athletes are being exploited for risking their lives, and that while judging has improved, it is still much too biased and inconsistent.

Regardless of specialization, "Do any professional surfers have college degrees? Any?" one of them provocatively asks me. Describing the economy of big wave surfing, Shane tells me:

> There's so many people doing it. It's very top-heavy. The bottom line is you should surf big waves because you love it, and that's the only reason you should surf big waves. It shouldn't have anything to do with your job or your sponsors or whatever, it should all come from that, that you love it. The surfing industry is very tough. There's a lot of guys who are on the World Tour who have no sponsors.

He adds that because of how well he has done, many big wave surfers ask him to divulge his "tricks." As if there could be any. "There's a lot of hungry guys out there . . . those guys always ask me: 'Oh, what's the secret to the whole sponsor game? How do you get a sponsor, like a good one? How do you negotiate? And how do you navigate the whole game?' and . . . (pauses, sighs) it's just, there's no good answer. You know value when you see it."

But what are the different modes of livelihood in this sport at this time? And how do big wave surfers increase their value through their performances? How are they generally evaluated? Besides sheer talent, luck, and timing, how have a handful of surfers succeeded in turning their passion into a career?

From Personalities to Athletes: For the Lifestyle toward Building a Sport

Brazilian Carlos Burle is in his early fifties. He was the first big wave world champion in 1998, at thirty years old; he won a second title at forty-two, and by the time he retired from the Tour he was the oldest competitor. One year later, at fifty-one years old, he was nominated for one of the five biggest waves ridden in 2019. Besides his athleticism and talent, which has been recognized in professional accolades, Carlos's success is grounded in his commercial savvy, work ethic, and intelligence. Describing him, a surfing judge says: "He's a thinker. Unlike other guys who surf big waves, he doesn't just go out and surf. He's analytical. He has a strategy." As in any surf contest, at its basic level strategy implies knowing how many waves there are per set and how frequently the waves are coming in. It involves learning how to read the ocean, but also knowing how your competitors are performing and how the judges are scoring, which varies day by day throughout the competition, and by event. Waves are not only changing day to day; they're changing throughout the day, as they're affected by tides, winds, and weather. This means that the playing field is constantly in flux—unlike in tennis or basketball—and athletes need to adapt their approach to changing conditions. Ocean awareness, the same judge tells me, depends on "understanding that there's a rhythm to the ocean and you got to be able to read it, understand it, and adapt." And these variables affect different surfing spots in different ways.

Carlos's world record tow-in wave at Nazaré in 2013, after he had saved and performed CPR on his tow-partner, Maya Gabeira, garnered him and the sport unprecedented media exposure: from CNN to Letterman to TV stations across the globe. It was like a "perfect script for a Hollywood movie," he says. But this episode also attracted criticism: was Maya trained and skilled enough to be out there in such conditions? Had Carlos been partially responsible for having selected the wave on which Maya wiped out? And should Carlos's wave count as a record, since he didn't complete the ride?

The incident triggered heated discussions on women's surfing more broadly, on the underlying machismo lurking beneath the sport, and on legitimate questions regarding equality, performance, risk, and fairness. "We have friends that have died already. And it didn't look bad. It looked good, because it's a man," Carlos says.

I first met Carlos one evening in 2016, at the house he usually rents for the season in Mokulēʻia on the North Shore. We begin talking while he's on the ground working on his back with a foam roll, and then he says he wants to continue our conversation in another room. We enter, he closes the door, and then lies down on the bed while I sit in a chair. He looks exhausted, and at one point he closes his eyes.

When I ask him why he pursued big wave surfing as a career, he invites me to look out the window of the beach house we're in. "For the lifestyle," he says. But the pace, the last-minute travel, and the injuries, he adds, "that's not living a good lifestyle. It's very hard." His vision revolved around making big wave surfing into a sport where a viable career could become a reality for future generations. Transforming a lifestyle and a commercial enterprise, eventually, into a sport. He says: "There are no half-professionals: either you are, or you are not a professional," pointing to the fact that his sport still has a long way to go to fully sustain its athletes.

And how did Carlos become a professional big wave rider? First, by dividing his time among different projects. When he was younger, he had to hustle: buying and selling clothes during his surf trips. Next, he developed into an entrepreneur, opening a series of restaurants in his native Brazil, hosting a television show, and giving motivational talks about risk management for large companies like Johnson & Johnson and Volkswagen. Later in life, by joining the big wave events and WSL Tour, and eventually coaching Maya Gabeira and his current protégé, Lucas Chianca. But his job has also involved promoting the sport, and he hopes that the work he's done with other surfers of his generation will pave the way for the younger ones.

Other surfers used to mock him, saying "Carlos is all about marketing," but his awards complicate the picture. Carlos is an exceptional competitor, and he also knows how, and is willing, to market himself. His first world title brought him prestige and attention, which he aptly capitalized on. When he got back to Brazil, the title enabled him to be introduced and framed as a champion. "You win things, people remember. You don't win things, people don't remember," he used to tell Maya and now says to Lucas.

He recalls how, years ago, he would get upset at other surfers who after an event would get hammered at the awards ceremony. His point was not about puritanism—it was about image, about the future, about a dream of professionalization, about building the sport. "What if someone who could sponsor the sport would be at the event?" He was an outsider in his own field, coming from the periphery of this social world, his life split between getting himself to competitions, surfing specific swells, and flying back home to work on other ventures, like opening a restaurant and a salad-dressing factory. He says he was the first surfer in the world to have his own PR agency, and that part of his strategy involves reaching beyond specialized media.

But there have been other surfers before and after him who have also put their energy into moving out of the surfing industry to tap into larger markets: Mark Foo in the late 1980s, Laird Hamilton in the 1990s and early 2000s, and Garrett McNamara most recently.

Besides working odd jobs on the side, receiving some kind of patronage, setting up entrepreneurial ventures such as speaking events, and winning awards or competitions, another way to make a living in this world consists of creating content. This strategy depends on producing promotional material. Examples include posting Instagram feeds, working with photographers and writers on articles, and creating videos.

Projects: Creating Stories to Sustain a Livelihood

When I met Nicole in 2016, she had been married to Garrett for six years. She used to be a schoolteacher. She didn't like the bureaucracy, and what she appreciates about her new life is the flexibility. Unlike other surfers' partners, she decided to travel with Garrett, ultimately assuming various roles, from manager to team member. She helped him surf Nazaré by spotting waves from the cliff and alerting him to them by walkie-talkie. Initially for safety, to help the jet-ski drivers find surfers after their rides, and then also to help surfers identify the best waves to ride.

She tells me that when she met Garrett, he was extremely disorganized, a man full of ideas, but having trouble focusing on one and making it happen. She became his manager, doing the PR and assisting him with marketing.

> I helped him make Portugal into a project: instead of just going and riding the waves, how can we make each mission a project? Your dream can be to surf big waves, but unless you make that dream different than the other guys, then you're not able to make it your life. We have to think of ideas to present to the sponsors to make them want to pay for us to go everywhere.

Turning each mission into a project means producing content—turning most of what athletes do on a daily basis into a story that can be successfully sold and consumed.

Garrett tells me that being a New Yorker rather than having been brought up entirely on the islands helped him in his career. "Somehow I kept the energy. I go full speed and stop." Then he adds:

> Look, I'm almost fifty and my career is at an all-time high with a broken arm (laughing). That's because I make projects, plans, always writing everything, focusing, manifesting, that's the only way I've done so well. Number one: meeting Nicole. Number two: reading the right books, writing things down. Focusing, manifesting, making things happen.

While talking about how hard work pays off, Carlos refers to Garrett as "the most radical traveler ever . . . looking for big waves everywhere . . .

he needed to come up with new waves." Before other surfers invested in chasing large swells and documenting them, "he needed news to feed." Delving further into what it takes to make it in this sport, Carlos tells me that "only a few can survive," and that those surfers have found their singularity: "they found the way—and it's here (pointing to his head with his right index finger). Garrett never stops working . . . he went everywhere. He had to." And then he talks about how busy his schedule is, and how much his wife has helped him with marketing and logistics.

Mention Garrett McNamara, and chances are many will associate him not only with the sport, but also with Portugal. Can you think of a better sponsorship situation than having a country supporting you? An ambassador for Portugal through the promotion of surfing. Besides his talent and courage, and the help he receives from Nicole, Garrett has benefited immensely from being in the right place at the right time. Paraphrasing Seneca (although he doesn't make the citation), he says: "Luck is when preparation meets opportunity," referring to the first professional contest he ever entered, when he was seventeen. At the last minute, contest organizer Randy Rarick asked him to compete, knowing that he would be capable. Garrett says: "I'd been surfing Sunset and Pipeline a lot, so I was prepared, and Randy put me in." And discovering Nazaré as Portugal was beginning to invest heavily in tourism also played a major role in his success.

In early 2005 a surfer from Nazaré contacted Garrett to inform him that there was a big wave spot in the middle of Portugal that had barely been ridden to its full potential. And while the two continued to discuss a visit through correspondence, it was only years later, when Nicole found an invitation by that surfer in their archives, that Garrett went there in 2010. Soon after he arrived, he understood how large waves there could get, and then surfed it for years almost alone. Not many surfers he contacted wanted to follow him. Eventually, as the popularity of large wave surfing climbed, and as a result of his performances and the popularization of Portugal as a tourist and surfing destination, Garrett was able to carve out a livelihood by promoting not only companies like Mercedes Benz, but also a country.

We started the Nazaré Project, the second year we got the world record. And then three years in a row the Project got CNN and BBC: 2012, 2013, and 2014. So, what it did, number one: it grew the sport of surfing. It put surfing into millions of homes three years in a row. So now we got all these . . . for lack of a better word, consumers that are going to be consuming surf products. And then Portugal became the number one destination in Europe. Nobody ever thought to go to Portugal. Every country has their little gems, but Nazaré has the biggest wave in the world.

Garrett is straightforward about a number of issues regarding the commercialization and professionalization of big wave surfing. First, about the inherent and apparent laziness of surfers in general: "The thing is, most surfers don't want to work, so they just complain. And if they do get sponsored, they don't want to do what the sponsor wants them to do, but they do it. Well, some of them do." Second, he tells me about how looking for sponsors outside the surf industry was the correct move.

I don't mess with surf. I stay as far away from surf as I can. I don't work with any surf companies. Their mentality is so . . . and it's all corporate war, and it's bullshit. It's all we're surfers, we're cool, we're zen, we're a surf company, but all they do is chew you up, spit you out, and take the next kid with blue eyes and blond hair. So, you get stuck in this . . . if you don't have a niche, then you're screwed. You'd better get a job. If you have a niche, you can have longevity, you can actually have a career. You can reinvent yourself.

Opportunity and Exposure

Big wave surfing is a rare-swell–dependent sport. As sociologist Daniel Chambliss[2] argues, at the top level exceptionally successful individuals don't necessarily practice more than their counterparts, but they practice differently. Meaning that they treat each practice session as if it's the day of competition, so that when the day arrives nothing is out of the ordinary, it's routine. And that includes being prepared for accidents and wipeouts—which, as I discussed in chapter 5, are unpredictable by definition. Further, as I found in a study[3] I conducted on professional freestyle BMXers, top athletes in lifestyle sports are also motivated to experience fun and defy boredom. By surrounding themselves with similarly skilled fellows whose company they deeply enjoy, they escalate their daring, which in turn can lead them to mastering very difficult and dangerous maneuvers, resulting in having them "dialed in." The athletes I studied relocated from different parts of the world to a remote town in North Carolina so that they could be near similarly talented riders who hold similar professional aspirations, and could build the infrastructures they needed to practice and improve during a period when most other locations lacked them.

Besides cross-training of various kinds, practicing in big wave surfing is challenging for a number of reasons, some of them related to the fact that big waves are both rare and seasonal. In Hawai'i, for example, the winter season typically starts around November and can go through March. But some winters don't produce any large swells, and even when these conditions do materialize it may be too windy. Further, the manifestation of the right conditions impacts not just an individual surfer's progression, but the well-being of the sport more broadly. As Jamie Mitchell says:

> I think the biggest thing in big wave surfing is just we don't get the swells consistent enough. It's not like the WSL (World Surf League) Tour has their events, their waiting periods, and they go no matter what. We have waiting periods but if the swell doesn't come, we don't run events. So it's very hard, I think, to potentially get sponsors. When they may be like: "Well, we might sponsor an event, but it may not run in three or four years."

And Aaron Gold concurs:

> It's such a swell-dependent sport. It's so intricate for it all to come together at the right time and be. . . . You know, we get swells like we had yesterday, giant swells, huge waves but not rideable.

Especially at this early stage in the sport's development, opportunities to travel and opportunities to hone your skills and get more exposure to surfing bigger waves go hand in hand. Missing a whole year stalls progress and negatively impacts surfers' confidence and trajectory. Especially early in a surfer's career, it's key to getting the attention of sponsors—as for example Jamie Sterling did through his wipeout—to get funding to travel, chasing swells nationally and internationally. Reflecting on his youth, Mark Healey says:

> You have to just seek the exposure, and if you're like us (Mark and Jamie), we were both poor growing up, we're not going to be traveling anywhere out of our pockets, so it was absolutely crucial to have moments like this for both of us to be able to get started, to try to get funding to be able to go . . . "OK, well, there's no giant swell here in Hawai'i, but we can go to Mavericks and there's a swell going on there, or in our summertime

we can go down to Mexico . . . somewhere else." And then once you start doing that, you get more exposure, then you get more opportunities, but they have to be happening at the same time. It's key. You can't get better at big wave surfing without experience.

Career Waves: Patience, Pacing, Knowledge, and Commitment

At the end of the day, at the end of the season, and throughout their career, surfers remember who caught the best wave. How long this memory lasts depends on the wave, the ride, and whether and how it was recorded and disseminated.

Additionally, specific waves and rides impact a surfer's reputation and value. A surfer's reputation hinges on memorable moments—"doing something that no one else has done." Waves of resonance. As they progress, successful surfers refine their target, so that instead of looking for the wave of the hour or the wave of the day, they look for the wave of the season or the wave of their life, hoping for an outstanding achievement that will be recognized by the community. This means that in general, the better and more experienced surfers become, the less waves they take per session and per year—because they know the danger, know what they're looking for, and want to maximize their chances of success while minimizing their chances of failure. Fewer but better is more valuable. But as Trevor tells me, "It's hard to sit still and let really good waves go by." And the same logic applies to deciding to pass on certain trips, or certain sessions.

Pushing the sport rather than just oneself, or gaining entry into the community of top surfers, entails *chasing* specific swells at specific locations and trying to catch the best outlier wave. Each swell typically produces one or two sets of waves larger than the others, and within those sets each wave is different, and one wave is bigger than all the others. But those opportunities are exceptional, and they take place sporadically at different locations around the globe, with short notice and no certainty. Plus, surfers trying to decide whether to chase a swell have different options in terms of location, and even when they make what in retrospect is the right choice, they may get there too late—when the swell has already peaked, or when the wind has picked up and ruined the conditions. And it's a matter of a few hours, against what might be a fourteen-hour flight. And even if they arrive at the right location at the right time, and are sitting in the right spot in the lineup to catch that exceptional wave, when the moment comes, they may not feel ready to commit to it. Courage may fail them. They may wipe out. Or someone else may be better positioned to take that wave.

Greg Long, for instance, is famous for sitting in the lineup for hours waiting for the wave he's looking for, and either catching it or paddling back in without having ridden a single wave. Many surfers I talked to look up to his approach as epitomizing the figure of the *sharpshooter* I introduced earlier.

Once a surfer has acquired a certain skill set, a reputation, and has aged and gotten hurt enough times, it can also become detrimental to chase too many swells, because it can produce fatigue and incrementally increase the chances of further injury by wipeout.

As Jamie Sterling puts it, "My motto is surf to surf another day," indicating that his approach has become more calculated and less reckless. Mentioning his concern about longevity and also about having become a father, he says: "And especially after I got injured eleven years ago surfing Waimea. I dislocated my right shoulder, and that day it was another lesson that I needed to train more, and I needed to be more careful." The calculation he talks about relates to wave selection, and waves successfully completed. Earlier in his career, though, he was falling more often, taking off on more waves that were close to impossible to ride successfully, and consequently breaking more boards.

Compared to other surfers at his level and career stage, Trevor Carlson has suffered many accidents. Like Jamie, he says that "injuries are kind of a blessing in disguise. They're like my secret motivation to come back from them, to prevent them," and also to know that at any moment he could have a really bad one and then never have the opportunity to surf big waves again. Put differently, injuries help him—and other surfers too—focus on the waves that really matter.

John, an acupuncturist who has been working with top athletes on the North Shore for decades, tells me that he thinks the hardest thing for older big wave surfers like Carlos is to keep going despite injuries. I ask Carlos to comment on this idea, and he tells me:

> That's true. I've had so many bad injuries. I have this feeling inside that you have two ways to cope with your challenges: either you fall, or you take them as opportunities to get stronger. And that's what I did with my injuries. I said: either I'm gonna fall into it and not be able to overcome, or I'm going to take it seriously and come back stronger. And I got motivated by the second choice, you know (laughing lightly, with a slight note

of pride). And said: I'm going to show everyone that I'm going to get back and get stronger (genuine laugh).

Then he reminds me of how a year ago he was in a lot of pain, while this year he's doing great because he has access to different kinds of trainers and he's working out with younger exceptional athletes like Lucas.

I'm joking with Lucas because the name of the TV show we're working on is "Burle train me." And I say: "Lucas train me," because now I'm feeling better than ever. And that's the beauty of life, of course you got to keep the light on, and how are you going to keep the light on? I don't know, I don't have the answer, but I'm willing to try. You got to have people in life to inspire you, and you got to have this kind of attitude, otherwise, what's the other option?

"Would that be one of the secrets of your longevity?" I ask.

It is. This way of sharing. You know, like: "OK, what can I get from you?" Like a good vampire. "Give me your energy." Accept. I'll change it into a good thing. I have something, we can fight together. And I love that.

Wednesday, January 27, 2016: Luke Shepardson riding the best wave of the day into The Eddie's Alternates List.

Risk and Reward

The principle underlying "risk and reward" is numerically reducing one's exposure to risk—number of waves ridden, number of swells chased—while increasing the amount of risk taken on each wave selected. But this refined approach can only work when a surfer has enough of a reputation, and especially when he has learned by experience how waves of different sizes move. And of course, how to surf them well.

With the development of safety devices and the push for progress, surfers overall are increasing the level of risk they commit themselves to. Take one example from the pre-leash era: Clark Abbey, one of the handful of surfers who never wore a leash at Waimea, remembers young Mark Healey and Shane Dorian taking off on a wave at Waimea that looked unmakeable. As Mark was paddling out, Clark asked him: "Why did you go?" The implied question was: Did you *really* think you were going to make it? Growing up, Mark recalls looking up to Shane and his early reckless approach. Describing how the approach of the top athletes has shifted toward a sharpshooting strategy, a pro surfer tells me:

> You trust your feelings much more. You got to be on top of your game so you can kind of cut the risks. After years of experience, you trust your feelings much more. It's not that you're not charging hard; in fact you can charge even harder, but you kind of concentrate and you give it a shot when you're one hundred per cent.
>
> I try to pick more carefully not only the waves that I ride, but also the travels that I do. You do change your approach, but you try to play it smarter because you catch bigger waves being smarter. It doesn't mean that you're going to go less. It's not only balls to the wall and just go for it, then you get hurt, you get fucked up. Time gives you opportunity to see things better, to know what's . . . to have a better approach.

Ian Masterson tells me that surfing without a leash is safer. First, he claims, it forces you not to rely on it, which means that unless you're prepared to swim back in after a wipeout, you won't paddle out. Second, it helps you to select waves you can ride out to the channel. And third, it helps you focus and operate at a hundred and ten percent of your ability, so that if you're about to fall, you may still choose to avoid it.

Describing a classic style of riding big waves in an era when surfers had to rely almost entirely on their ability and strength—getting in and out of the water on their own—Clark says: "Falling is a sin." Most of the waves that older figures like he or Eddie Aikau or James Jones took looked makeable—not maybe makeable, or unmakeable. And within this style, making a wave meant riding it out while still standing and moving forward diagonally, not going straight toward the beach with the white water behind you.

But because of the safety features like the leash, jet skis, and vests, the new generation of surfers can take more risks and gamble more on whether they will make the wave or not. And such gambles may pay off—they may pull off a memorable ride. They live with greater confidence that they won't drown, even though they can still get hurt, or the technology may fail. Older surfers say that this approach is based on a "false sense of security" that also increases the risk for others in the lineup. When younger surfers adopt this style, they rely more on their courage than on their skills. This is the style being referred to when, for instance, one of those surfers tells me that big wave surfing is "all about playing mind games with yourself"—choosing to take more courageous lines of action. Older surfers are more calculated. Because they grew up in an era when they had to be.

Jamie Sterling calls the style of those who rely too much on safety equipment "go straight and inflate," meaning not making the wave, and inflating a safety vest during wipeout, or even before it happens. Ian, who has been working with water safety on Oʻahu, recalls a surfer at Waimea who, after a wipeout, started yelling in desperation and frustration: "Where's the jet ski?!" And Ian told him: "Start swimming toward the beach!" while paddling alongside him to make sure he was OK. Recalling the style of the older era in which he lived, he adds: "Surfers from back then would have pride and try to make it on their own." Jamie and the lifeguards I talked to confirmed that.

Mark Healey, who has molded his approach from studying Shane's later sharpshooting approach, and Greg's, says:

> You just learn that if you expose yourself to risk too many, enough times, your number comes up. Yeah, if I enter a lottery three billion times I'm probably going to win . . . once. So it's a numbers game as well. I'm more selective on the waves that I catch, but I take a lot more risk once I catch them than I used to. Because that's where the opportunity lies to push the level of big wave surfing. Because a lot of times you have to make a decision. If you're going to try to pull into a twenty-foot tube, you have to make a decision halfway down that wave if you're going to try to put your rail in the water and start turning and take a very aggressive turn, it's

about a fifty-fifty chance that's gonna end up putting you in the worst spot and that wave is gonna land directly on you. Which is like . . . then you're talking about like . . . besides thinking about drowning and all that, you're thinking about real injuries: backs breaking, concussions—real mechanical body issues. So I take those risks more. I pick my waves so that I can tell myself to take that risk more.

Talking with Shane Dorian about his career and how his approach to risk-taking has changed toward sharpshooting, he tells me that:

I don't need to surf any more fifteen-foot waves, you know? For me that's fun and everything, but for my job that does nothing for me to go and surf . . . to go to Jaws when it's fifteen to eighteen feet, it doesn't really do anything besides keep me sharp and have fun. As far as like the value and whatever, yeah, I still . . . it's those waves that resonate with people that, the impact lasts a long time—those are the waves that people remember ten years later: "Oh wow, that ride was incredible. . . . That changed something," or "that influenced a whole generation."

I think of the career thing just in terms of trying to lower my risk level and not try to catch a hundred big waves. I want to catch two or three big waves a year, or one if it's good enough. Like if I paddle out, if I go all the way to Jaws, pack all my gear up and take time away from my family and do the whole thing, and I get out there and my first wave is amazing, I'm done for the day. I just pack everything up. I'm not: "I came all the way here, it's only seven thirty in the morning, I got the rest of the day." I just go: "Hey, that's what I came for."

In contrast, a younger surfer who recently turned professional reflects on his approach before he had earned peer respect and a number of accolades. He's surprised that he got to a point where he doesn't have anything to prove anymore. Thinking about the characteristics of his earlier *charger* approach and about carving out a career, he says:

There's no clear path, but you have to find a way to do it by pushing. You have to prove to the world that you're willing and able and have the ability to really do things that everybody's been talking about for a long time. Four years ago . . . what was it? Four or five years ago, my first year at Jaws, I was, in my head, like pretty willing to die to prove myself. There were certain waves, you'd see the wave, you'd turn, and you'd just decide: I'm going to go no matter what. Even if I have very little chance of making it, because I need to catch this wave because I need to prove to all these fucking guys that I'm not a fucking kook. And it's a weird game that you play with your head then. Then there's this whole other game, you hope that you play that game hard enough that you just stop caring about proving yourself. For myself, I played that game for so long that eventually I kind of proved myself more than I actually thought I wanted to.

Chasing

Randall Collins writes provocatively that highly successful individuals are so energetic that they don't sleep.[4] They don't need to because they're charged up with what he calls *emotional energy*, which is the drive and confidence that derive from participating in a series of successful rituals at fairly regular intervals. More accurately, there is a body of research and anecdotal evidence showing that highly successful individuals sleep less than average. Collins focuses on high-achieving adults rather than average people: high-energy entrepreneurs like Steve Jobs, round-the-clock politicians, and up-all-night generals. In his book *Interaction Rituals* he calls these kinds of individuals "energy stars." In addition to favorable network positions connected with other highly creative persons, the big intellectual stars shared many accounts of staying up all night, concentrating on their work, on a roll, generating new ideas. Subjectively, this kind of self-entrainment is energizing because it immerses you in a trajectory where you feel yourself moving forward, attaining a goal; and if highly creative persons have internalized the social field of colleagues, rivals, and audiences in their specialty, they are subjectively getting a train of successful interaction rituals.

Put another way, because stars are embedded in tight networks, they are so locked into their trajectory that they almost can't derail. Their social circles, reciprocal obligations, and interactions ensure that they will persist almost through inertia. In such optimal scenarios there is little time to waste on second-guessing oneself, and little energy spent on creating networks as contenders have to do. Talking about his success, Jamie Sterling refers to "a reliable network of people who are just as serious as you are" and the importance of having "no weak links in your network."

If you think of *emotional energy* as fuel that sustains you and motivates you to move forcefully forward, once it's used up, it needs to be replenished. At the opposite end we find boredom, apathy, and at its extreme, depression. Successful individuals have a trajectory and are able to maintain it over a long period—in rare cases, throughout their lifetime. This brings to mind Garrett and Carlos, as well as two-time world champion Billy Kemper, who told me just after he had won his first championship at Jaws:

> Now my life revolves around Jaws. I train, for it, I sleep and eat *all* aimed toward Jaws in preparation. Me, I want to get the biggest, best wave ever ridden. I wanna . . . I haven't been content with what I've done yet. Every session I come in and I haven't got what I wanted. Not even close. I have fun and I've been somewhat safe and I've made it back to my family, but it's still out there, what I'm looking for. I'm looking for a feeling in my heart and in my body to just be content with like: "What, holy shit, that's what I've been searching for." And it's a feeling more than a certain wave, and it's a feeling of overcoming and conquering something that maybe I thought wasn't possible. That's the whole goal, is to keep going until it's not doable (his voice trembling) and make what's impossible, possible.

By looking at Billy's close networks, one can easily discern the kind of relationships described by Collins and by Michael Farrell when they respectively discuss successful individuals and collaborative circles. For Billy, it's the older members of the Strapped Crew, his own circle of peers, his medical doctors helping him overcome injuries, and his personal trainer and former pro surfer, Kahea Hart. Billy recently asked rhetorically if there could even be a Billy Kemper without a Kahea Hart. And one can try to fathom the strong networks Billy is part of by how he survived a near-death wipeout in Morocco in early 2020 and managed to get back to surfing Jaws in early December of the same year. Among the many injuries he suffered, he had broken his pelvis and severely damaged one of his knees. Yet in less than twelve months he was back charging.

Or recall Clark Abbey, who devoted thirty-one years of his life to surfing the Bay religiously. "Do you call that suicidal?" he asks me. "I was willing to die out there. Fear tamed me. How many thirty-five-foot waves do I want to take before I lose everything I worked so hard for—my wife and my job?" Clark retired from the Bay at fifty. By then, older guys had already left, and by having not missed a swell and having increased his skills, Clark retired at the top of the pecking order. Status. Respect. Meaning. A powerful trajectory imbued with ritualistic opportunities for *emotional energy*. Adding to the social dimension related to drive, writer Daniel Duane[5] says: "Until someone figures out how to ride sound or light, surfing will remain the only way to ride energy." *Emotional energy* is both mind- and body-related and tends to fluctuate synchronically—when you're feeling physically strong, your mind will follow, and *vice versa*. But riding the surf, especially the wild surf, is also connected to spiritual energy. A number of neuroscientists argue that near-death episodes produce out-of-body experiences similar to religious experiences.[6]

The next swell and the wave of your life are almost always ahead of you, at least as long as the desire and trajectory are maintained and your mind and body can sustain it. Think of the North Shore as a *magnet place*—a place that attracts novices and is rich in the resources that matter for what you aspire to accomplish.[7] Such a place generally offers many of the situations and interactions that have the potential to keep an aspirant, as well as a professional, motivated and charged up. Yet, as I pointed out earlier, these occasions—in this instance, large swells—vary by year and are limited to the winter season, and meaningful networks are not evenly distributed.

A number of big wave surfers who can afford it, or manage to by some other means, chase swells across continents. They do so for multiple reasons. As Jamie and Mark suggested, one reason relates to practicing and being noticed. Another has to do with trying to get on the World Tour and maintain visibility and sponsor interest. Yet another is linked to continuing to fuel their passion—or, for some, their obsession. Within a few days a surfer can not only chase different swells, but also chase the same swell to different coastlines at different times. Striking a mission is what Jamie Mitchell is talking about when he mentions feeling like James Bond.

A Contender

At twenty-three years old, after one successful year of being a door knocker and replacing roofs after a particularly ferocious hurricane season, Californian transplant to O'ahu Trevor Carlson amasses a large sum of money. His work schedule is six days a week from seven a.m. until six p.m. During this time he learns that one of his friends who was recreationally chasing waves in Oregon was allowed to participate in a big wave competition because there weren't enough athletes on site. And he made it to the final. "What? Are you telling me that if I just show up and keep showing up they're going to let me in?" The next competition is to be held in either Peru or Chile. A few days before the decision is made, Trevor flies from O'ahu to Los Angeles and sleeps near the airport. When he finds out that the contest will be held in Peru, he buys the next ticket there. He jumps in the water before the competition starts, and in front of athletes, judges, and the media, manages to score a truly outstanding wave. "Are you the guy who got that fricking barrel?" many ask him when he walks up on the cliff. But there are already enough athletes in the event.

Over the years many have tried this strategy, and when they got denied by the organizers they quit trying. Trevor persists. He employs a partner to keep his business running for another year, collecting 50 percent of the revenues. He tells everyone, including the organizer, Gary Linden, that he's going to keep showing up until they let him into an event. The next one is held in Oregon, and again he surfs before the competition and catches the only barrel wave of the day. Story repeats itself until he shows up to another event and the organizers finally tell him: "We get it: please stop showing up at these events. We're gonna let you in, but the next one is in Europe, please don't fly all the way there. Don't waste your money and time. We're not gonna let you in this year, but don't worry: you've already proved your point."

A few months later the organizers of the Tour put out the "prove it wildcard." It's based on a video competition in which a surfer has to provide video documentation of five twenty-foot Hawaiian-scale waves caught in at least three locations on the current Big Wave Tour. Trevor is one of the few who correctly follows the guidelines, collecting waves he's ridden from four locations on the Tour at the required size. He does a very good job not only catching waves, but also gathering clips and photographs from local photographers. That same year he's nominated for the "Performance of the Year Award." Afterward, he finds out that the Tour has only two wild-card spots that year, and he's won one. After sharing this story of how he made it on Tour, he tells me: "I was lucky I set this goal before it was really a goal for anybody." What he means is that big wave surfing at the time was less professionalized and publicized, which meant less competition and fewer contenders. Also, the main way to get on tour now—being nominated for the Performance of the Year award—didn't exist then. One wave is not enough. "What gets you on Tour is an entire year of chasing waves," he says, because while some surfers may be exceptional at one particular break, they need to demonstrate that they can perform in different conditions and on the types of waves found in locations where the tour holds competitions.

During his acceptance speech for his Performance of the Year award, Shane Dorian—one of Trevor's heroes—allegedly says: "I don't know how

I got this award because it's really hard to compete with kids like Trevor coming out of nowhere these days. I didn't expect to win. Thank you for letting me win. You know, it's not for long." The whole crowd erupts. Trevor tells me: "It blew my mind. Who am I? The craziest thing I've heard in my life." Trevor is ecstatic and filled with enthusiasm to continue his quest. One week later he flies to Puerto Escondido, where he has a near-death experience surfing.

Much has changed since 2016. Now there are more surfers chasing not only swells, but also an opportunity to get on the Tour and stay there—which at this writing has been suspended, in part because of COVID-19. This means that big wave lineups—especially in those spots where competitions are held—are more crowded, and more surfers are looking to catch the special wave or waves that could put them in the spotlight. "The next generation is going to have wild big wave surfers," Trevor says.

Fear of Missing Out (FOMO)

"FOMO is fucking real!" Mark Healey tells me. And Nicole McNamara warns me not to mention the Tahiti swell to Garrett. Fear of missing out[8] is a malady peculiar to our contemporary, overly connected lives. We're constantly exposed to someone else's staged experiences from anywhere in the world at any time. This means that often we're not living in the moment, but questioning whether someone else's life is better than ours. We miss out on fully experiencing the present because we're distracted by the idea of someone else's reality—or staged present. We're not fully here, and not fully there either. This constant over-supply of information leaves some of us deeply dissatisfied, worrying that our lives aren't as exciting or worth living as someone else's. Maybe for those who can afford to choose among multiple options, that very economic privilege is actually a handicap. Regret. Second, third, fourth guessing. Blockage—like you have too many windows open at the same time on your computer.

In 1654 the scientist, philosopher, and writer Blaise Pascal wrote that "All of humanity's problems stem from man's inability to sit quietly in a room alone." Now that room is replete with perfect pictures and moving images of someone else having fun and looking successful, and it leaves some of us paralyzed, scattered, depressed—arguably more than before, or at least in a new way. A self-inflicted torture? Silence is a prized commodity, but also a double-edged sword, as philosopher Aaron Ben-Ze'Ev says of imagination. As he writes: "The capacity to imagine, which unchains us from the present, also chains us to the possible. . . . [I]t is a gift, but one that can cut deeply."

Sociologists like Gerhard Shulze[9] and Andreas Reckwitz[10] refer to post-materialist values, or what the psychologist Abraham Maslow termed self-actualization, in discussing the increasing importance of experiences as opposed to material belongings. More recently, sociologist Stephen Lyng[11] writes about the growing appeal of excitement as an emotion, and living an exciting life as almost an imperative. Following the intellectual work of sociologists Norbert Elias and Eric Dunning,[12] Lyng argues that "the same modernizing forces that have produced the privileged status of excitement among human emotions have also worked to diminish opportunities to experience 'true' excitement."[13] As excitement becomes popularized, commodified, sold, and often safely consumed, it loses value and some individuals yearn for a more authentic experience. Concomitantly, truly exciting experiences, often connected to risk-taking, increase in value. Pair that with the increasing number of "bullshit jobs"[14]—jobs that workers are not invested in because they know they have no relevance to them or anyone else— and secularization, and you have a recipe for what Bron Taylor[15] calls *dark green religion*: "religion that considers nature to be sacred, imbued with intrinsic value, and worthy of reverent care." And surfing big waves is not only an opportunity to acquire status, enjoy the thrill, and feel accomplished, but also an opportunity to be humbled by Mother Nature. A chance to have those silent moments "when you realize that there must be something bigger than us," as Aaron Gold tells me. Or have a chance to reconsider both your insignificance and your wrongdoings. How many of us can get that close to dying—by choice and at the peak of our fitness—and then get a second chance to make it better? Or at least to temporarily reconsider our life priorities? Or just live another day? Being hit by a massive wave may be akin to kneeling and asking for forgiveness.

Matt Rode is almost as skilled as some of the best big wave surfers in the world. And he travels for waves just as much, even more than some of them. He's the son of a Christian pastor, an environmentalist, a mountain biker, a climber, a snowboarder, and a thinker who writes for a living to chase the dream. Stunned by his fitness, a kid who sees him bouldering at Waimea Beach Park asks him: "How often do you exercise?" Speaking in his customary soft and playful tones, Matt replies: "Each day" (with some amusement and pride). His dream is not making it onto the Tour—even though, as some of his friends tell him, that could be just one exceptional wave away. His dream is to surf perfect and often gigantic waves with only a handful of friends. A well-established big wave surfer once told him: "You have the best job. If we have a bad season, we're out. But if you have one, then you can just go home and write an article about it."

Growing up, he remembers loving "anything fast and crazy" and telling his friends that "heaven—or at least the construct of heaven—is bullshit, because in heaven you can't die. If there's no death, there's no injury, then where's the fun? Where's the thrill if you can't fucking get hurt? And if you're not scared of getting hurt, then what's the point of surfing big waves?"

There are currently about thirty guys in the world who are able to regularly chase large swells across the planet. When he's chasing them, Matt sees the same thirty guys—and they include those who are on the Tour and a handful of others who are underground.

Matt is aware of having an addictive personality, and growing up he purposely veered away from drugs. Today he doesn't even drink coffee. He recalls the first time he experienced FOMO. He was on O'ahu, where he surfed the outer reefs and Waimea. Then he flew to Mavericks in Northern California to catch the same swell. Then he drove overnight to Nelscott in Oregon for another swell the next day. He drove back to Mavericks thirty-six hours later, but he missed that session because he was sick. And then he flew to Maui the next day to surf Jaws, and then to O'ahu that evening. How long did it take him to do all this traveling and intense surfing? One week. After the chasing ended, he remembers feeling not only understandably disoriented, but also depressed. Looking at the forecast, he couldn't see any massive swell anywhere on the globe. That's when he experienced a week-long depression—the first in his life. Some surfers have mentioned suicidal thoughts related to FOMO, and these could be caused or aggravated by undiagnosed concussions and chronic traumatic encephalopathy (CTE).

Another surfer tells me that it's difficult to imagine anyone whose main focus is surfing big waves and chasing them globally as being a balanced individual. While surfers may not consciously supplement their big wave addiction with other high-adrenaline pursuits, many of them do. One tells me: "You can't judge, you can only try to understand their behavior."

FOMO may relate to missing a particularly outstanding swell, failing to take off on a wave or taking a safer route while riding it, or realizing come the end of the winter that you haven't worked as hard as you could have. And will the next winter be as good as this one? As Trevor tells me, surfers then can start questioning:

> What's my purpose? Why am I here? I spent my whole life training for this one thing, and then I miss the swell of the decade. The swell of the year, of the month. I missed this amazing swell. It's like being a NASCAR driver and missing the race. You spent your whole life. You drive because you like to drive, but you really drive because you want to go do the race. For us the race is the swell, and your whole life training, but you got to show up on the right day too. The hardest part of the sport at this level is being an amateur forecaster so knowing when to be where.

As surfers experience depression, some may stop taking care of themselves and training, slipping into a tailspin that causes them to lose trajectory as well as mental and physical fortitude. One surfer tells me that "people just spiral downwards and stop chasing the dream," and others tell me it's very difficult to maintain the desire and focus as long as some giants of the sport like Carlos Burle have, especially if you lack a network of peers and support personnel.

Several surfers have also mentioned how easy it is to miss a swell by simply not paying attention to the forecast for even a handful of days. Trevor recalls:

> I missed a Mavs swell this year because I wasn't paying attention. It wasn't big, it was small, but it was pretty, and I was rock climbing (laughing). I wasn't even . . . I was rock climbing and I left my phone and I was like: "Oh! Mavs is firing." I was like: "What the fuck?" I stopped paying attention for like five days? A week? and all of a sudden what was like a little bump on the swell, bumped up, and it became a Mavericks swell. And I was in Makapu'u climbing the most beautiful place in the world and for some reason I have FOMO that I'm not surfing cold water Mavs, even though I was having just as much fun doing what I was doing . . . but I still have this like: I spent my life dedicated to this thing, when those days come, that are rare, I should be there.

Mark Healey, who is seven years older than Trevor, tells me about a swell he missed at Cloudbreak in Fiji while he was working a stunt job on Kaua'i for a movie. He had already been on set for a couple of weeks, and he had only one day left to film when the swell appeared on the forecast.

He asked his stunt coordinator if he would be needed, and if not, if he could leave to chase the swell. But the answer was no. One of his big wave surfing friends who was also working on the movie was able to go. Mark says:

> I was in a dark place mentally. I was so bummed. Because if there was ever one thing that my surfing is suited to, where I really feel good, is giant left barrels, especially at Cloudbreak. If I was going to pick one place that I feel like I can compete with anybody in the world, it'd be there on a huge day. And it was just like . . . it hurt, man. But you know what? As I got older I noticed—I couldn't totally see it before, but it's things like Jamie getting that wave and me missing that day (when they were teenagers). I've noticed that every time I miss one of these swells and have crazy FOMO it gets me so fired up that the next time something comes around I have my best performance ever. Because I'm just so like bottled energy from that (nervous laughter). So nowadays I try to look at it as a positive: well, it's just feeding the fire. Next swell it's on, you know. So that definitely . . . it factors in.

Mark also explains that while that particular swell, like the one Garrett McNamara missed in Tahiti, was truly special, many of them are not. And at this point in his career his livelihood doesn't entirely depend on always being there and performing well at every big swell, regardless of their size. When he was younger he used to think that certain swells would be a once-in-a-lifetime opportunity, but now he understands that most of them "end up coming back around," while certain social events certainly won't.

> The thing is that I found too is from going so hard for years and just traveling my ass off and . . . you get fatigued. And for every giant, amazing swell you go to, there were five that you travel across the world for that were highly forgettable. It's a shot on *Surfline* and people forgot about it next week. They didn't really move the needle for you. Now, being more focused, you actually do better. I found that I do better from the goals of progressing what I have done, what big wave surfing has done, and doing things that matter to the people who allowed me to do this and paid my living by being more targeted and having that energy, and having that fire for those days that really count. And you go and do those things that are timeless, that will be just as relevant in two years and not just a blip on an Instagram feed, you know?

Yet, as Billy Kemper (who is younger) tells me: "big wave surfing is all about opportunities. When an opportunity presents itself, if you don't capitalize on that situation you might never see that wave for the rest of your life. Every wave is different. Every swell is different; if you lose that chance at that one wave, you might never see it again."

Judging Aquatic Performances

"It's not a diving contest," a few people say, referring to the controversial 2018 Jaws competition on Maui when the World Surf League (WSL) "got a lot of flats" for their judging. The winners in both the men's and the women's divisions wiped out during their rides in the finals, while those who came in second completed them. The performances of those who won, though, were noticeably more spectacular than those of the other competitors. Keala's wipeouts as she attempted to take off looked dramatic, and Billy Kemper's tube rides were "next level," but none of them were foolish—both had a shot at making their waves. But ultimately the wind was just too strong, which contributed significantly to their falls. If completed, both attempts could have elevated the sport. And looking at the progress of the sport between then and 2021, some argue that they did anyway. Regardless, they certainly caused the audience to hold their breath and shake their heads, on either disapproval or disbelief—or both. Ultimately, both were failed attempts, yet both led to victory. Can you fail and still win? Can you fall on every one of your waves throughout the entire event and still be world champion? Keala reflected openly on both of these questions, and especially so because this was the first event in which women and men were paid equally.

While watching the contest, two male teenage pro surfers tell me that women surfing big waves is "clueless" and "fucking retarded," and that most women were indeed faking to try to take off on waves. Later, others point out that the competition shouldn't have opened with the women, because the "waves started to pump" right as they jumped into the water. It was a "wrong call" by the contest organizers, and further proof of how unpredictable the ocean is despite the quantum improvements in forecasting. Yet the rationale was the opposite: the organizers thought they'd be "sending the women out" when conditions were supposed to be the mildest in the day. None of the women would have surfed Jaws that day if the competition wasn't on—too windy no matter the wave size—and some of the men wouldn't have either. Keala is the first one (but by no means the only one) to reassure me of that. And after a few of the guys' heats, the competition was called off because conditions were too dangerous. Even Grant Baker, one of the top guys, was puking out blood on the rescue boat after his heat. Keala was crowned women's world champion at that event, and Billy Kemper men's world champion. That year the World Tour had merely one event for the women, at Jaws; the women weren't included in the competitions at Mavericks and Nazaré. This meant that the women's world championship was based on a single contest, where not only did the winner not complete a single ride in the final, but most rides by women—and many by the men as well— were essentially wipeouts of one kind or another.

Disagreements over surfing competition results are not unusual, but this episode, especially if considered alongside The Eddie, helps us better understand the current state of big wave surfing from a sociohistorical perspective. It also provides us with more information to gauge the commercialization and professionalization of the sport.

During the last edition of The Eddie in 2016, organizers made sure to tell competitors that the judging criteria would be emphasizing "complete rides." A judge also tells me that the judges were instructed to stop watching surfers once they passed a certain point closer to the beach. By this he meant that crowd-pleasing bravado displayed by riding into the shore break—and potentially even getting barreled there—wouldn't count.

A judge tells me that George Downing's son, Keoni—who was the main organizer of the event until 2017, when Eddie's brother, Clyde Aikau, took over—wanted to highlight the fact that The Eddie represents and rewards how Waimea Bay pioneers like Eddie surfed it. And while those surfers ventured into a partially unridden realm with no safety devices—no leashes and certainly no jet skis or flotation vests— and surfboards that weren't optimal for large waves, they were "surfers of a different caliber" compared to the majority of those who now regularly surf the Bay. They were watermen who would dive and fish, and who relied on their own strength and ocean knowledge to get in and out of the water. Essentially because they had to. "They had pride," more than a few, including lifeguards, tell me, to underscore how self-reliant they were. Putting it bluntly, and referring to modern big wave surfers in general, the same judge tells me, "They didn't ride deep and eat shit," and even though they wiped out a lot, that had more to do with the surfboards they used at the time.

The difference in judging criteria between events like Jaws that are on the Big Wave World Tour and The Eddie—which is a single event not connected to the tour—provides us with a lens to look deeper into the genealogy of this activity. To begin with, it leads us to consider the different reasons for having a contest. While the tour, and other competitions, are concerned with the professionalization, commercialization, and advancement of the sport, The Eddie's goal is to gather the surfing community in what is widely considered its most prestigious surfing event. But it is also focused on preserving Hawaiian cultural heritage and the Hawaiian style of surfing.

While the forecast needed for the competition to run is rare, meaning the event takes place on average only once every four years, its opening ceremony is held every year in early December at the Bay. To run The Eddie, waves need to be at least twenty feet Hawaiian size for eight consecutive hours during daylight. George Downing—a pioneer of big wave surfing in Hawai'i since the early 1950s—conceptualized and honed the event over the years, from its parameters to the holding period, the selection of the participants, and the forecasting. During a time when forecasting was in its infancy, the organization relied on having a three-month waiting period from December 1 to February 28 or 29 every year, a condition that persists to this day.

The Eddie usually consists of seven judges, of whom five are on shift at any given time, with two rotating out for breaks. The judging panel consists of an eclectic mix of professional judges who work internationally evaluating regular surf contests, surfers who have surfed big waves and previously competed in The Eddie, and some of the early professional surfers from the mid-1970s. There are also two spotters, who yell short messages about conditions such as a set of larger waves approaching from the horizon, surfers taking off, or a contestant falling.

Each year, whether the contest ultimately runs or not, twenty-eight surfers are selected as invitees, along with a number of alternates. The invitees are selected by a committee of previous invitees and the main sponsor of the event, and a few are picked by the Aikau family. Unofficially, one of the main selection criteria is having consistently surfed well at the Bay on truly big days, but this criterion is only nominal now. As with most matters in the surfing industry, "there's a lot of politics involved," but nearly all of the surfers are outstanding big wave athletes from different parts of the world.

Per George Downing's design, and in contrast to the Olympic-style zero-to-ten scoring system now used in professional surfing, surfers in The Eddie are evaluated on a zero-to-twenty-point scale, like the Duke Kahanamoku contests of the 1960s and 1970s. With the zero-to-ten scale, judges are thinking within a tightly compressed package, so they're often in "very close proximity agreement." With the larger scale, the scoring spread can get broader "just because the opportunity is there." Bernie Baker, who has been the contest director for the prestigious three-competition Triple Crown of Surfing since 1983, served as a judge in the 2016 Eddie. With his proven expertise, he tells me: "You will never get all judges giving a five, but occasionally you'll get all judges giving a ten when you see something that's outrageously fantastic. The hardest part of all the Eddies is the takeoff and bottom turn. Completing the wave adds to the total."

As the competitions unfolded, George would periodically walk up to the top of the tower to instruct judges in how certain waves and rides should be evaluated, basically telling them "what they should be looking for, and what not worry about. What a high score would be about, and what a low score would be about." Then, to increase consistency, Jack Shipley's son Davey would remind judges of rides as the competition unfolded. For instance, as Bernie tells me, sometimes the waves would soften during the competition, and judges then had to "keep those scores down compared to a guy who's going to do a beautiful bottom turn, or coming off the top, or maybe take off twenty yards deeper into the face of the swell so they're charging at an angle and not (riding) straight down" toward the beach. Because they have to get around this huge body of water that's going to come crashing down—referring to the surfers taking off *beyond the boil* and toward the Church. "These are the guys who are going to put their life on the line. They're challenging it—by it, meaning the Bay. Committing themselves and their ability to the highest order, and that's where the seventeen, eighteen, nineteen, or twenty-point score comes into play." According to Bernie, "risk is everything," covering commitment, challenge, and ability—a reflection of every aspect of a surfer's style. Risk in the end is almost always going to determine who wins.

Historically, surf judging has moved from "distance"—length of ride while standing up—to an Olympic style reflecting ability, maneuvers, and risk. Bernie adds that for any surfing event, but especially for The Eddie, scoring depends on: first, where a surfer takes off—generally the closer to the curl of the wave, the better; second, how steep his drop is; and third, where he initially places himself as a competitor on the wave—the more critical his position is—meaning further away from the lower part of the wave (in the case of Waimea, toward the deep water channel in the direction of the middle of the Bay).

Judges are usually informally briefed by the head judge weeks ahead of the competition, but those in the first heat of the contest set the standard by which surfers will be evaluated. Also, as waves change throughout the day, judges have to modify their scoring criteria somewhat. How different criteria are weighted depends on the day, but also on the surf spot. Puerto Escondido, for example, is heavy barrels. Nazaré (for paddling, not for tow-in) is a "survival test," where just making the wave will give you a high score, while at Waimea, judging would generally be on these three factors: "biggest, deepest, and making the wave."

On the morning before most big wave events, competitors are debriefed on the parameters by which they will be evaluated, further signifying that they are dependent not only on the contest organizers and the head judge, but also on the idiosyncratic surfing conditions of each contest—conditions that often change over the course of a few hours. Scoring rules influence riders' approaches. For instance, in some competitions your best wave counts double the points, pushing surfers to be patient and wait for a "bomb" of a wave.

Challenges in Scoring

Often during The Eddie, as in a regular session at Waimea, surfers take off together on the same wave without being penalized for interference. But it's a challenge for judges to keep track of how each surfer rides. First, even though judges are sitting in a twenty-foot-tall tower on the beach, their view can still be blocked by waves in the same set. Second, surfers in the same heat may all be riding different waves of a set at the same time, further complicating the task of keeping track of what's happening.

A third challenge relates to setting the scoring scale in the first heat of the contest, which will be used for the rest of the day, with some minor adaptations. Dennis Pang tells me how much he wanted to be on the judging panel for the first heat: "Every heat is going to be different— waves are going to change. Conditions are going to change. But at least a general scale is set for the first one," implying that it will function as a standard for the other heats. Yet athletes competing in the first heat are usually at a disadvantage, because judges tend to keep scores low early in the competition.

A fourth challenge judges face concerns "keeping the scale" throughout the contest by being able to recall how they scored earlier in the day, and also remembering guys' waves. And then, Bernie says, they have to "be able to say: 'this guy's wave now was better or worse.' So judges have to try to place rides in comparison with the first rides evaluated during the day, which work as reference scores." They have to gauge where rides stand in comparison: were they better or worse?

A fifth challenge usually pertains to position rather than wave size. Each rider in the competition is a great surfer, and most waves are giant—around forty feet face or bigger—and in the course of a few hours you may have three or four waves that are virtually identical. So how do you evaluate surfers' rides? According to Bernie, the variation in scoring depends on subtle differences in surfers' styles and position on the wave. As he says:

> A lot in the beginning of that moment has to do with: where is he on the wave? Is he on the shoulder, but coming down toward the breaking part of the wave at an angle? Or is he further over—as we say, to the point— and taking off and running across this giant, giant folding wall and coming from behind? I, personally, have felt that anybody coming from behind and making that initial . . . making the drop, and getting around the section and then going into the maneuver was definitely going to be on my higher side of my scale just because . . . again, risk. Risk and skill.

Each of the twenty-eight invited athletes surfs for two sessions. They can catch a maximum of four waves per heat, and only their top two waves in each heat will count. If by the end of the contest their best rides are all in one heat, then these are the ones that count toward their final score. Greg Long won the 2009 edition of The Eddie by riding four exceptional waves in his second heat, which was the last of the contest. One of those rides earned him a perfect score.

A judge tells me that it's easier to grade outstanding rides than the "middle stuff." There are two types of outstanding rides: the "mathematical ten" and the "chicken skin." The latter infuses judges and spectators with "an intense in-the-moment feeling." These performances usually have the whole audience gathered at the natural amphitheater of Waimea Bay erupting. The same judge tells me how he feels then: "Crap, I just witnessed this having the whole thirty thousand spectators scream and yell on the beach for the guy I'm about to put down the score for." He further refers to it as that "in-the-moment feeling" when he knows he just witnessed a memorable performance. Yet when this scenario plays out, judges have to try to objectively analyze the ride, because it may or may not have been amazing. The cheering of the audience may have been influenced by a hometown favorite. Or the announcer may have hyped up a particular rider or wave, and then gotten the crowd behind it. The same judge tells me: "We have to tune that out. We're all emotional, we're not robots. We can get swayed or pulled into that kind of stuff to some degree occasionally, but collectively, as long as you have enough judges, it works. Three judges, it wouldn't work." Again, the comparison to previous rides is key: "Was it much better than the one we already gave a 78 or an 81?" Those chicken-skin performances are "memorable moments."

Now let's conceptualize these evaluative moments using Collins's framework. The "middle stuff" and the "mathematical ten" this judge mentions seem not to be problematic. What seems more difficult to score fairly are the rides that generate "chicken skin" in the judges. Those are moments when the whole community, both spectators and judges, is focused intently on a single event—the particular ride, the surfer, and the crowd participation. When successful, these kinds of occasions generate collective effervescence and emotional energy, which may positively influence how a judge scores the surfing performance. If he lets the occasion sway his emotions, then his evaluation may not be objective. Building on Émile Durkheim and Erving Goffman's emphasis on the importance of synchronized bodily movements for group formation, Collins contends that rhythmic synchronization not only stimulates solidarity, but also generates emotional energy—and both of these emotions are highly pleasurable. By focusing on the same object (the athlete and his ride) and becoming entrained in the audience's bodily movements and positive emotions, the judge may start to feel what the crowd feels, and may therefore be influenced by their enthusiasm, possibly leading to biased scoring.

Put another way, if the judge is seduced by the solidarity and emotional energy into feeling what the crowd feels—which may be affected not just by the athlete's performance, but also by such unrelated factors as his being a local hero or a celebrity—then the "high" produced by the experience could impact how he scores the performance.

Many psychological studies demonstrate that the display of emotions is contagious, and that rhythm is infectious.[16] And while recent experimental research in sport psychology finds that judges and audiences are positively influenced by surfers' claims[17] (post-performance nonverbal emotional expressions), this work does not take into consideration the entrainment that can sometimes take place *in situ*. But as that research shows, athletes' claims may bias—or in my view, sometimes even help— judges in making sense of a performance that depends on rather fluid evaluative criteria rather than objective measurements and scoring. On seeing an athlete display a claim—for instance, raising his fist or throwing both arms overhead—judges may infer that the athlete felt that his ride was an outstanding one, and thus might be influenced in their scoring of it. Whether the claim was a genuine expression of the athlete's excitement or a false expression intended to influence judges is a variable that needs to be weighted.

While shared rhythm is key for successful group performances of various kinds, such as sacred harp singing and rowing,[18] in judging it can have a detrimental effect.

Judges assign scores independently of one another, and they may ask questions of the head judge. But they're under time constraints to punch in their scores, which in the most recent contests are then immediately averaged by a tabulator program and announced. The highest and lowest scores are dropped, and the average is calculated from the remaining scores.

As a judge tells me, evaluating surfing is "a subjective thing and surfing is a personal thing. There's never a clear definition, but the scoring is always based on interpretation. Generally, when you do it enough, and you work with the same people enough, you'd think it would be all over the place all the time, but through the experience we've all had judging together, we usually navigate it pretty well."

Collective judging entails the "blending of opinions and subjectivity" to produce an average score. The judge continues: "You have to have something tangible from it all. A recorded score. In that middle there's that cohesion, coalescing of everyone's opinion that then becomes the average, or the score. In that sense it just kind of works, and overall you have that subjective mind come together."

Intention

Casual observers are impressed by any big wave ride, perhaps even more so when it leads to a wipeout. Expert observers, on the other hand, are trying to put themselves in surfers' trunks to evaluate whether their exploits are just bravado or well-thought-out decisions and deftly applied skills that, even if they ultimately result in a wipeout, could have culminated in a completed ride, or one that pushes the sport forward. While the athlete's statement of intention is not overtly communicated, sometimes it can be read by a trained eye.

Did the surfer in the black jersey, for instance, take off on a wave obviously knowing that he had no chance of riding it, still standing, through the kick-off in the channel, and then straighten up and ride it toward the beach? Regardless of how large the wave was, the scoring of that ride should be lower than the score of another surfer who took off on a smaller wave, but ended up in the channel still standing—a "complete ride." The second surfer showed better wave selection and better adherence to The Eddie's criteria. Bravado is not enough—and is too easy, given the quality and quantity of safety measures in place. Courage needs to be coupled with good judgment and ability.

Reflecting on how big wave surfing has changed since its beginning, Dennis Pang, who competed in the second edition of The Eddie in 1986 and served as a judge at the 2016 Eddie, tells me:

> Guys have more confidence they're gonna come to the surface with that flotation, and they're more trained up than when we were doing it thirty years ago. Everybody's more aware of their body, and all the breathing techniques. Everything about preparing yourself for Waimea. So what was happening is that surfers were just going for it more, some foolish stuff, because they knew they were gonna come to the surface and they're trained up for it. They're prepared very well mentally and physically for it. Big difference from how it was in the first Eddies. And jet skis are all over the place, that's a huge confidence booster for a surfer in the event. There are guys who are gonna get you out as soon as they can. Plus, you have the personal flotation devices that's gonna bring you to the surface, and you're prepared physically to withstand the wipeouts, and you're strong, and your limbs aren't gonna be ripped apart 'cuz you're physically prepared. So that made the surfing more dramatic. Guys were taking off foolishly. That's the difference between then and now.

The Nature of Aesthetic Judgment

Big wave surfing, like surfing more generally or skateboarding, is a field with highly uncertain value criteria. Just like any art form or artistic occupation—photography, fiction writing, cooking, fashion—these sports are characterized by personal expression, chance, timing, network alliances, and reputation rather than by clear standards of evaluation (as in swimming, high jumping, paddle board racing, physics, or mathematics). Like the social sciences, these are low-consensus fields.[19] Bias is inherent in the evaluation process because individual judges hold and sometimes strategically highlight different factors as key, and are emotionally moved both by their personal taste and by the evaluative experience itself.[20] Beauty and quality are in the eye of the beholder. And because of the vagueness of evaluation standards, the opinions of judges are hard to predict and objectively dispute. Also, in these fields there's no way of knowing what the next breakthrough is going to be. Even just measuring wave height, which should be the clearest evaluative parameter, is contested and regularly leads to disputes. Waves differ, and so do the framing of the video and photographic points of view from which assessments are averaged to derive an estimate for Big Wave Awards: "land versus water, up high versus down low, and the height of the surfer."[21] As in any review process, much can be done backstage to make sure your favorite wins. Ben Wilkinson contends that his linebacker size, underground status, and no-bullshit attitude have often worked against him. And the very selection of documentary material to show the public for evaluation—for instance, online polls or to display and justify rankings—already entails a built-in and some would say intentional bias that gives well-known names backed by sponsorship an invisible upper hand. Visibility generates more visibility. Following Matthew's parable, sociologist Robert Merton[22] argued that more credit and opportunities will be given to those who already have them. Seemingly inconsequential advantages at early career stages pay off exponentially and pave the way for future success in a "self-reinforcing virtuous circle,"[23] which in some fields can lead to a sharpshooting approach in later career stages.

Where exactly are the bottom and the crest of the wave? And should we take into official consideration wave height alone, or also its thickness and thus its power? Laird Hamilton's tow-in "Wave of the Millennium" in 2000 at Teahupo'o in Tahiti redefined what was possible. Yet it wasn't size alone that distinguished that rogue wave during an already memorable swell, but also its thickness, its highway-tunnel–like cylindrical shape, and the way Laird successfully rode it—all of which put it on the cover of several magazines both in and outside the surf industry and drove it to overflow into other media outlets. A mistake or bad luck could have vaporized him, sent him into another world. Ushering us into a new epoch, *Surfer Magazine* captioned Laird's cover shot "oh my god . . ." It was impossible to miss, and wave height wasn't the determining factor. Albeit probably even harder to calculate, wave volume would arguably have been a better indicator. No one could even imagine dismissing, however, that it was an unbelievable ride on an outlandish kind of wave that no one had ever even seen. But it was just that—an outlier; especially at the time. And Laird was certainly no outsider. That ride paved the way for many accomplishments in the sport, including Keala Kennelly's award-winning wave at the same spot.

As Douglas Booth notes, surfing debates over style have "fueled dissension over judging methods and scoring, and led to accusations of bias, corruption, cronyism and nepotism"[24] since the early days of professional surfing.

I first met Aaron Gold in the winter of 2016. He tells me how much it meant to get respect from his peers and achieve his goals—which resulted in his invitation to The Eddie. Back when he was seventeen, one of his dreams was to be the first to ride a hundred-foot wave. He adds that now he's comfortable saying to himself, "I don't know if I want to catch a hundred-foot wave. I want to look at it from the water, and then I'll decide. When that happens, those times come, those limits, you're in the moment of it, but you're not looking to prove anything."

On January 14, 2018, Aaron flies from O'ahu to Maui and catches, at Jaws, what is to date the largest wave ever paddled. Two years later we look back at that experience. At the end of the ride—which some criticize because after having made the takeoff, he didn't bottom turn into the shoulder—he didn't know how special it was.

Three-quarters of the way down the wave, he realized it was different, but by then he was already on autopilot, telling himself: "Don't fall. Make the wave. Ride it 'til the end." A wild, bumpy ride for sure, hanging on by having one of his feet wrapped around one of his board's rails. Paddling back out, he saw people on the various boats clapping and cheering. "It must have been something special," he thought.

Shaking his head, one of his friends tells him: "You know you can go in, right? That's the biggest wave I've ever seen in my life." By this point he still doesn't realize the magnitude of his accomplishment. After all, his friend Jeff has just gotten back into Jaws and has missed all the sport's latest progression.

But the very next person he paddles over to is Shane Dorian, who says (Aaron's voice now trembling with excitement as he tells me the story): "Straight off the rocks into the history books." Aaron had just paddled out, and that was his first wave.

"Did you see a picture? That thing was cartoonish," Shane adds. The picture looks photoshopped.

The photo gets printed on the cover of *Freesurf*, the Hawaiian magazine (which is free), but other publications don't give it as much importance. *Surfer Magazine* prints it small, captioning it "The Big Wave Working Class," and beginning the accompanying short piece by stating that the beauty of the sport is that even a regular Joe can paddle out, catch a huge wave, have a photo taken, and then have it "showcased in a photo gallery, virtually indistinguishable" from professionals[25]—yet perhaps distinguishable enough to keep it off the cover. The author roughly estimates the wave as a 72-footer, and predicts that the surfer who tops it may be another underground name because the majority of serious big wave surfers aren't professionals. As I argued earlier, there isn't yet enough money in the industry to support more than a handful of guys, and arguably no women at all.

The Guinness World Records grants Aaron the accolade of biggest wave ever paddled, yet they measure it at only 63 feet. Many of Aaron's peers think that's under-sizing it. Maybe it's closer to 80 feet? Aaron thinks that registering it for its actual size would be "political bad business." "What if it takes twenty years to break the record?" he asks me. Then he answers his own question: "That's bad marketing." The previous Guinness record, held by another underground charger named Shawn Dollar, was just two feet less.

Then he explains that he tried arguing with those who made the measurement, but his voice went unheard for the same reasons most surf publications didn't give much attention to his ride (and those of other underground surfers): not having sponsors behind him who regularly advertise in those magazines. "My sponsors aren't paying them money to put it on. And I'm not in with the boys over there" (meaning in California, where the *Surfer* and *Surfing Magazine* editorial offices used to be before they folded).

While Aaron's ride is unique, a similar disagreement about another record takes place in 2020 between the Brazilian Maya Gabeira and the French Justine Dupont. Maya has earned the Guinness World Record next to Aaron for biggest wave towed-in by a woman. Unlike Aaron or Maya, Justine successfully completed her ride still standing.[26] Yet Maya surfed her wave closer to the peak, taking a more critical line and thus meeting a key parameter in evaluating big wave rides: commitment. Plus, as the Big Wave Surfing evaluative guidelines stipulate, she completed the "meaningful portion of the wave while in control."

Adding to the complexity of evaluation, there are tensions among practitioners based on the use of various technologies and their impact on different riding styles and approaches to risk. Those tensions are also grounded on generational differences that are inseparably, intricately connected to technological advancements that, along with other factors, impact the broader culture and demographics of this social world. If the first generation of modern big wave surfers in the 1950s resembled the archetypical model of Hawaiian watermen, the latest developments in surfing technology have had three main effects on how the sport is practiced and judged.

First, they have lowered the threshold of participation in this activity, allowing those who are not physically, mentally, technically prepared enough to try it. Many of these individuals, as well as many who tried their hand at tow-in surfing in the 2000s and still do so today, rely on a "false sense of security." They can enjoy the activity, true, yet they often put themselves and others in danger when things inevitably go south. Skipping steps eventually has a cost. And as journalist Taylor Paul puts it: "Your flaws can hide so easily in the shadow of a massive wave. . . . [B]ut eventually, the ocean reveals all frauds."[27] As Mark Healey explained earlier in this chapter, while social life can be unfair, Mother Nature is both fair and ruthless. A blind deity who can whimsically turn into a cold murderer.

Second, these changes (along with the renewed hype) have brought younger surfers into a sport that for decades was primarily the arena of middle-aged men, and we are slowly beginning to see a handful (but growing number) of women. Like the recreational type described before, many in this new aspiring breed lack the physical, mental, and technical preparation that used to, and still can, come from having to be self-reliant—making calculated decisions while trying to be vigilant and in control of as many factors as possible. The fewer factors in the risk equation, the better. If technology fails, it can mess up your mental game, and that's why some surfers, for instance, try never to inflate their vests. Echoing what I have heard from many other veterans, Aaron Gold says: "If you don't need it, don't use it. Treat safety as a backup tool. Don't rely on it."

Because judging competitions is partly in the hands of people who are not proficient in this sport, new tensions arise. Younger surfers, fully equipped with "wing suits," can take unnecessary risks without really feeling the consequences of their decisions that surfers from previous generations would have suffered (e.g., brutal wipeouts with no vests or jet skis for safety)—but because of the technology they can also sometimes innovate in the field. Earlier surfers, however, had to be able to read the water well in order to get a wave "you can ride, and not kill yourself"—and then make it back to shore largely on their own. The younger surfers can also dare more than they should, in situations where *at times* they display only their bravado and not their technical judgment. Often those rides get rewarded during competitions, upsetting those with a deep knowledge of the sport, who instead pursue a more "calculated approach," wanting to complete rides (e.g., kicking off while still standing) rather than take a gamble, potentially fall, or complete the drop but then end up in the white water in front of the wave.

While surfing Chuns Reef, I spot the always gregarious Buzzy Kerbox, a former member of the Strapped Crew who pioneered tow-in surfing at Jaws in the 1990s. While we're waiting for the next set of waves, I ask him to comment on the Big Wave Awards event that had unfolded the previous night. Knowing that this is a heated topic, I begin our conversation by noting that more than a few surfers had been rewarded for their efforts on rides that ultimately ended in wipeouts. Buzzy says: "To me those are great wipeouts, not great rides," highlighting a generational difference as to what counts as a ride and what shouldn't because it's not a make.[28] Days later, during an interview, I ask him what he thinks makes for an outstanding ride, and he says:

> For me if a guy just takes off on a huge wave, super deep, goes to the bottom and straightens out, that's not that exciting. To me that's an exciting drop, the guy went on the big one. I like to see a wave that's actually made, so the guy takes off and positions himself, maybe halfway to the end, not behind the bowl, maybe from the middle of the bowl, a critical takeoff, get to the bottom and be able to work around some open face and make it to the end and complete the ride. I've grown up in an era, a complete ride is an amazing takeoff, something good happens in the middle, and you finish that ride. A ride to me finishing horribly, getting annihilated in the white water, is not a fantastic ride.

Jamie Sterling, who is twenty-five years younger than Buzzy and started riding big waves before most of the current safety devices had been invented and popularized, explains further:

> They're rewarding guys with Ride of the Year nomination for going straight and not even making the wave. And guys are doing that nowadays because they have a life vest on. They have a jet ski rescuing them. And I think that's pretty lame to have that approach. You're in the wrong spot, and you're not going to make the wave even though I'm in the right spot, and I'm going to make the wave. They're going to give you Ride of the Year because you were deeper than me, even though you wiped out.

People are pushing it. But you're pushing it recklessly, and it's a false sense of security you have.

Even during regular sessions, those surfers can impact and escalate the overall risk level of other surfers, sometimes with negative outcomes. Dennis explains to me that some of those new big wave surfers are taking more chances compared to previous generations of surfers, but that doesn't necessarily mean they're "reading the wave better." Before the leash—one of the first of many safety innovations—"surfers had to be pretty astute . . . you had to be pretty wise in reading the ocean."

Interestingly, new technological advancements coupled with a renewed push toward the professionalization of big wave surfing have led to a *renaissance* of the Hawaiian waterman ethos. This newer breed of big wave surfers is taking the sport to unprecedented heights by integrating the improved technology (including board design and forecasting) and their modern professional-sport-like training regimen (which is partially afforded by sponsorships and based on the latest physiological advancements) with what they've learned from previous generations. Currently considered the most complete well-known waterman, Kai Lenny often credits his accomplishments to having grown up on Maui doing all sorts of water activities, having been mentored by members of the Strapped Crew, and having learned and developed alongside a small number of peers like Billy Kemper, Ian Walsh, and Albee Layer, some of the best big wave surfers.

From Chargers to Sharpshooters: Between Play, Entertainment, and Sport

Taking an art world perspective, this chapter has analyzed the evolution of the sport by identifying several different career strategies and two approaches to risk-taking—charging and sharpshooting—and their related challenges.

It has also discussed the role of judges and their evaluative criteria in shaping a surfer's reputation. As in Becker's work on ballet performances or Claudio Benzecry's research on opera fans, there is a mix of members of the big wave surfing audience: naïve members who are influenced by the media, and expert members who judge the performances based on their intimate knowledge of the activity. The latter don't just listen, or just watch; they have instead learned how to listen, what to tune into (and how), and what to focus on while looking closely. Big wave surfing is a relatively new social world that has seen much evolution over a relatively short period. And while it's moving toward becoming a sport, it still operates partly as entertainment, where quality of performance and what quality means are not necessarily the most important factors, and are not fully agreed upon among gatekeepers and athletes. Standards of evaluation are changing as the sport is changing. Judges oscillate between rewarding courage and emphasizing skills, and between highlighting or quietly ignoring underground figures or those who might help promote the sport by reaching a larger public and garnering vital resources to help maintain the functioning of this social world.

Additionally, judges need to insulate their evaluations against the collective effervescence that can energize an audience that is focusing on athletes who function as sacred objects. Judges can't simply experience the collective effervescence; they also have to produce a fair evaluation based on athletic performance and untainted by the enthusiasm of the crowd.

As Becker writes, "value depends on the achievement of consensus."[29] But as this new, low-consensus field is changing, the elements that constitute consensus are unstable. This makes for an exciting period in the sport, but a moment in which disagreement is likely to arise and athletes must devise different strategies to be noticed, to become and try to remain relevant, and to impact their sport by distinguishing themselves, modifying their approach to risk, and managing their public personae.

Reaching beyond the surfing world requires a strategy that not only entails performing well, but also depends on creating an image that can be recognized and sold to a public experiencing the sport vicariously through athletes who also are personalities. The ubiquity of communication technologies allows for the creation and dissemination of these types of careers, which we experience through a form of "parasocial interaction"[30] akin to how we experience celebrities in other fields. As Fine writes: "They enter into our personal universe, where we respond to them as if they were part of our personal circle and as if we knew their motivations and values."[31]

CHAPTER SEVEN
One Last Ride

"He's-da-man-brah," Clyde tells me, qualifying what he warned Kai Lenny and others about. "Don't be a high makamaka." Don't be stuck up holding your eyes high above the others. Be humble no matter how successful, rich, and famous you may be now. "Your legacy is in what you give back, not in what you have accomplished." Be regal and proud as a Hawaiian. Surfing here was the serious leisure of kings, chiefs, queens, and commoners. All classes. All ages. In an apparently much simpler society where nature, spirituality, rules, respect, and reciprocity governed life.

Aloha: a value that imbues all aspects of life, including surfing, but largely lost in translation with the internationalization of surfing. Not to mention the disappearance of those who carried it. "Take, take, but never give back," a local says of those coming to the islands with the wrong attitude. And when Ian Masterson meets me, his nose almost touches mine so that we breathe the same air and share it. *Hā'ole*: a term introduced in Hawaiian at the time of Western contact to signify those white foreigners who, as literally translated, have "no breath"—no knowledge of local customs, and therefore are not to be trusted.

The sacrality of surfing has been commodified and profaned in many ways, too. Norms based on sharing, excitement, and wonder have partially given in to selfishness and a claim to property rights of waves or entire surf spots—"place-based localism." Partly a countermovement. "I've paid thousands of dollars to come here so I deserve those waves, mate." "I'm an American goddamn it, I have expectations!" The water, the surf: a last, partially preserved vestige of stolen islands, land, culture.

Powerful rituals entailing an obdurate number of intricacies and codes. Powerful, religious, collective joy. Not just pleasure and enjoyment, but fun, camaraderie, passion/obsession, wonder.

Someone else will ride a bigger wave. Someone else will make more money. But did you help that old lady across the street when you saw her struggling with heavy bags? Did you do something cool for someone else without telling them, as Jock Sutherland mischievously enjoys doing? As Jock says: "Sometimes you do something for somebody and they don't know it was you, but you watch them from a distance. 'Gee, somebody helped me out here. Did I . . . I didn't know I deserved that.' And you go (making a wheezing laughter à la Muttley of *Wacky Races*)." Clyde adds, "Tell that teacher or coach you appreciate their work. Tell your dad that you love him. It may be the last chance you get; you *just never know*. Lots of egos, especially with males," while admitting that it took him thirty-five years to say, "Pops: I love you." "A little unsure of themselves," Jock calmly says, naming my timidity while referring to egos and singling out a male bully from older days at Waimea.

Stevo mentions an interesting paradox: you can spot those who surf big waves because they walk a little tall, but are also humble. They've been to that place where they temporarily dodged death. Many times over. "It's a spiritual thing," he adds. "It shows from within."

"Been there, done that, brah." That's Clyde closing out his sixties. Is there anything left to prove at that dire age? If so, to whom? Or anything else to experience? Clyde pauses, and then says: "For me, I still want to drop a couple [of waves] at Jaws, ah, and also master kitesurfing." Which challenges do you still look forward to and why? Simple questions. Deep questions; perhaps especially so if you voluntary put yourself in harm's way while your body is inadvertently, unintentionally, relentlessly . . . breaking apart. And how did you get here so fast? Stevo reflects on now being the older guy.

> The other day I'm looking around for the guy with the pot belly and the bald spot on the single fin and it's all these young kids. I'm the fat guy with the belly and the bald spot on the single fin. And I'm the old guy now. I have twenty-five years experience at this, and now I go off my experience rather than my youthful enthusiasm and my personal muscle strength. I don't have so much of the paddling power or the strength that I used to. I have to come to terms with that and pick my battles.

All the accumulated injuries finally meet you all at once. How do they converge so as to keep you stuck at home? And how do you

Clyde today and at thirty-six years old, about to paddle out and win the first edition of
The Eddie, held at Waimea Bay in 1986.

change your approach if you want to keep doing what you dedicated your life to? How and when do you completely retire from your avo-cation? Is there such a thing as perfect timing, or lingering on too long?

In big wave surfing there are two main philosophies on disengage-ment. You either retire on top, as Clark Abbey did when he hit fifty and never showed up at the Bay again. Or you fade away gradually, taking a more and more conservative and safer approach, as James Jones or Jock Sutherland are doing.

Throughout his life, decades before Kai, Clyde had mastered several water sports: surfing, big wave riding, windsurfing, diving, catching fish, sailing, too. Windsurfing every day for two years brought him healing from the tragic loss of his brother. He tells me that "the worst thing you can do is stay home staring at your four walls. You have to get yourself physically exhausted." Like his seniors, Peter Cole, Jock Sutherland, and a few others, a waterman before it became *en vogue*. Training as a boxer like Tony Moniz, believing conditioning was key. A man of the islands from another era, invoking reverence and some fear too. Short-fused, perhaps. "Quiet!" Stubborn, some might say. Highly emotional. True. Religiously charismatic. Listen. But also authentic, and beneath the sur-face and between the lines, humorous, intelligent, and loving. Just don't mess with him. "Waimānalo," he tells me, "the true hidden gem of Oʻahu." "Waimānalo? That's such a shitty place," another spits out, but not con-fronting him. Clyde picks me up by the gate where he lives with his wife of thirty-five years, Eleni, who runs a dog-training compound. Besides giving inspirational talks, Clyde works with the Department of Educa-tion as a homeless concerns liaison. In this capacity he monitors about three hundred students and their families who, as they used to say in Hawaiʻi before homelessness became the tragedy it now is, have "no more house." His job primarily consists in making sure that these elementary, middle, and high school students are properly fed at least one decent meal per day, and that their families fill out the proper paperwork so that they can get aid. His job is more difficult and shattering than any big wave he has ever taken or been overwhelmed by.

He drives by me on his ATV without coming to a complete stop. Intui-tively, I guess that all I have to do is just jump on its back. A rescue? Some entertainment? A test? Impatience? All of the above?

By 2021 humble Kai, as many call him, arguably the best waterman in the world now, has taken it further than most others before him. And that includes Uncle Clyde, who is proud of him. That's how progression goes in any field, "ah?" Stand on the shoulders of giants to see further, go further. But let's glance back now to see where we ended up here.

Clyde didn't win the last Eddie he competed in, in 2016. Officially, John John Florence did. But judging from the crowd's reaction as he first paddled out, came back on shore heavily injured after his first heat, and went back out for his second and final heat, he probably did. "Uncle Clyde, Uncle Clyde, Uncle Clyde." Even if only a tenth of the twenty-five thousand people congregated on the beach chanted, that would have been enough. A first. His last ride. Waimea Bay as a stadium celebrating one of the day's heroes, and by proxy Hawaiian culture and Eddie's legacy. Mother Nature at its best, in the best conditions The Eddie has ever had.

The Bay with waves so large they're closing out every ten minutes or so. A handful of surfers so scared to be out there they didn't even catch one wave during any of their forty-five-minute heats. No one had enough courage to listen to Clyde's speech on the morning of the event inviting anyone who didn't feel comfortable to decline paddling out. The fear of being called a chicken apparently required more strength. A pandemonium of a day.

The underdog by age who got hurt real bad in the first round, but kept going "no matter what," perhaps recklessly, as others do swayed by emotions and adrenaline, during competitions and free surf. A Rocky Balboa. At sixty-five years old, the oldest competitor. The last one from the old entourage still competing here.

His win at The Eddie in 1986 during its inaugural edition at the Bay, in memory of his older brother lost at sea in 1978 at thirty-one years old. A life of fun and adventure, but also of service, tragedy, and hard work growing up poor. Eddie: the first lifeguard at the Bay. Almost full-blooded Hawaiian, yet looking and holding himself as one hundred percent Hawaiian. Eddie: the archetypal religious story of departing while trying to save innocent others. Clyde's living legacy of Eddie-forever-young. Gone and never forgotten. A persistent symbol. Clyde: his brother's spokesperson. The Eddie: reminding the world of how deeply Hawaiian surfing is. Eddie's reputation[1] and The Eddie demarcate a collective identity that reminds members of the community who they are, who they aspire to be, and perhaps where they're going or should be going back to. But the event is also a celebration, almost like a music festival, as spectators camp out on the beach or in their cars the night before.

If it hadn't been for Eddie's inspiration, Clyde probably wouldn't have dropped into his first serious wave at Waimea—a forty-footer—in 1969. When Waimea was big, a lot of the established surfers from the first generation of big wave riders—George Downing, Mike Doyle, Mikey Muñoz, Mike Stang—were already getting a little older. "And as you get a little older," Clyde tells me, "you get a little apprehensive." Every time Eddie paddled into the lineup, especially when it was massive, everybody felt more comfortable. Clyde likes to remember his brother riding down giant waves with a smile, and he says: "Awesome attribute that a big wave rider can do that: you got twenty people, they're a little jittery, but when Eddie comes into the lineup they're all calm. How's that? Laird Hamilton probably had that touch at Jaws." More recently, others like Phil and Chris play that role for many at the Bay. And on a smaller scale, many who surf big waves draw comfort from their friends' presence. That's why they often paddle out in groups, or even sometimes deliberately take off on the same wave together. And lifeguards' patrolling, of course, also provides reassurance.

Eddie's reputation was born on November 19, 1967, at Waimea Bay. That was the day his life changed forever. Clyde shows me a picture of Eddie. His board is eleven feet and in the picture there's room for seven of it end to end down the face of the wave. According to Clyde, that was the biggest wave ridden at Waimea Bay until recently—a record that held for over forty years. Besides the accuracy with which the feat is recorded and remembered, what matters most is how such epic stories provide the cement for group cultures. A means to bond and a compass by which to navigate.

Clyde didn't want to be invited to the 2016 edition of The Eddie because he was Eddie's brother. That's not how he wanted to go out. He wanted to go out on as high a level as he could. And at sixty-five years old, he realized it was time to pass the torch.

> If you're a responsible athlete, you'll know when it's time to pass that mantle on. The problem with athletes is that they don't know when it's time and they hang on, and they hang on, and they get beat up, they get stomped on and they look really terrible. And I don't think that's the right way for an athlete to go out. And this was my last ride, at sixty-five years old, and a lot of people don't know that I trained for seven months.

He ran and regularly paddled to Rabbit Island and back through shark-infested waters. As Clyde tells me, the training involved not just conditioning, but also trying "to get in the right frame of mind because I was gonna ride Waimea Bay as big as it gets for the last time." Yet, as a couple of his friends tell me, years prior he had physically let himself go a little bit, and he should have been in better shape for the contest. But keeping in shape for so many years while holding a job and not living on the North Shore is no easy feat. Intuitively, at least, everyone can imagine that.

Four weeks before The Eddie, there were two swells that were just as big, and Clyde confidently surfed them by pitting his skills against anyone else that was out there. During those days I posted up at the *heiau* on top of Waimea, about three hundred feet above the sea, armed with an 800-millimeter zoom lens, taking pictures from early morning until late in the afternoon. I captured a handful of Clyde's rides. Looking back at his performances, he concedes: "Uncle Clyde was doing pretty good." "I have proof," I say. And Noa Ginella, who was in the water with him that day with his friend Mo, tells me: "He was sitting on the boil way more inside than anyone, and a set caught him inside and totally smoked him. And when he came up he was smiling. It was calming how comfortable he was, and it definitely helped me relax." Yet, during one of these sessions he broke one of his favorite boards, one he planned to use at the competition, and that likely undermined both his confidence and the quality of his performance.

The day before The Eddie went, Clyde and his son Ha'a slept in the park by the Bay. Ha'a wakes him up: "Dad, Dad, waves are coming up into the park!"

Still half-asleep, Clyde says: "What? The waves are coming up into the park?" He elaborates for me: "When that happens, you know it's monstrous, brah. That never happened since 1969, when the waves washed all the way back up to the road," when many of the houses were being carried across the street on Ke Nui Road.

Then he tells me: "You may think that I'm talking bubbles, but even at sixty-five years old, I believed that I could have took—could have took, the contest. Ah! (in wondrous disbelief)."

Two years prior to the contest, the media were making a big deal about the young John John Florence challenging the old Uncle Clyde. "I looked at that and I took it on as a challenge," says Clyde.

When he and John John paddled out on the day of the competition, they both went for the deepest and most challenging spot at Waimea, "where you really want the juice to be, so he and I were in the right spot." Then he adds:

> But prior to paddling out I had my game plan set already. Like a football player. Like a basketball player, or like a boxer: you have your plan before you even step on the court.

Every athlete has a plan before they step on the golf course, because they've done their homework—personalities are different, so you got to do your homework. Golf courses are different, so you got to do your homework. Football players you're playing against are different players, so you need to know their strengths and their weaknesses so you attack their weaknesses, ah?

It's like The Eddie. I was ready to go. I was ready to go. And my plan was: (self-talking) "When I paddle out there, no matter what happens, the first biggest set that pulls in I'm going. It's a go. No matter what. No matter what." The first big set that comes, I'm going. So me and John and everybody else out there see a set rolling in—one line from Hale'iwa to Velzyland. One line coming in. Everybody on the beach screaming, horns going nuts, and me man, I'm going into my mode: "No matter what, no matter what happens, I'm gonna go."

"Why on the first set?" I ask. "Because there could be no other set?"

No, no (his tone expressing frustration at my second question). It's because you have your confidence . . . your confidence level is so high that you could catch a tidal wave and feel comfortable about it. You've done the training. You've done the sacrifices. You have forty years of experience behind you. You've ridden Waimea Bay every single big wave that ever came in for forty years, this is your last ride for Eddie. Say no more. You're ready to go.

On the beach his team suits him up, psyches him up, and puts wax on his board. Next, Clyde comes over in front of the scaffolding where old George Downing—the mind behind the contest—and the various officials, the judges, the governor, the mayor are sitting. And he yells out: "Uncle George, Uncle George!"

George finally sticks his head out and Clyde tells him: "Uncle George! (still yelling) I'm gonna go out and I'm gonna catch a big one for you!"

"The whole place went nuts, brah. The whole scaffold went crazy," he says. Then he turns around, goes down the beach, and paddles out by the corner of the Bay beneath the Church and Phil's home. Out in the lineup, the wave he was expecting comes soon after, and both he and John paddle out to be in position to take it. Clyde tells me:

It didn't matter what John was gonna do. It didn't matter what Nathan Fletcher was gonna do. It didn't matter. All that mattered was: this big wave is coming, and I'm swinging it around and I'm going. Either they're

in the inside of me. They are in the outside of me. Under me. I'm going. I
paddle. I take off.

As he takes off alone on the wave, the tail of his board loses contact
with the water and gets in the air—looking at photographs you can see
the fins. Half of his board is in the air and somehow Clyde momentarily
brings the board back into the face of the wave. Then he drops another
ten feet and the whole fin comes out again. And after that, he wipes out.
The wave drills him down (*pam!*) and he can't come up. So he decides to
inflate his vest to get back to the surface. Lifeguards can't get to him in
time, so the next wave just smashes him up, and by the third wave they
come and get him into the channel, where he puts another canister into
his vest and gets ready to ride some more waves. In that fall he seriously
injured his shoulder and knee. Two-inch screws. Nine hours surgery.
Nine months recovery. But right then Clyde didn't know how severe the
injury was.

In his first round, the biggest set of waves of the day pull through. It's
a set of waves that closes out the entire Bay. Rescue jet skis, trying to save
themselves, bolt toward the beach since they have no chance of escaping
toward the horizon. It's an exciting moment for all of us on the beach,
and a moment of fear for both the drivers and the athletes. The first wave
of that set catches Clyde inside, overwhelming him. It rags him like a doll
and then it pushes him down to the very bottom of Waimea Bay, on the
sand. Remembering that moment, Clyde says:

And it wouldn't let me go. That wave. Wouldn't. Let me. Go. I was on the
very bottom of Waimea Bay and I was going: "Oh, whoa . . . this is the
moment." So I pulled all my canisters and inflated my vest and I started
coming up, but I still got to fight to come up because it's just so big, it was
actually the biggest wave of the day. . . . I'm coming up, and all this time
I'm being worked by the force of the wave. I'm going this way. I'm going
that way. I can't come up. It's pushing me down. It's holding me down. I
can't come up. It's like: "That's it, man." When I'm like twenty feet from
the very top of the water, my air is gone—everything is gone. I finally
come up above the water and I look around and as far as I can see the
entire area is white. Waimea Bay is white. Waimea rock is white. Waimea
mountain is white. Everything is white. I feel like I'm in a church. I'm
not scared—not even one bit. I'm not excited. I'm just so calm. All of a
sudden. I shake it off. Then my eyes open again. And then the water turns
blue. I see the mountain and there's nobody around. I'm in the water all

by myself and there's nobody around. Nobody. No other surfer. No other lifeguard. Nothing. And then finally after two, three minutes the ski comes and picks me up.

After his heat is over, Clyde is dropped near the shore break by a jet ski operated by lifeguard Terry Ahue. In the meantime, his board caddy, Ian Masterson, and three other lifeguards run toward the right corner of the Bay to help him get out of the water. It's a fraught scenario: while the waves are pushing him in, the back current is pushing him back out. Putting twenty years of experience to work, Ian manages to grab Clyde by the shoulder and help him out of the water, making it look like it wasn't even a rescue. Just before that, Clyde almost hits a big rock. As Ian puts it: "It's like his brother put his hands under him, lifting him up and moving him over about ten feet to the side, preventing a catastrophic collision." Carrying Clyde's board over his head across the beach, Ian announces: "Ladies and gentlemen: Eddie Aikau's brother, Clyde Aikau!" The crowd goes wild.

Clyde is then taken to the doctors' tent, where he's given oxygen and has an IV placed on his left arm to numb the pain. He hasn't successfully completed one ride yet, and he's determined to go back out.

Some of the judges and organizers pull Ian aside, forming a circle around him and asking him to prevent Clyde from going back out. "Ian, you got to tell him not to surf," one says. "You got to tell him: Don't go out," another reaffirms. "He went out already. He got waves. He got injured. He's hurt. He can't go back there again. Man, he's going to get killed. Tell him not to do it," another says.

Then Ian looks at them and says:

I'm a lifeguard and I understand exactly what you're telling me, and in any normal circumstance, I'd probably say that. But I'm his surf caddy—that's my role here today. My job is to support Uncle Clyde one hundred and fifty percent, no matter what he chooses to do. So if he decides he wants to go out, am I supporting that? Absolutely! Without question. In every way I can.

The others look at each other, they all nod their heads, and they break the circle.

The lifeguards then put Clyde on their cart to take him to the church corner of the beach, where he can get back into the water for his second and final heat. As the crowd sees him coming back, people on the beach gradually stand up and chant: "Un-cle Clyde! Un-cle Clyde!" When he reaches the corner, more voices have joined, and it sounds like a stadium. Clyde tells me: "I swear I look up at the mountain and it looks like the mountain was gonna collapse. It was so much. So much vibes . . . so much energy at that moment." While his body is shattered, the chant feeds his powerful soul. Clyde rides another handful of waves with basically only one arm and a damaged knee.

As Ian later tells me: "You got to end with grace. It was a big risk for me telling the organizers I supported Clyde's decision. But there was no way I was going to tell Uncle Clyde Aikau: 'I'm your board caddy, don't go out, I'm telling you.' Fuck that. That's not Waimea. That's not what you'd tell Clark Abbey."

Fading, Scaling Down, Changing Approach, and Losing the Edge

Kaipo stopped riding big waves recently. He's in his late fifties now. As he got older, and visibly out of shape, he experienced a number of clearly dangerous situations in the water, and finally he decided to quit. He thinks that three of those situations were "close calls," and they all took place in the same year. In one of them he had to swim in without his board at night after a wipeout at an outer reef on the North Shore called Himalayas. He describes that incident as being "kind of weird." He wore a leash he thought was almost unbreakable. He fell off and heard this sound underwater: *bin!* He knew his leash had snapped and he had to figure out the current to swim in. Next, he saw his board start coming back toward him in the rip current. And he said to himself: "Oh, I'm going to make it." And he got really close to his board. Then a big set came in, and his board was gone. "Oh man, I thought I was going to make it. Now I'm not sure I'm going to," he thought. And it was getting real dark. He eventually found his board washed up on the beach, and he started walking back to his car. In the meantime, a guy he had been surfing with noticed that all the other cars were gone, but Kaipo's van was still parked. He started walking up and down the beach looking for him. And when he met him, he said: "I was ready to call the Coast Guard." "That was one time that really got me thinking: I could have missed the beach and swam somewhere else," Kaipo tells me. And he adds: "You begin to think: I could be unlucky. Something could happen."

In essence, surfing big waves is a form of calculated gambling, where there are only so many variables one can control. The rest is chance. And the odds are usually against you. When I ask him why he quit, Kaipo says he thinks many will consider stopping when they realize that it could *actually* happen to them—that it could be them dying and not someone else. Then he adds that in his case, another reason is knowing that drowning is a very painful death. As writer Philip Hoare[2] says about drowning: "You're there one minute, in another world the next; a transition rather than a destruction." Yet as Janet Murray[3] says about being submerged in water, "the sensation of being surrounded by a completely other reality, as different as water is from air, that takes over all of our attention, our whole perceptual apparatus," is already being in another world. This means that drowning is a sort of double transition to yet another world we still don't know enough about.

Kaipo reasoned—or rationalized—that he was being too selfish, and that instead it was time to focus on his son's surfing rather than his own. Plus, reflecting on some of his friends who died too young (not from surfing, but in a few cases from drugs), he lowers his voice and tells me he wanted to see "what's next . . . I just wanted to live." Yet, like me, he also says he's been wondering why other big wave surfers do what they do, and continue doing it at higher levels than he ever did. He tells me he'd be interested in knowing: "Why did they do it? Why did they push it that far? What were they expecting to get out of it?" He remembered asking one of those older individuals, who answered quickly, which for him indicated an honest response: "What was I gonna do?" To this day, Kaipo doesn't know if what the surfer meant is that there was nothing else that he could have done, or that he had no choice. A prisoner perhaps, like Clark Abbey, whose obsession with and dedication to the Bay almost shattered his work life and social relations. One of his friends describes Clark's relationship with Waimea: "His whole life was clocking in and cataloging every single swell. He sacrificed everything to surf . . . *the* Bay. But we never saw him unless country (the North Shore of O'ahu) was fifteen to twenty feet plus. He would piss off the whole world to go surfing—especially his wife and his boss. He found every way out. It didn't matter what was happening." Yet, having talked with Clark, I'm sure that looking back with a smirk, he thinks it was all worth it.

Surfers on the North Shore generally scale up through steps—for example, setting goals like going up two feet in wave height every winter, or surfing certain spots before others (for example, Sunset before Waimea, Waimea before the outer reefs or Jaws). And they also eventually scale down. But skipping steps is becoming more common, in large part because of the development and popularization of safety equipment. Risk levels grow along with confidence over the course of a winter, usually peaking toward its end; they also go up within a single session, and throughout an entire career or life cycle. The risks surfers take are related not only to their own mental and physical preparation, but also to the individuals that surround them in the lineup, as well as those on the beach or at home waiting for them. Plus, there's clearly an aging curve related to the decline in physical fitness and the accumulation of injuries, coupled with an increase in experience. Surfers talk about how as they age they learn to listen to their bodies better, and "surf with their minds"—having "an eye" for which waves are safe to take. But physical decay is unavoidable.

I'm being treated with an acupuncture technique that uses a light electric current to stimulate my muscles, because I can barely lift my left arm after having fought the current to get out of the water at Waimea after a session in which I caught no waves. Waves were clearly too big for me, and if it hadn't been for Dan, who helped me get out of the impact zone, dodging a much larger set that was approaching, I shudder to think of what might have happened.

John Abramson, a therapist in his late fifties who is also a good surfer—tall, lanky, and lean, with spirited eyes—has treated many professional surfers. He tells me that eventually surfers figure out the parameters within which they feel comfortable. He says they learn specific numbers relating to the size of the waves out at sea—read by the buoys—and specific swell directions for each spot. As he learned from one of his friends, Milton Willis, and as I would hear from others, a general rule is that unless you're comfortable taking off on the biggest wave of the day, then you shouldn't be out there. Otherwise, "You're a danger to yourself and to everybody else." You have to be ready for such an occurrence. And there's always a rogue set—like the one I just described that caught me off guard—no matter how accurate forecasting has become. Clearly, I've broken this rule more than once, but luckily it's only resulted in minor injuries—which nevertheless persist years after those sessions as a reminder of my mistakes.

"What are the common injuries in big wave surfing?" I ask. "Mostly neck, back, and shoulders," he answers. But brain injuries, while also common, mostly go undetected. Then I explain to him that when I wiped out earlier at Waimea, the nose of my board went underwater, I was catapulted in front of it, and my body was stopped when I hit the water first on my neck, before the wave hit me. I was surprised that what hurt me afterward was not my neck, but my back. John explains to me:

Once you're in the water, the water gets heavy and just twists your body, and wherever the weakness is . . . some people it's the shoulders, back, knee, wherever the weakest part is, the ocean is gonna twist the whole body . . . in your case it's the back . . . once you have that, you know the area you need to strengthen to get ready for the next wave.

We talk about confidence, how much of it is in your mind and how it's also related to how hard you train. Recalling an image from years back, he tells me of sitting by the lifeguard tower at Waimea Bay with George Downing, Peter Cole, and the head judge of The Eddie. A woman who seemed overly excited started saying how much she wanted to surf big Waimea, and how she was training by lifting weights, swimming, and carrying rocks underwater. After about five minutes she stopped. George commented: "But how's your brain?"

John tells me of having surfed big Sunset thirty years ago, when it was the first time for Carlos Burle as well, and how scared they both were, and how they didn't know how to surf such large waves. Talking about Carlos's career, but also the careers of many others who practice the sport, John says he thinks that what's truly impressive is how they paddle back out to the surf after they get hurt. Not necessarily on the same day, but year after year. How mentally and physically taxing it is. And people like Carlos paddle out after not just one major injury, but a series of them. The North Shore of Oʻahu produces large waves only during the late fall and winter, sometimes through the spring. As summer turns to fall, waves typically increase in size and consistency on the North Shore, until by spring the sea turns flat, and the new swells hit the South Shore instead. John says:

The North Shore is very tricky, it's very insidious because you can come over here and you start in September, and you surf the first swell, and you surf every swell and you go up . . . you know, from six, eight, ten feet, and all of a sudden you get away with it and you can go along for a couple of months and think you really know what you're doing. And all of a sudden, it's big and then it just takes one mistake and you have an injury that takes two, three, four months, or two, three, four years to get over. And then comes a point when you collect enough of these types of injuries; it's just not really worth it anymore because you might get that one great wave, but if you mess up you're out, for how long? And so, you reach a point where you just surf your capabilities, wherever that is. Like Randy Rarick said: "You're in it for the long haul" . . . you can surf ten feet, but you surf six feet because you want to keep surfing your whole life and you want to have fun out there. And you surf what makes you happy.

He likes to say that when people ask him about his plans for the winter he replies, "Try not to be a lifeguard incident report," then laughs. "Conditioning is extremely important for surfing the North Shore." When people tell him they want to surf it, he responds:

Number one: make sure your health insurance is paid up. Number two: be ready to say goodbye to any equipment you have—it could get broken, destroyed, caught in a rip and just disappear. And then be prepared for an injury that may take you out anywhere from a few days, to a few weeks to a few months. If you're not ready for all of that, don't paddle out. Just wait for a smaller day.

He mentions two big injuries he suffered over the last ten years:

One is from 1999, that was a bad one, a wipeout at Sunset, just double overhead Sunset, you know? (ironically) I just hit my face on the water. Got to the bottom and fell off. Hit the side of my head on the water and had a concussion and two herniated disks.

Then our friend Dave steps into the conversation, saying: "Did you break your eardrum?"

And John says: "Yes, I was lucky about that one . . . then I got to the car, looked into the rearview mirror, and the rearview mirror was melting like [I was on] an LSD trip, so on one whole side I couldn't really see out one eye for like four hours."

Not having heard the beginning of our conversation, Dave asks: "How big was it?"

A little bit more than double overhead. Not three times overhead, but more than double. Way too big for me. That's when I learned I shouldn't be out there trying to surf that stuff. It was a glassy sunny day with no wind, but I just lost my balance at the bottom because it was too fast. I don't have that skill level to go that fast. You have to have a lot of good conditioning. You have to know your limits.

"How long did it take to recover from that injury?" I ask.

Three years. Once you know the right exercises, your body will recover fast, but do what the doctor says. Don't overdo it, but don't underdo it. I always say: "No sacrificing body parts for sports anymore." When you're young you think you can keep going, but sooner or later you get wise, you pick your waves. You need to be physically fit enough to swim under three big waves. If you get caught inside, and you can't make it under three comfortably, then go in. Don't stay out there anymore, just turn around and catch one in.

Felipe Pomar, who was a champion, wrote that anyone can come to the North Shore to surf, and surf for a few days or a few weeks, but if you stay for the whole season sooner or later you're gonna get a really bad wipeout, and that's when you find out who you are. Can you overcome that fear, paddle back out, and get another one?

And how long can you actually do it? I wonder. At ninety years old, Peter Cole may be the oldest big wave surfer alive today. Peter likes to recall a saying from one of his friends: "You start as a kook, and you end as a kook." Like others, he clearly remembers when and how he decided to stop, and it happened on two occasions—and note he's one of the handful of surfers who always went in without a leash.

I stopped surfing Waimea at Thanksgiving in 1995.

"Because it was too crowded?" I ask.

Ah, ah, yeah (reluctantly) . . . and because I wasn't good (raising his voice slightly). I think what basically happens is that you don't maintain that peak surfing for very long, you know? Your peak is probably between twenty-five and . . . well, I surfed Waimea until I was sixty-five, but I wasn't surfing it like when I was fifty (coughs). And I was backing out on waves that I usually wouldn't be backing off, and the crowd was bothering me. And a combination of all these things, so I decided, the heck with it. It's not worth it. I'm not having fun and I think that what happens is you don't do that well, you don't have fun. I think surfing is a matter of fun, and at Sunset I was having fun until I quit, until I had problems with my shoulder.

Brendan Shea, a lifeguard who also surfs without a leash, was out with Peter on that Thanksgiving session. He says: "Peter would only surf

Waimea or Sunset. He wouldn't lower himself to Chuns, Kamis, or softer breaks. He used to say: 'I'm surfing until I'm not surfing. And it's going to be those two waves.' He quit surfing Waimea in his sixties, and rode Sunset into his seventies. At the end he struggled. He just didn't have the strength."

Mike Takahashi explains how he stopped riding the Bay. He's scaling down, but he still surfs Sunset, which in his younger years was a stepping-stone toward the Bay. I ask how he's disengaging from big wave surfing, and he says:

> The fear of dying. The fear of getting hurt. My rule was: If I don't want to go out and catch the biggest, ugliest, thickest wave, you better stay on the beach because you're going to be put in that position. You're going to get tested. Something big, ugly, and crazy is going to come your way, and you'd better be able to swing around and go. Once you lose that, you don't go out. You know? So, until I was about my late forties, I would still go out when it's twenty feet and swing, go. But I think . . . just something happens incrementally. As a recreational guy you go: well, this is just supposed to be fun. I don't want to worry about getting hurt and not being able to provide for my family. I got kids that need me. So, around fifty I would go out and I would start going: "Oh no, it's twenty feet and up. I'll wait till it's just eighteen feet." Then you gradually start bringing your way down until finally it's like . . . I think when I was fifty-eight I caught my last like eighteen-foot wave. After that it was only fifteen-foot days. Eventually you just bring it down slowly and calm down.

Individuation

Building on the work of psychologist Heinz Kohut,[4] Michael Farrell discusses the importance of friendship groups to complement and complete early life socialization.[5] Idealizing significant friends we can interact with over a long period helps us feel more grounded and secure in ourselves. Like a good parental figure, such friends serve as supportive audiences to our attempts to master a skill—encouraging us to succeed, consoling us when we fail. With their belief in us, they help to stabilize our equilibrium, our belief in ourselves, when we have doubts. Once the process is complete and the new skill is mastered and integrated into our self-concept, we are ready to individuate, to break free from the dependent relationship. But at the end of a career, when it is time to lay down those skills, other processes are needed to maintain equilibrium. Surfers report that working through this process often involves having talks with the self. For example, Shane Dorian told me:

> I'm way less competitive than I was. Now I'm not competitive, like I'm surf-ing Jaws and Mark Healey gets an insane wave and I'm just stoked for him, I don't need to go: "OK, well I'll just sit here and wait to get a super giant one and try to outdo his wave" or anything like that. I'm just like plain simply happy for people if they get a great wave and they get a good ride and they're safe. We all come home at the end of the day, that's the most impor-tant thing. And if I get a really incredible ride, that's like icing on the cake.

For Fun

There's a plurality of answers to the question of why anyone would surf big waves, and none of them are definitive. Sociologists have long dis-cussed the complexity of understanding motivation for action, especially taken as retrospective accounts decoupled from lived experience. Plus, motivations can change as our circumstances and selves do. Sociologist Everett Hughes[6] conceptualized the idea of career as a moving perspec-tive in someone's life. When I talk about this matter with Matt Rode, we identify a handful of reasons that, at least theoretically, could explain surfing big waves. Yet Matt surfs big waves and knows most of the top surfers well, and I have met and talked with many of them for my project. But how honest can you be with yourself when trying to understand why you would voluntarily put yourself in such risky environments?

First, surfers might engage in big wave surfing for fame or money. According to Clyde, as many as eight out of ten surfers who are chasing big waves professionally do so for these reasons. Checking Clyde's opin-ion with other surfers I'd met, I find that while his count is probably an exaggeration (albeit one with truth in it), without the safety devices that have been developed, even the top athletes would probably not take the risks they take. They might not quit if there was no potential to make "livable money," but they certainly wouldn't take the risks they do with-out it and without the safety devices that have been developed.

Second, surfers could pursue this activity to seek approval or accep-tance from their peers. Based on the need to be recognized by others and develop and sustain self-confidence. Yet, as Matt points out, doing it for the money, fame, or acceptance is doing it for the wrong reasons, and that's irresponsible because there's not much money to be made and because you're risking your life. As Jock Sutherland puts it:

A lot of people are unsure of themselves. They don't have a good sense of self-confidence. They don't have a sense of being worthwhile, of being valuable human beings. They've got to do this. They've got to accomplish this. They're worried. And you shouldn't be, because it takes away from . . . the human condition is usually one of happiness—mostly. . . . Human beings have a good nature to begin with.

Without claiming to have fully transcended these "wrong" motivations, Matt reflects:

Why do we need anyone's approval for anything? It's ego. It's lack of self-confidence. If you're truly self-aware and self-confident, you really value yourself as an individual, it doesn't matter how big a wave you catch. Doesn't matter who thinks you're a big wave guy. . . .

Why do you want the approval or the respect? Why do you want someone to respect you because of how good a surfer you are, instead of just respecting you for how good a person you are? We're pretty confused. We're pretty lost. But it seems more important. But how many people do you know that are going around really trying to be good people so that people will think they're a nice person? Nobody. They're going around trying to do the biggest wave, do the biggest air, whatever. . . .

I think it always comes down to self-worth, and like how much do you value yourself. If someone is completely comfortable in who they are, and they love themselves for who they are, it doesn't matter to them if other people know they charge, it doesn't matter if they have other people's respect.

They don't even need to charge to prove to themselves that they charge. And that's my struggle. And to the point where I don't give a fuck what other people think about me, but I still will judge myself by why am I not catching as big of a wave as the other guys . . . or I'm not accepting myself, am I? Still struggling.

Similarly, Shane Dorian says:

Probably the hardest thing is to know when to stop, when to go: "You know what? I don't want it anymore." That's because it has to come from . . . a lot of big wave surfing has a lot to do with ego. A lot of times when you turn around to catch a wave it's your ego telling you to go. It's your ego telling you not to puss out. It's your ego telling you that your friends are watching, and you need to go because of that. Or because you need to go back to Brazil to have everyone think you're a hero, or you need to get a shot in a magazine, or you need to get that video clip. Or someone is filming and you pretty much have to catch a wave because that guy's there. There's just so much ego involved.

Finally, we discuss a third reason: fun. Matt says, "That's the point! If you're doing it purely for fun, that's fucking great, man. Do whatever you want. I respect that."

"I met some guys who told me they're doing it just for fun," I say.

"Those underground guys are proud of being the underground," Matt replies, "and so I would love to have a moment when they're completely honest with themselves; that's the moment I'm interested in with everyone. Because I think that it's easy to say, 'I just do it for fun and fuck all those silly guys.'"

Then, we hypothesize that one way to understand the real motivations behind big wave surfing might be to see how often people surf spots with cameras, or how often they post images of their feats on social media. The less often they do any of those things, the more likely they're doing it for themselves rather than to impress someone else.

I mention to Peter Cole what Shane Dorian said about the "right reasons" for surfing big waves, and he says: "He's right, and the right reason is fun—the camaraderie. To me the best part, also about competitive sports—and I was into competitive swimming—is the camaraderie." Camaraderie and fun—implicitly merged by Peter to mean the same thing—are built on mutual respect among a select group of individuals you end up spending lots of time with, voluntarily doing something you love while growing together through communal experiences.

Then we talk about his last session at Sunset. The large windows of his beach house overlook Rocky Point, but if you look to the right you can see Sunset at a distance. One morning late in the season, the waves suddenly picked up and it was unusually uncrowded. And while Peter hadn't surfed for a while, the sight was too alluring for him to let it pass by. So he decides to paddle out, but ends up surfing "terribly" because first, he can barely see—an old surf injury left him blind in his right eye—but more significantly, because his shoulder isn't strong enough for him to get up on his board taking off. Also, none of his friends are there. "It wasn't fun," he recalls, with frustration and nostalgia. "And I sure miss it," he adds, referring to surfing in general. Then he reaches for his wallet, picks out a small piece of paper, and unfolds a faded black-and-white photograph of a giant wave he caught at Waimea in 1967. It's a film still from one of Bud Browne's movies that was used as a poster promoting the film. Peter no longer surfs; now he just swims. Essentially, he's reversed the steps of engagement with big waves and the ocean. Back to basics. Based on the theory of fun I formulated with Gary Alan Fine, fun depends on daring to risk in the company of friends, on enjoying failures and successes, sometimes outwitting fate together, and then telling and retelling stories of the adventures group members had together. Further, as Walter Podilchak[7] argues in one of the first articles on the sociology of fun, one of the conditions that inhibit fun is the inability to participate in the activity, which in Peter's case is due to physical decline.

The 2019 Underground Awards

One day in April, toward the end of the winter season, members of the Waimea underground group meet at a restaurant in Hale'iwa for a small gathering organized by Tracy and Ricardo. When we've eaten, Ricardo gets up at one end of the table, calls for everyone's attention, and says:

> We used to have a surfer we all looked up to at the Bay, Clark Abbey. Because of my mistake Clark ended up hurting his eardrum that day twelve years ago. I was just trying to surf that wave that I loved so much. Since then I felt obliged to teach others because I've experienced it. I look up to you guys so much because you've shared your knowledge with me over all these years.

Seizing a pause, Chris steps in and says, while looking at Ricardo:

> He's become a mentor to me the past year. He's taught hundreds of us now how to hold our breath properly. And let me tell you that the wipe-out I had at Mavericks last December, I owe a lot of it to him. Unless I'd done my breathing exercises weeks before that swell, I wouldn't have survived it.

Ricardo smiles and continues:

> I was already a diving instructor and I wanted to be a better big wave surfer, so I started to swim more and to train to hold my breath longer, but also to help others. That mistake I made helped me want to train, and also help others not to make the same mistake.

So, you guys are my brothers. You guys, I look up to you so much. I love you guys. Every single wave you guys go down, if I don't catch the next wave, my job is to watch after you guys and make sure you come up safe, or do the best I can to get you as fast as possible, and everybody knows that's a situation. I learned from my mistakes and I'll keep teaching the younger people who come surfing the Bay, and I'll try to help them open their eyes about the lineup to keep everybody safe.

Next, Ricardo introduces the season's winners, handing them each a trophy and a medallion of the same size. Chris Owens first, and Phil Owen second. Then he reaches into the bottom of the white plastic bag from which he has pulled out their awards. He holds a silver plastic statuette about twenty inches high and weighing little more than an envelope. He says a few words about meeting me three years earlier, my book project, how I started to surf the Bay to better understand big wave surfing, and then says I've become part of the group. I feel slightly embarrassed, because I feel like I still have much work to do both on the book and on getting stronger and more courageous surfing bigger waves. I know I have enough skill to step it up, but I need better conditioning and more strength; I need to train to feel as strong and confident as I did when I first surfed the Bay in 2016 and 2017. I stand up and thank Ricardo, and after requesting a chance to speak, I say: "If it wouldn't have been for Phil, none of this would have happened. He took me out at the Bay against my will. Thank you, Phil, and to all of you guys."

EPILOGUE

Gone but Here, Yet Barely in Sight

While our existence is limited or cut short against our will, sometimes our horizons expand beyond our imagination. If we look back on those periods when we felt larger than ourselves, we often find small groups of *significant others* nearby. Those few who danced, sang, and talked within our frequency, amplifying and expanding what we thought and did. Those memorable occasions. Unique, powerful blending of minds and souls. The miracle of the right individuals at the right time, through moments that matter.

Our lives can be conceptualized as a series of conversations, experiences, interactions, and accidents. Philosopher Charles Sanders Pierce stated that "life is a train of thought."[1] Sociologists like Randall Collins theorize that our life trajectories are constituted and determined by different series of encounters we go through, each propelling us toward the next. We all can look back and recall pivotal moments and periods of our existence when everything just clicked. Like stones rolling through life, amassing energy, seducing some to join, while bouncing off or confusing others.

Boundaries matter, and members of the self-formed groups I discuss are not easily interchanged. And it should be this way. Exclusivity maximizes reciprocity and underlines the sacrality of the unit and its force. Fun, as powerful in action as in its recollection, is based exactly on this means of letting go without fear of reprimand just to test and expand the realm of possibilities.[2] As a dynamic it's rooted in the freedom and exhilaration[3] of not having to worry about being judged, in the fear of letting down those you love and admire, and in the desire to daze those you oppose and resent. It's a theatre of the possible where the impossible can become a new reality. A play that is often more real than many of the pantomimes we engage in as part of our daily lives. During these instances we want and sometimes need to be fully present, and we know that those around us are as alert as we are, sharing the same communal project. Goals and dreams intersecting in a blending of egos. While it's pleasurable and mighty to momentarily lose one's ego, and it's exciting and powerful to experience communion, it's also gratifying to feel as if we have improved ourselves. And activities involving both *flow* and *edge-work* are characterized by internal growth and by taking authorship of the result of our actions, regardless of how ephemeral or inconsequential they may be.

Much of our lives is not chosen. It happens. Many of our interactions, and the people involved in them, are dictated by forces beyond anyone's full understanding and by chance. Yet there are times when we can control what we do and how and with whom we affiliate; and our free time is one of those instances. Lifestyle sports[4] like surfing, skateboarding, or mountaineering provide us with opportunities to live realities where spontaneity is both rewarded and punished, but also expected.

These activities are as much social as they are physical, physiological, and cognitive. Yet the occasions within which we practice them vary depending on their level of sociality, solidarity, and intensity. Intensity is based on our personal life history, the history of the groups with whom we partake on those occasions, and the history of the communities within which they fit. But it also depends on the amount of synchronization and mutual awareness between ourselves and our collaborators, and the situations we face. As familiarity can be connected to acceptance and trust, it can also be a predictor of mutual attunement. Sometimes we experience the *fateful moments* I described in this book: distinct, highly intense interactions that change our self-concept and profoundly alter the course of our lives—interactions that can also affect history.

Lifestyle sports are constituted by what theorist Michel Maffesoli[5] calls neo tribes: microcosms to which some of us can turn as an alternate reality, an antidote to the tedium of everyday life, and a surrogate system within which to realize oneself within the social sphere. In Collins's terms they provide *pockets of solidarity*—situations that produce high rhythmic entrainment.[6]

To paraphrase one of my informants: my job is not who I am, it's a means to do what I love. These enclaves enable excitement in a partially disenchanted world in which this emotion, and its authentic experience, are increasingly sought after, manufactured, and sold.[7] A mental, social, and temporal escape from the mundanity and drudgery of modern life that also has a strong physiological element—the chemicals released during highly stressful, yet ultimately enjoyable situations.

Being "out there" in the ocean and catching a giant wave, or seeing one of your friends succeed or fail at the feat, and then making it back safe to shore, is fighting for meaning and belonging;[8] it's dying to live, living to be amazed by life.

As Shane Dorian says, "Big wave surfing is not a sport at all," and maybe it isn't just yet. As in play-like activities like skateboarding, freestyle BMX, or music-making, the success of a session depends on each participant's contribution, and whether or not their own performance is acknowledged, appreciated, and reworked by other group members. While efforts are singular, the outcome is collective. As Phil says, most surfers, most of the time, are too focused on themselves, and fail to grasp the broader picture. They fail to integrate into their performance mutual focus and mimicry through sharing—two key ingredients of a successful ritual (even though overcrowding is certainly a confounding factor). By taking themselves and what they do too seriously and competitively, surfers tend to miss out on the fun. Often, even amateurs don't play around, but instead fixate on their *own* performance—in Dennis Pang's words, "Hey, look at me, I'm ripping . . . compared to you, and I surf better than you." As another surfer puts it, regular surfing sometimes feels like a job where aggression and competition foment interpersonal strains. While it may seem counterintuitive, big wave surfing instead is a stress-release kind of venture, helping you yearn for and savor basic human needs like food, air, and shelter. Additionally, it provides ample opportunities to generate collective effervescence, emotional energy, and bonding. Evolutionarily speaking, when successful these play-like activities build on archetypical forms of rituals in which each individual represents a distinct character within the social group.

Belonging together and sharing memorable experiences witnessed, told, and retold across time bind us, divide us, and essentially make us humans who can sometimes find meaning and joy in life. We can keep searching and dreaming while being barely in sight, ever on the move, looking ahead while thinking back.

Acknowledgments

I want to begin by thanking my informants who shared parts of their lives with me. Jukka Gronow, Gary Alan Fine, and Randall Collins read and commented on two drafts of this manuscript. Additionally, Jukka discussed the project with me at different phases, always offering sharp suggestions. I'm also grateful to Doug Mitchell for having recognized the project's potential. The two external reviewers complemented each other's perspectives particularly well, and ultimately contributed to improving the quality of the book. My editor, Elizabeth Branch Dyson, ensured that the publication process flowed smoothly. "Onward!" she recently wrote to me, and so it will be from now as well; on, full on, toward the next adventure. At the Press I also want to thank Mollie McFee, Dylan Montanari, Evan Young, Carrie Olivia Adams, Lindsy Rice, and Eleanor Ford.

In Stockholm I'm grateful to Maria Karin Walczuk, Igor Di Marco, Patrik Aspers, Eskil and Anders Österling, and Alex Hammarstrand.

The Helsinki Collegium for Advanced Studies was an ideal intellectual home. And even though nine months weren't enough to finish the manuscript, they sufficed to produce a first draft.

At the University of Hawai'i at Mānoa I am beholden to the friendship of David Johnson and his wife, Adrienne, Nick Chagnon, and Kathy Irwin, and to the support I could always count on from Patricia Steinhoff and Patti Chan.

On O'ahu Mason Beutel, Kevin Seid, and the McGill family not only brokered introductions to the local community, but also functioned as a sounding board for my evolving ideas and challenges. Additionally, thanks are due to Brian Robbins, John Clark, Ian Masterson, Tom Farber, Luca Patrone, Marco Contati, Antti Gronow, Paolo Corte, and Pat Matsueda.

I received generous support through the Erik Allardt Fellowship, Uppsala University, and from the University of Stavanger. At my home institution I thank Espen Mathiesen, Cato Wittusen, Turid Rødne, and Nicoló Daniotti.

To my father for showing me how to catch marlins. To my mother for teaching me to notice the details.

U. C.
Albisola Capo, Italy
Stavanger, Norway

Notes

Prologue

1   Leila Fujimori (2016) writes about this.

Introduction

1   Stranger 2011, 140.
2   "Late Drop—The Big Wave Podcast: Jamie Mitchell Hosts Nathan Fletcher," 2020.
3   Émile Durkheim ([1912] 1995) defines *collective effervescence* as a kind of social electricity that transports those participating in a ritual to "an extraordinary degree of exaltation." The main precursory element required to experience this state is shared rhythm, achieved for example by singing or dancing in unison. During these peak moments we feel larger than ourselves because we are a collectivity who knows and feels its existence: physiologically and spiritually as well as cognitively. But according to Durkheim's theory this state is temporary and is limited to those gatherings, and this fact explains the need to regulate their periodic reoccurrence. Paraphrasing Durkheim, in the company of others we can rise above ourselves, and when the assembly disbands we go back to our ordinary state of living, looking forward to experiencing those feelings again.
4   Fine (2003, 655) writes: "We care about our audience, but not in the amorphous and astructural way suggested by Goffman (1959) in *Presentation of Self in Everyday Life*, a caring, apparently, for everyone and no one. Goffman suggests a desire to conform to an audience which one barely knows and into which one has never been bred, implying control without a model of socialization or identification. We conform, we strive to organize our impressions, because those with whom we belong—structurally, behaviorally, and

psychologically—have demonstrated in a dance of threats and tricks that the performance of a good impression has consequences."

5 See Farrell 2001; Parker and Corte 2017.

6 Farrell 2001.

7 See the work on creative pairs by psychologist Vera John-Steiner (2001), in which she discusses the paramount importance of believing in a partner's capabilities to establish and maintain highly successful collaboration. In this respect John-Steiner refers to Chadwick and de Courtivron (1993) and their concept of the *gift of confidence*. Complementarily, in his book on mountaineering, sociologist Richard Mitchell (1983, 81) says (in line with symbolic interactionism—e.g., Mead 1964; Cooley 1972) that "it is by the opinion of others that progress is marked and accomplishment gauged. Yet, not just any others will do. Special qualities are required of those who judge. These significant others are expected to know, in general, the purposes, rules, precedents, and other subtleties of the games being played." I call such individuals *specialized others*, to emphasize their level of expertise while drawing on the concepts of *specialized play* (see Kjølsrød 2003) and *edgework* (see Lyng 1990).

8 Collins 2004.

9 Collins 2018, 257.

10 If Erving Goffman extends Durkheim's ideas on formal religious rituals to include everyday rituals as fulfilling the same functions, Collins pushes the idea forward by focusing on local situations and identifying the characteristics of successful rituals—a topic I will discuss and illustrate in chapter 2. Contrastingly, he also identifies how others don't work. In his words, "individual lives are chains of interaction rituals" (Collins 1998, 24). In his view, and in Goffman's, if we want to understand anything about society, we must start by examining its smallest unit of analysis, which is not individuals, but the situations within which they behave. Following Durkheim, this version of ritual theory suggests that morality, and thus social order, is established and preserved not through faith or socialization but through institutionalized group rituals that produce high *emotional energy*. Yet ritual participation also has the potential to create new meanings and energy that can change existing social structures, rather than just reproducing them.

11 Collins 1998, 19–53.

12 Describing the most classic antagonism in big wave surfing to date, between Ken Bradshaw and Mark Foo, Andy Martin narrates their conflict as "a clash of civilizations," adding that "Hawaii, like all islands, is a natural arena of pure Darwinian conflict" (Martin 2007, 245).

13 According to Erving Goffman (1967, 185), *action* refers to "activities that are consequential, problematic, and undertaken for what is felt to be its own sake."

14 See Giddens 1991, 113. In his study on parkour, culture, and the meaning of risk, Jeffrey Kidder uses the phrase "fateful moments of adventure" (2017, 73) to describe how individuals in contemporary Western societies value taking chances as a way to test themselves and assess masculinity. In this respect his analysis is based on previous studies of masculinity, and on Goffman's use of the term *action*. My use of the concept is different because it's both more specific and of more general use. In my definition a fateful moment entails irrevocable changes to the self-concept. See Goffman (1961; 1967) for a discussion of the concept of fatefulness. And see the work by Alice Goffman on what she terms "fateful situations: forms of experience that pull us out of our routines and open us to bursts of change going in many directions" (2019, 69). In her article she argues that this level of analysis should be included in sociologists' life-course models. While there are similarities between her concept, my use of the concept partially grounded in Giddens's work, and the importance of such moments as "turning points," there are also differences. One is that rather than situations, I focus on and examine moments. My unit of analysis is smaller. Situations are made up of moments. *Fateful situations* can be broken down into *fateful moments*. I make a similar distinction later in the book between *edgework* situations and *flow* moments. Situations are the largest of these units, while moments are smaller. There are other uses of the term moments in sociology. In their research on scientific collaboration Parker and Hackett use the concepts "hot spots and hot moments" to describe "places and times of high emotion, creativity, and performance where transformative science is done" (2012, 39), which they also define as "brief but intense periods of collaboration undertaken in remote and isolated settings" (21). And writing about creative collaboration in pairs, Michael Farrell refers to "collaborative moments" to identify consequential exchanges of ideas dependent on openness and high trust that ultimately lead to discovery (2001, 23). And even while not exactly focusing on moments, I want to mention that Jooyoung Lee defines *momentous interactions* as "encounters that leave people feeling excited and hopeful about their future" (2017, 153). An example of these interactions is a fleeting encounter with a celebrity that can lead an amateur musician to believe that her professional success is near.

15 Like any theory, Collins's idea of *interaction ritual chains* has been criticized on various grounds, but it has also been praised for its originality and for how intuitive and applicable it is. Further, research on entrainment in other fields (e.g., experimental psychology, evolutionary biology, and anthropology) has demonstrated how synchrony during exertive rhythmic activities generates endorphins and bonding (e.g., Tarr, Launay, and Dunbar 2014). Gary Alan Fine (2012, 23) argues that Collins and Goffman do not pay enough attention to groups' shared pasts. Situations matter, as do vestiges of *emotional energy*; but if we do not consider reciprocal expectations, group culture, and informal roles established among group members, we are likely to miss significant details and nuances, as often happens to those who pursue experimental work by studying groups in artificial settings. In such settings little is at stake, because those groups not only don't share a past, but also lack a common future.

16 *Edgework* refers to working an edge, crossing back and forth over a consequential boundary. It requires not only courage, but also skills. Stephen Lyng (1990) adapted the term from Hunter S. Thompson's famous book *Fear and Loathing in Las Vegas* (1971), in which the author describes a wide range of drug-addled mischief. Thompson (1967) first mentioned the idea of "edge" in relation to pushing the limits while speeding on a motorcycle.

17 Lyng 2004b, 18; see also Katz 1988.

18 See Jeffrey Kidder and his description of how traceurs goad one another through a reciprocal influence (Kidder 2017, 83). For a concept that captures this dynamic see Farrell's *escalating reciprocity* (2001). Jason Laurendeau and Erin G. Van Brunschot (2006) argue that the interactional setting of *edgework*

needs to be further researched, as does Stephen Lyng (personal communication, June 7, 2021).

19 In a chapter on the science of surfing and the biology of sensation-seeking, sport historian Douglas Booth describes the production of specific hormones in relation to extreme sports and their addictive qualities: "Some neurophysiologists propose that chronic elevation of dopamine reduces the availability of dopamine receptors, which in turn limits their ability to respond to chemical signaling. Dulling the responsiveness of the brain's reward pathways may produce desensitization to a stimulus whereby the individual requires more dopamine to maintain the same physiological response. These findings help explain apparent addictions to physical activity and why some surfers constantly seek bigger, faster, steeper, longer waves, just as drug addicts seek more frequent and higher doses" (2011, 53–54). Booth cites and relies on the work of Franken, Zijlstra, and Muris (2006, 299) and Esch and Stefano (2004, 242).

20 Katz 1988.

21 See Farrell 2001 and Kohut 1977.

22 Dixon 2011, 126.

23 Casey 2010, 385.

24 Becker 2008.

25 See Wacquant 2004.

26 See Wacquant 2004; for a critique of this work see Collins 2015.

27 McCall and Simmons 1969.

28 Davis 2015, 19.

29 Davis 2015.

30 Taylor 2007.

31 See Clark 2011.

32 Finney and Houston 1996, 36–38; Thrum 1896; Masterson 2018. The original reference to women surfing better than men is in Finney and Houston (1996, 36–38), where they discuss women in surfing and quote Thrum (1896): "the gentler sex carried off the highest honors."

33 For instance, see Westwick and Neushul 2013.

34 Westwick and Neushul 2013.

35 Corbin 1994.

36 See Westwick and Neushul 2013, 8.

37 Finney and James Houston 1966, 59.

38 Lodge 1992, cited in Davis 2015.

39 Silva 2004.

40 Walker 2011.

41 Walker 2011, 143.

42 Finney and Houston 1966, 73.

43 As Andy Martin (2009, 255) writes: "It was no coincidence that the renaissance of surfing at the end of the nineteenth century and its relentless expansion in the twentieth precisely coincided with the cinematic revolution. Surfing and celluloid were made for one another."

44 See Booth 2011, 37–46.

45 Warshaw 2000, xi.

46 Farber 1994, 60.

47 See Clark 2011.

48 Finney and Houston 1966, 38.

49 Dawson 2017, 143.

50 As Mark Stranger writes: "Any pleasure found in sharing a wave with another surfer virtually disappeared in the 1960s as advances in surfboard technology allowed surfers to carve turns all over the face of the wave" (2011, 60).

51 Stranger 2011.

52 Nazer 2004, 656.

53 See Partington, Partington, and Olivier 2009.

54 Brisick 2016.

55 Warshaw 2010, 300.

56 Booth 2011.

57 Fine and Corte 2017.

58 Booth 2011, xiv.

59 See Lyng 1990.

60 Booth 2011.

61 Booth 2011, 100–103.

62 Warshaw 2000, 108.

63 Warshaw 2010, 403.

64 The Quiksilver Big Wave Invitational in Memory of Eddie Aikau—now The Eddie Aikau Big Wave Invitational—is a celebration of surfing, of Hawaiian culture, and of the skills and courage of the late Eddie Aikau. A Hawaiian who in 1968 became the first lifeguard at Waimea Bay, Aikau was also an outstanding surfer at the Bay and Sunset. He died at sea in 1978 while attempting to save his crew mates during a voyage of the *Hōkūleʻa*.

65 Citing William Ellis (1826, 209, 304–5), Kevin Dawson writes: "The communal thrill of Hawaiian surfing was 'heightened by the shouts and laughter' as people shared waves, perpetuating childhood joys into adulthood" (Dawson 2017, 39).

Chapter Two

1 As Jeff Divine puts it in the *Encyclopedia of Surfing*: "A circular pattern on the wave face, formed as a swell passes over a raised area on the bottom—usually a large rock or cluster of rocks. Boils are generally a red flag, as they indicate shallow water. They can also be difficult to traverse, as the boil's perimeter will often grab the rail of a surfboard, and because the water within can be unstable" (Warshaw n.d., https://eos.surf/entries/boil/).

2 Finnegan 2015.

3 Morrill and Snow 2005, 18.

4 Wireman 1984, cited in Morrill and Snow 2005, 18.

5 Nazer 2004.

6 Kaffine 2009, 741.

7 Taylor 2010; Hartig et al. 2014. Relatedly, Aristotle talks of the restorative and pleasurable effects of leisure activities. In this line, Norbert Elias and Eric Dunning (1986, 46) argue that leisure activities fulfill functions similar to those of religious activities.

8 Fine 1998, 250.

9 Author Thad Ziolkowski, for instance, argues that surf therapy is part of a broader movement of outdoor psychological approaches grounded in the positive effects of "being physically active in stimulus-rich natural settings" (2021, 193).

10 Collins 2015, 16.
11 Collins and McConnell 2015.
12 Collins 2020.
13 Burt 2005.
14 Collins 2004, 35; Durkheim (1912) 1995.
15 Collins 2004; Peter Baehr 2005.
16 Collins 1998, 35.
17 Parker, Cardenas, Dorr, and Hackett 2020, 1072.
18 Fine 2012.
19 Mead (1934) 2015, 213.
20 Collins 2004, 124; Summers-Effler 2010, 126.
21 Collins discusses mentorship in much of his published work and in relation to different fields, including philosophy, war, violence, and business. Mentors do more than just function as paragons; they also share with novices their networks and resources. In Collins's words, they are not "cheerleaders" but "facilitators" who put their reputation on the line, and in fields like business they also invest money in their protégés (see also Villette and Vuillermot 2009). Further, in fields like science, by regularly interacting with a mentor a protégé learns the structures of the field within which he operates, and thus how to best combine ideas—to which they have access before those who are not as tightly connected to the core of a discipline—and win legitimacy for his creative products.
22 See Farrell 2001 and John-Steiner 2000.
23 In his study on the micro-sociology of charisma, Collins (2020, 116) describes leaders' interactional style and a handful of characteristics related to this role. One of them is what he terms *emotional domination*, which he says is typical for instance of Jesus's style. Both Phil and (especially) Chris also benefit from what Collins terms *reputational charisma*. This mechanism pertains to the authority to set and maintain interactional rhythm in a situation, whether overtly or subtly.

Chapter Three

1 Walker 2011, 18.
2 *Surfer Magazine* 49 (4), April 2008.
3 Irwin and Umemoto 2016.
4 Cook 1846, 216–17.
5 Warshaw 2016.
6 Beckman 2014, xix.
7 Beckman 2014.
8 Collins 2004
9 See Katz (1999), cited by Collins (2004, 381) while discussing "happy laughter."
10 Huizinga 1955, 3.
11 Fine and Corte 2017, 66.
12 Snow and Moss 2014.
13 Goffman (1961) writes that there has to be uncertainty of outcome for a game to be fun.
14 Collins 2008; Jackson-Jacobs 2004.

15 Tuomela 2007.

16 Simmel 1984.

17 Collins 2015, 15.

18 Booth 2011, 53–56.

19 Ziolkowski 2021, 142.

20 Collins 2004, 51.

21 Mitchell 1983, 156.

22 Mitchell 1983, 222.

23 Csikszentmihalyi 1982.

24 Katz 1988.

25 James 2012.

26 Csikszentmihalyi 1996.

27 Girard 1972.

28 Katz 1988, Collins 2008.

29 Kaffine 2009.

30 Brisick 2016.

31 Geertz 1973, 416.

32 Lyng 2018.

33 Reith (2006, 264) is referring to de Jonge's ideas on the "syndrome of intensity" (1975).

34 Writing about extreme sports and the "quest for sensation," Le Breton says: "the more intense the suffering, the more the achievement has a reassuring personal significance" (2000, 1).

35 Toohey 2011.

36 Lyng 2004a, 18.

37 Kidder forthcoming.

38 Lyng 2016.

39 Martin 2007, 224.

40 My theory and Collins's interaction ritual theory share the rudiments of a theory of drug addiction. In Becker's theory of drug consumption (1963) as well as in others' work, addiction involves a social group focusing on a particular physiological experience it has singled out (those who can't focus on the part that is the "high" do not continue in the group); the group then develops a rhythm of behavior around its consecrated sacred objects, which individuals even away from the group can use as reminders of the peak experience they want to repeat, more than anything else in their life.

Chapter Four

1 Chambliss 1989, 85.

2 Wiley 1994.

3 Collins 2004, 201.

4 Laurendeau and Van Brunschot 2006.

5 Many surfers talk about how taking one wave can change their perspective, propelling them to paddle back out wanting more. For more examples, see my description of my first experience at Waimea in the introduction, and Kawika's account in chapter 2.

6 See Mitchell 2021.

7 Fine 1998, 250.

8 Dubin 1992.

9 Best 2011.

10 On surfing and addiction, see Ziolkowski 2021.

11 Farber 2020, 86.

12 Collins 2008.

13 Mead and Baldwin 1971.

14 Goffman 1967.

15 Sawyer 2007.

16 On acquiring and recombining ideas, see also the work by Ronald Burt (2005) and other network and organizational scholars.

17 Collins 1998, 49.

18 Collins 2004, 181.

Chapter Five

1 Farrell 2001.

2 Menger 2014.

3 For example, Mead (1934) 2015.

4 Farrell 2001, 155.

5 Parker and Corte 2017, 35.

6 Farrell 2001, 185.

7 Collins 1998, 73.

8 Collins 2004.

9 See Westwick and Neushul 2013, 261.

10 Westwick and Neushul 2013, 266.

11 Masterson 2018.

12 Thrum (1896, 110), cited in Finney and Houston (1966).

13 See Booth 2001, 100–106.

14 See John Loy (1995), who coined the concept of *agonal fratriarchy* to describe a brotherhood status system in which men direct performances of physical courage toward one another.

15 Wiley 2016, 2.

16 Fernyhough 2016, 7.

17 Wiley 2016, 9.

18 Fernyhough 2016, 38.

19 Collins 2011, 161.

20 Wiley 1994, 220.

21 Wiley 1994, 215.

22 Wiley 1994, 216.

23 Wiley 2016, 6.

24 Wiley 2016.

25 Archer 2007, 63.

26 Collins 2004.

27 Collins 1998, 52.

28 Collins 2004, 197; Wiley 2016, 11.

29 Collins 2004, 198.

30 Wiley (1994, 67), cited in Collins (2004, 201).

31 See Parker and Hackett 2012.

Chapter Six

1 Becker (2008) uses the term *integrated professionals* to refer to those who have internalized the rules of their field and know what is worth doing within them. Not all sharpshooters are equally integrated in their field, and my emphasis is on the kinds of risks they take in relation to their occupational phase, the level of their expertise and experience, and their personal development, including what sociologist Everett Hughes (1997) refers to as a career—a moving perspective in someone's life.
2 Chambliss 1989.
3 Corte 2013.
4 See Collins and McConnell 2015.
5 Duane 1996, 143–44.
6 For a simple overview of this literature connected to surfing, see Kotler (2006, 192–203).
7 See Farrell 2001, Corte 2013.
8 Psychologists Franchina et al. define it as being related to "feelings of anxiety that arise from the realization that you may be missing out on rewarding experiences that others are having" (2018, 1). While it is not a new concept, a number of scholars argue that it has significantly increased with the rise of social media. Previous research finds that it leads to irritability, anxiety, and feelings of inadequacy.
9 Shulze 1996.
10 Reckwitz 2020.
11 Lyng 2018.
12 Elias and Dunning 1986.
13 Lyng 2018.
14 Graeber 2019.
15 Taylor 2010.
16 See Asma 2017, 58.
17 Furley, Thrien, Klinge, and Dörr 2020.
18 Heider and Warner 2010; King and De Rond 2011.
19 Parker and Corte 2017; Fuchs 1992; Collins 1994.
20 Fürst 2018.
21 Morton 2020.
22 Merton 1968.
23 Collins 2015, 110.
24 Booth 2001, 106.
25 Paul 2016.
26 As the company behind big wave surfing specifies in its rule book for the sport: "For a ride to be deemed successful and eligible to be considered as a Submission to the Big Wave Awards, a surfer must be standing only on their feet on a board and complete the meaningful portion of the wave while in control and under the power of only the wave and gravity ('Ride')." Journalist Zander Morton (2020) points out that: "'the meaningful portion of the wave' is a gray area."
27 Paul 2016.
28 See also Kerbox 2019.
29 Becker 2008, 134.

30 Caughey 1984; Fine 1977.
31 Fine 2001, 4.

Chapter Seven

1 See Fine 2001, 11.
2 Hoare 2017, 85.
3 Murray 1997, 124.
4 Kohut 1977.
5 See Heinz Kohut's work on the *selfobject*, a significant other that one sees as possessing the strength and abilities one wishes to embody and master. In psychological terms, he/she works as a mirror. Farrell writes: "Under the spell of the *selfobject*, the creative person invests more energy in an inner life and is able to carry out sustained periods of creative work" less distracted by guilt and self-doubt (2001, 17). As Farrell argues, in collaborative circles this dynamic typically takes place in dyads wherein at first only one member plays this role; later in the group's development both members may alternate in this role. Farrell draws examples from a number of fields, but in this respect his data documents particularly well the relationship between Joseph Conrad and Ford Madox Ford in the Rye Circle.
6 Hughes 1997. For an illustrative application of this concept, see Lee's study on aspiring rap artists (2016).
7 Podilchak 1985.

Epilogue

1 Peirce (1934, para. 314), cited in Wiley (2016, 8).
2 Describing the interactions among the French Impressionists, Farrell (2001, 54) argues that "part of the fun was pricking the ego of your opponent, but with humor and goodwill so as not to provoke his anger. . . . The exchanges were open, loud, and merciless, but generally remained within limits that allowed most members to maintain their dignity and self-esteem."
3 The fun situation, as in any situation involving the "I," lends itself to self-expression and gratification. In these intense instances one can simultaneously impulsively let go of inhibiting normal restrictions and enjoy belonging to a community of like-minded others (see Mead [1934] 2015, 213, 219).
4 Wheaton 2004.
5 Maffesoli 1995.
6 Collins 2004; Draper 2019.
7 Lyng 2018; Holyfield, Jonas, and Zajicek 2005.
8 Baumeister and Leary 1995.

References

Archer, Margaret S. 2007. *Making Our Way through the World: Human Reflexivity and Social Mobility*. Cambridge: Cambridge University Press.

Aristotle. 1996. *Poetics*. Translated and with an introduction by Malcolm Heath. London: Penguin Books.

Asma, Stephen T. 2017. *The Evolution of Imagination*. Chicago: University of Chicago Press.

Baehr, Peter. 2005. "Review Forum—The Sociology of Almost Everything: Four Questions to Randall Collins about Interaction Ritual Chains." *Canadian Journal of Sociology Online* (January/February): 1–11.

Baumeister, Roy F., and Mark R. Leary. 1995. "The Need to Belong: Desire for Interpersonal Attachments as a Fundamental Human Motivation." *Psychological Bulletin* 117 (3): 497–529.

Becker, Howard S. 1963. *Outsiders. Studies in the Sociology of Deviance*. New York: The Free Press.

———. 2008. *Art Worlds*. 25th anniversary edition, updated and expanded. Berkeley: University of California Press.

Beckman, John. 2014. *American Fun: Four Centuries of Joyous Revolt*. New York: Pantheon.

Benzecry, Claudio. 2011. *The Opera Fanatic: Ethnography of an Obsession*. Chicago: University of Chicago Press.

Best, Joel. 2011. *Everyone's a Winner: Life in Our Congratulatory Culture*. Berkeley: University of California Press.

Booth, Douglas. 2001. *Australian Beach Cultures: The History of Sun, Sand and Surf*. London: Frank Cass.

———.2006. "Politics and Pleasure: The Philosophy of Physical Education Revisited." *Quest* 61 (2): 133–53.

———. 2011. *Surfing: The Ultimate Guide*. Santa Barbara, CA: Greenwood Publishing.

Brisick, Jamie. 2016. *The Big Wave Riders of Hawaii; Aloha Spirit, Heritage & Respect*. Huntington Beach, CA: Quiksilver.

Burt, Ronald S. 2005. *Brokerage and Closure: An Introduction to Social Capital*. New York: Oxford University Press.

Canetti, Elias. 1984. *Crowds and Power*. New York: Farrar Straus Giroux.

Casey, Susan. 2010. *The Wave: In Pursuit of the Pursuit of the Rogues, Freaks and Giants of the Ocean*. New York: Anchor.

Caughey, John L. 1984. *Imaginary Social Worlds: A Cultural Approach*. Lincoln: University of Nebraska Press.

Chadwick, Whitney, and Isabelle de Courtivron, eds. 1993. *Significant Others: Creativity and Intimate Partnership*. London: Thames and Hudson.

Chambliss, Daniel F. 1989. "The Mundanity of Excellence: An Ethnographic Report on Stratification and Olympic Swimmers." *Sociological Theory* 7 (1): 70–86.

Clark, John. 2011. *Hawaiian Surfing: Traditions from the Past*. Honolulu: University of Hawai'i Press.

Collins, Randall. 1994. "Why the Social Sciences Won't Become High-consensus, Rapid-discovery Science." *Sociological Forum* 9 (2): 155–77.

———. 1998. *The Sociology of Philosophies: A Global Theory of Intellectual Change*. Cambridge, MA: Belknap Press of Harvard University Press.

———. 2004. *Interaction Ritual Chains*. Princeton, NJ: Princeton University Press.

———. 2008. *Violence: A Micro-Sociological Theory*. Princeton, NJ: Princeton University Press.

———. 2011. "Wiley's Contribution to Symbolic Interactionist Theory." *The American Sociologist* 42 (2): 156–67.

———. 2015. "Visual Micro-Sociology and the Sociology of Flesh and Blood: Comment on Wacquant." *Qualitative Sociology* 38 (1): 13–17.

———. 2018. "What Has Microsociology Accomplished?" In *Ritual, Emotion, Violence: Studies on the Micro-sociology of Randall Collins*, ed. E. Weininger, Annette Lareau, and Omar Lizardo, 243–61. New York: Routledge.

———. 2020. *Charisma: Micro-Sociology of Power and Influence*. New York: Routledge.

Collins, Randall, and Maren McConnell. 2015. *Napoleon Never Slept: How Great Leaders Leverage Social Energy*. Maren Ink. E-book (PDF).

Contreras, Randol. 2013. *The Stickup Kids: Race, Drugs, Violence, and the American Dream*. Berkeley: University of California Press.

Cook, James. 1846. *The Voyages of Captain James Cook: With an Appendix, Giving an Account of the Present Condition of the South Sea Islands*. London: William Smith.

Cooley, Charles Horton. 1972. "Looking-glass Self." In *Symbolic Interaction*, 2nd edition, edited by Jerome G. Manis and Bernard N. Meltzer, 231–33. Boston: Allyn and Bacon.

Corbin, Alain. *The Lure of the Sea: The Discovery of the Seaside in the Western World, 1750–1840*. 1994. Berkeley: University of California Press.

Corte, Ugo. 2013. "A Refinement of Collaborative Circles Theory: Resource Mobilization and Innovation in an Emerging Sport." *Social Psychology Quarterly* 76 (1): 25–51.

Csikszentmihalyi, Mihaly. 1982. *Beyond Boredom and Anxiety*. San Francisco: Jossey-Bass.

———. 1996. *Creativity: Flow and the Psychology of Discovery and Invention*. New York: Harper Perennial.

Davis, David. 2015. *Waterman: The Life and Times of Duke Kahanamoku*. Lincoln: University of Nebraska Press.

Dawson, Kevin. 2017. "Surfing beyond Racial and Colonial Imperatives in Early Modern Atlantic Africa and Oceania." In *The Critical Surf Studies Reader*, edited by D. Z. Hough-Snee and A. S. Eastman, 135–54. Durham, NC: Duke University Press.

de Jonge, Alex. 1975. *Dostoevsky and the Age of Intensity*. London: Faber and Faber.

Dixon, Chris. 2011. *Ghost Wave: The Discovery of Cortes Bank and the Biggest Wave on Earth*. San Francisco: Chronicle Books.

Draper, Scott. 2019. *Religious Interaction Ritual*. New York: Lexington Books.

Duane, Daniel. 1996. *Caught Inside: A Surfer's Year on the California Coast*. New York: North Point Press.

Dubin, Robert. 1992. *Central Life Interests: Creative Individualism in a Complex World*. New Brunswick, NJ: Transaction Publishers.

Durkheim, Émile. (1912) 1995. *The Elementary Forms of Religious Life*. Translated by Karen E. Fields. New York: Free Press.

Edwards, Bob, and Ugo Corte. 2010. "Commercialization and Lifetime Sport: Lessons from 20 Years of Freestyle BMX in 'Pro-town, USA.'" *Sport in Society* 13 (7/8): 1135–51.

Elias, Norbert, and Eric Dunning. 1986. *Quest for Excitement: Sport and Leisure in the Civilising Process*. Dublin, Ireland: University College Dublin Press.

Ellis, William. 1826. *Narrative of a Tour through Hawaii*. London: Fisher, Son, and P. Jackson.

Esch, Tobias, and George B. Stefano. 2004. "The Neurobiology of Pleasure, Reward Processes, Addiction and Their Health Implications." *Neuroendocrinology Letters* 25 (4): 235–51.

Farber, Thomas. 1994. *On Water*. Hopewell, NJ: The Ecco Press.

———. 2020. *Acting My Age*. Honolulu: University of Hawai'i Press.

Farrell, Michael P. 2001. *Collaborative Circles: Friendship Dynamics and Creative Work*. Chicago: University of Chicago Press.

Fernyhough, Charles. 2016. *The Voices Within: The History and Science of How We Talk to Ourselves*. New York: Basic Books.

Fine, Gary Alan. 1977. "Popular Culture and Social Interaction: Production, Consumption, and Usage." *Journal of Popular Culture* 11 (2): 453–66.

———. 1998. *Morel Tales: The Culture of Mushrooming*. Cambridge, MA: Harvard University Press.

———. 2001. *Difficult Reputations: Collective Memories of the Evil, Inept, and Controversial*. Chicago: University of Chicago Press.

———. 2003. "Review Essay: On the Trail of Tribal Sociology." *Sociological Forum* 18 (4): 653–65.

———. 2012. *Tiny Publics: A Theory of Group Action and Culture*. New York: Russell Sage Foundation Publications.

———. 2015. *Players and Pawns: How Chess Creates Community and Culture*. Chicago: University of Chicago Press.

Fine, Gary Alan, and Ugo Corte. 2017. "Group Pleasures: Collaborative Commitments, Shared Narrative, and the Sociology of Fun." *Sociological Theory* 35 (1): 64–86.

Finnegan, William. 2015. *Barbarian Days: A Surfing Life*. New York: Penguin.

Finney, Ben R., and James D. Houston. 1966. *Surfing: The Sport of Hawaiian Kings*. Tokyo: The Voyager's Press.

Franchina, Vittoria, Mariek Vanden Abeele, Antonius J. Van Rooij, Gianluca Lo Coco, and Lieven De Marez. 2018. "Fear of Missing Out as a Predictor of Problematic Social Media Use and Phubbing Behavior among Flemish Adolescents." *International Journal of Environmental Research and Public Health* 15 (10): 2319.

Franken, Ingmar H. A., Corien Zijlstra, and Peter Muris. 2006. "Are Nonpharmacological Induced Rewards Related to Anhedonia? A Study among Skydivers." *Progress in Neuro-Psychopharmacology & Biological Psychiatry* 30 (2): 297–300.

Fuchs, Stephan. 1992. *The Professional Quest for Truth*. New York: SUNY Press.

Fujimori, Leila. "11.5 Miles of Road Closed as Sizable Surf Advances." *Star Advertiser*, February 23, 2016.

Furley, Philip, Fanny Thrien, Johannes Klinge, and Jannik Dörr. 2020. "Claims in Surfing: The Influence of Emotional Postperformance Expressions on Performance Evaluations." *Journal of Sport and Exercise Psychology* 42 (1): 26–33.

Fürst, Henrik. 2018. "Making the Discovery: The Creativity of Selecting Fiction Manuscripts from the Slush Pile." *Symbolic Interaction* 41 (4): 513–32.

Geertz, Clifford. 1973. *The Interpretation of Cultures*. New York: Basic Books.

Giddens, Anthony. 1991. *Modernity and Self-identity: Self and Society in the Late Modern Age*. Redwood City, CA: Stanford University Press.

Girard, René. 1972. *La Violence et le Sacré*. Paris: Hachette.

Goffman, Alice. 2019. "Go to More Parties? Social Occasions as Home to Unexpected Turning Points in Life Trajectories." *Social Psychology Quarterly* 82 (1): 51–74.

Goffman, Erving. 1959. *The Presentation of Self in Everyday Life*. New York: Anchor.

———. 1961. *Encounters: Two Studies in the Sociology of Interaction*. Indianapolis: Bobbs-Merrill.

———. 1967. "Where the Action Is." In *Interaction Ritual: Essays on Face-to-Face Behavior*, 149–270. Garden City, NY: Doubleday.

———. 1983. "The Interaction Order." *American Sociological Review* 48 (1):1–17.

Graeber, David. 2019. *Bullshit Jobs: A Theory*. London: Penguin Books.

Hartig, Terry, Richard Mitchell, Sjerp de Vries, and Howard Frumkin. 2014. "Nature and Health." *Annual Review of Public Health* 35 (1): 207–28.

Heider, Anne, and R. Stephen Warner. 2010. "Bodies in Sync: Interaction Ritual Theory Applied to Sacred Harp Singing." *Sociology of Religion* 71 (1): 76–97.

Hoare, Philip. 2017. *RISINGTIDEFALLINGSTAR: In Search of the Soul of the Sea*. Chicago: University of Chicago Press.

Holyfield, Lori, Lilian Jonas, and Anna Zajicek. 2005. "Adventure without Risk Is Like Disneyland." In *Edgework: The Sociology of Risk Taking*, ed. Stephen Lyng, 173–85. New York: Routledge.

Hughes, Everett. 1997. "Careers." *Qualitative Sociology* 20 (3): 389–97.

Huizinga, Johan. 1955. *Homo Ludens: A Study of the Play-Element in Culture*. Boston: Beacon Press.

Irwin, Katherine, and Karen Umemoto. 2016. *Jacked Up and Unjust: Pacific Islander Teens Confront Violent Legacies*. Berkeley: University of California Press.

Jackson-Jacobs, Curtis. 2004. "Taking a Beating: The Narrative Gratifications of Fighting as an Underdog." In *Cultural Criminology Unleashed*, ed. Jeff Ferrell, Keith Hayward, Wayne Morrison, and Mike Presdee, 231–44. London: Glasshouse Press.

James, Aaron. 2012. *Assholes: A Theory*. New York: Doubleday.

Johnson, David T., Nicholas Chagnon, and Meda Chesney-Lind. 2019. "Honolulu Police Are Using Lethal Force Far Too Often." *Honolulu Civil Beat*. https://www.civilbeat.org/2019/01/honolulu-police-are-using-lethal-force-far-too-often/.

John-Steiner, Vera. 2000. *Creative Collaboration*. Oxford: Oxford University Press.

Kaffine, Daniel T. 2009. "Quality and the Commons: The Surf Gangs of California." *The Journal of Law and Economics* 52 (4): 727–43.

Katz, Jack. 1988. *Seductions of Crime: Moral and Sensual Attractions in Doing Evil*. New York: Basic Books.

———. 1999. *How Emotions Work*. Chicago: University of Chicago Press.

Kerbox, Buzzy. 2019. *Making Waves*. Honolulu, HI: Watermark Publishing.

Kidder, Jeffrey L. 2017. *Parkour and the City: Risk, Masculinity, and Meaning in a Postmodern Sport*. New Brunswick, NJ: Rutgers University Press.

———. Forthcoming. "Reconsidering Edgework Theory: Practices, Experiences, and Structures." *International Review for the Sociology of Sport*.

King, Anthony, and Mark de Rond. 2011. "Boat Race: Rhythm and the Possibility of Collective Performance." *The British Journal of Sociology* 62 (4): 565–85.

Kjølsrød, Lise. 2003. "Adventure Revisited: On Structure and Metaphor in Specialized Play." *Sociology* 37 (3): 459–76.

Kohut, Heinz. 1977. *The Restoration of the Self*. New York: International Universities Press.

Kotler, Steven. 2006. *West of Jesus*. New York: Bloomsbury USA.

Laurendeau, Jason, and Erin Gibbs Van Brunschot. 2006. "Policing the Edge: Risk and Social Control in Skydiving." *Deviant Behavior* 27 (2): 173–201.

Le Breton, David. 2000. "Playing Symbolically with Death in Extreme Sports." *Body & Society* 6 (1): 1–11.

Lee, Jooyoung. 2016. *Blowin' Up: Rap Dreams in South Central*. Chicago: University of Chicago Press.

Lodge, David. 1992. *Paradise News*. New York: Viking Press.

Loy, John W. 1995. "The Dark Side of Agon: Fratriarchies, Performative Masculinities, Sport Involvement and the Phenomenon of Gang Rape." In *International Sociology of Sport: Contemporary Issues*, ed. K. H. Bette and A. Rutten, 263–81. Stuttgart: Naglschmid.

Lyng, Stephen. 1990. "Edgework: A Social Psychological Analysis of Voluntary Risk-taking." *American Journal of Sociology* 95 (4): 851–86.

———. 1998. "Dangerous Methods: Risk Taking and the Research Process." In *Ethnography at the Edge: Crime, Deviance, and Field Research*, ed. J. Ferrell and M. Hamm, 221–51. Boston: Northeastern University Press.

———. 2004a. *Edgework: The Sociology of Risk-taking*. New York: Routledge.

———. 2004b. "Sociology at the Edge: Social Theory and Voluntary Risk Taking." In S. Lyng, ed. (2004a), 18–39.

———. 2016. "Goffman, Action, and Risk Society: Aesthetic Reflexivity in Late Modernity." *UNLV Gaming Research & Review Journal* 20 (1): 61–78.

———. 2018. "Excitement—Risk and Authentic Emotion." In *Emotions, Everyday Life and Sociology*, ed. M. H. Jacobsen London: Routledge.

Maffesoli, Michel. 1995. *The Time of the Tribes: The Decline of Individualism in Mass Society*. London: Sage.

Martin, Andy. 2007. *Stealing the Wave: The Epic Struggle between Ken Bradshaw and Mark Foo*. New York: Bloomsbury.

———. 2009. "Surfing, Lies and Videotape: Two Perspectives on the Role of the Media in Sport." *Sport in History* 29 (2): 243–58.

Masterson, Ian 'Akahi. 2018. "Surfing Ali'i, Kahuna, Kupua and Akua. Female Presence in Surfing's Past." In *Surfing, Sex, Genders and Sexualities*, ed. lisahunter, 191–207. London: Routledge.

McCall, George, and J. L. Simmons. 1969. *Issues in Participant Observation: A Text and Reader*. Reading, MA: Addison-Wesley.

Mead, George Herbert. (1934) 2015. *Mind, Self and Society*. Edited by Charles W. Morris. Chicago: University of Chicago Press.

———. 1964. *On Social Psychology*. Edited by Anselm Strauss. Chicago: University of Chicago Press.

Mead, Margaret, and James Baldwin. 1971. "Margaret Mead & James Baldwin: A Rap on Race." *YouTube*, January 9, 2017. https://www.youtube.com/watch?v=3WNO6f7rjEO.

Menger, Pierre-Michel. 2014. *The Economics of Creativity. Art and Achievement under Uncertainty*. Cambridge, MA: Harvard University Press.

Merton, Robert K. 1968. "The Matthew Effect in Science." *Science* 159 (3810): 56–63.

Mitchell, Jamie. 2020. "Late Drop—The Big Wave Podcast: Jamie Mitchell Hosts Nathan Fletcher." *YouTube*, November 12. https://www.youtube.com/watch?v=gdC7q8wFQ5Y.

———. 2021. "Late Drop Big Wave Podcast with Shane Dorian." *YouTube*, April 7. https://www.youtube.com/watch?v=WDmtIiPXIes.

Mitchell, Richard G. Jr. 1983. *Mountain Experience: The Psychology and Sociology of Adventure*. Chicago: University of Chicago Press.

Morrill, Calvin and David A. Snow. 2005. "The Study of Personal Relationships in Public Places." In *Together Alone: Personal Relationships in Public Places*, edited by Calvin Morrill, David A. Snow, and Cindy White, 1–22. Berkeley: University of California Press.

Morton, Zander. 2020. "Why Measuring Big Waves Will Always Lead to Controversy: The Recent Debate over the 2020 CBDMD XXL Biggest Wave Award Is Par for the Course." *Surfer*, September 18. https://www.surfer.com/features/why-measuring-big-waves-will-always-lead-to-controversy/.

Murray, Janet H. 1997. *Hamlet on the Holodeck: The Future of Narrative in Cyberspace*. New York: Free Press.

Nazer, Daniel. 2004. "The Tragicomedy of the Surfers' Common." *Deakin Law Review* 9 (2): 655–713.

Parker, John, Edgar Cardenas, Alexander Dorr, and Edward Hackett. 2020. "Using Sociometers to Advance Small Group Research." *Sociological Methods and Research* 49 (4): 1064–1102.

Parker, John, and Ugo Corte. 2017. "Placing Collaborative Circles in Strategic Action Fields Explaining Differences between Highly Creative Groups." *Sociological Theory* 35 (4): 261–87.

Parker, John N., and Edward J. Hackett. 2012. "Hot Spots and Hot Moments in Scientific Collaborations and Social Movements." *American Sociological Review* 77 (1): 21–44.

Partington, Sarah, Elizabeth Partington, and Steve Olivier. 2009. "The Dark Side of Flow: A Qualitative Study of Dependence in Big Wave Surfing." *The Sport Psychologist* 23 (2): 170–85.

Paul, Taylor. 2016. "The Big Wave Working Class." *Surfing Magazine*, February 1. https://www.surfer.com/surfing-magazine-archive/surfing-originals/the-big-wave-working-class/.

Peirce, Charles Sanders. 1934. *Collected Papers of Charles Peirce*. Vol. 5, *Pragmatism and Pragmaticism*, and vol. 6, *Scientific Metaphysics*, edited by Charles Hartshorne and Paul Weiss. Cambridge, MA: Harvard University Press.

Podilchak, Walter. 1985. "The Social Organization of Fun." *Leisure and Society* 8 (2): 685–92.

Reckwitz, Andreas. 2020. *The Society of Singularities*. Cambridge: Polity Press.

Reith, Gerda. 2006. "The Experience of Play." In *The Sociology of Risk and Gambling Reader*, ed. J. F. Cosgrave, 255–90. New York: Routledge.

Roth, Randall W. 1992. *The Price of Paradise: Lucky We Live in Hawaii?* Honolulu, HI: Mutual Publishing.

Sawyer, Keith. 2007. *Group Genius: The Creative Power of Collaboration*. New York: Basic Books.

Shulze, Gerhard. 1996. *The Experience Society*. London: Sage.

Silva, Noenoe K. 2004. *Aloha Betrayed: Native Hawaiian Resistance to American Colonialism*. Durham, NC: Duke University Press.

Simmel, Georg. 1984. *Georg Simmel: On Women, Sexuality, and Love*. New Haven, CT: Yale University Press.

Snow, David, and Dana Moss. 2014. "Protest on the Fly: Towards a Theory of Spontaneity in the Dynamics of Protest and Social Movements." *American Sociological Review* 79 (6): 1122–43.

Stranger, Mark. 2011. *Surfing Life: Surface, Substructure and the Commodification of the Sublime*. Surrey, UK: Ashgate.

Summers Effler, Erika. 2010. *Laughing Saints and Righteous Heroes: Emotional Rhythms in Social Movement Groups*. Chicago: University of Chicago Press.

Tarr, Bronwyn, Jacques Launay, and Robin I. Dunbar. 2014. "Music and Social Bonding: 'Self-Other' Merging and Neurohormonal Mechanisms." *Frontiers in Psychology: Auditory Cognitive Neuroscience* 5: 1096.

Taylor, Bron. 2007. "Surfing into Spirituality and a New, Aquatic Nature Religion." *Journal of the American Academy of Religion* 75 (4): 923–51.

———. 2010. *Dark Green Religion: Nature Spirituality and the Planetary Future*. Berkeley: University of California Press.

Thompson, Hunter S. 1967. *Hell's Angels: A Strange and Terrible Saga*. New York: Random House.

———. 1971. *Fear and Loathing in Las Vegas: A Savage Journey to the Heart of the American Dream*. New York: Random House.

Thrum, Thomas G. 1896. "Hawaiian Surf Riding." In *Hawaiian Almanac and Annual for 1896*, 106–13. Honolulu.

Toohey, Peter. 2011. *Boredom: A Lively History*. New Haven, CT: Yale University Press.

Tuomela, Raimo. 2007. *The Philosophy of Sociality: The Shared Point of View*. Oxford: Oxford University Press.

Villette, Michel, and Catherine Vuillermot. 2009. *From Predators to Icons: Exposing the Myth of the Business Hero*. Ithaca, NY: Cornell University Press.

Wacquant, Loïc. 2004. *Body & Soul* Oxford: Oxford University Press.

Walker, Isaiah Helekunihi. 2011. *Waves of Resistance: Surfing and History in Twentieth-Century Hawai'i*. Honolulu: University of Hawai'i Press.

Warshaw, Matt. N.d. "Boil." In *Encyclopedia of Surfing*. https://eos.surf/entries/boil/.

———. 2000. *Maverick's: The Story of Big-Wave Surfing*. San Francisco, CA: Chronicle Books.

———. 2010. *The History of Surfing*. San Francisco, CA: Chronicle Books.

———. 2016. "Obituary: Big-Wave Surfer Brock Little (1967-2016)." *Outside*, February 19. https://www.outsideonline.com/outdoor-adventure/water-activities/obituary-big-wave-surfer-brock-little-1967-2016/.

Westwick, Peter, and Peter Neushul. 2013. *The World in the Curl: An Unconventional History of Surfing*. New York: Crown Publishers.

Wheaton, Belinda. 2004. "Introduction: Mapping the Lifestyle Sport-scape." In *Understanding Lifestyle Sports: Consumption, Identity and Difference*, ed. B. Wheaton, 1–28. London: Routledge.

Wiley, Norbert. 1994. *The Semiotic Self*. Cambridge: Polity Press.

———. 2016. *Inner Speech and the Dialogical Self*. Philadelphia, PA: Temple University Press.

Wireman, Peggy. 1984. *Urban Neighborhoods, Networks, and Families: New Forms for Old Values*. Lexington, MA: Lexington Books.

Ziolkowski, Thad. 2021. *The Drop: How the Most Addictive Sport Can Help Us Understand Addiction and Recovery*. New York: HarperCollins Publishers.

Index